W9-BPJ-868

LEGO MINDSTORMS
NXT-G Programming Guide

Second Edition

Ela Area Public Library District
275 Mohawk Trail, Lake Zurich, IL 60047
(847) 438-3433
www.eapl.org

31241007587317

JUL   2012

James Floyd Kelly

Apress®

LEGO MINDSTORMS NXT-G Programming Guide, Second Edition

Copyright © 2010 by James Floyd Kelly

All rights reserved. No part of this work may be reproduced or transmitted in any form or by any means, electronic or mechanical, including photocopying, recording, or by any information storage or retrieval system, without the prior written permission of the copyright owner and the publisher.

ISBN-13 (pbk): 978-1-4302-2976-6

ISBN-13 (electronic): 978-1-4302-2977-3

Printed and bound in the United States of America 9 8 7 6 5 4 3 2 1

Trademarked names, logos, and images may appear in this book. Rather than use a trademark symbol with every occurrence of a trademarked name, logo, or image we use the names, logos, and images only in an editorial fashion and to the benefit of the trademark owner, with no intention of infringement of the trademark.

The use in this publication of trade names, trademarks, service marks, and similar terms, even if they are not identified as such, is not to be taken as an expression of opinion as to whether or not they are subject to proprietary rights.

President and Publisher: Paul Manning
Lead Editor: Jonathan Gennick
Technical Reviewer: Fay Rhodes
Editorial Board: Clay Andres, Steve Anglin, Mark Beckner, Ewan Buckingham, Gary Cornell, Jonathan Gennick, Jonathan Hassell, Michelle Lowman, Matthew Moodie, Duncan Parkes, Jeffrey Pepper, Frank Pohlmann, Douglas Pundick, Ben Renow-Clarke, Dominic Shakeshaft, Matt Wade, Tom Welsh
Coordinating Editor: Laurin Becker
Copy Editor: Mary Ann Fugate, Katie Stence
Compositor: Mary Sudul
Indexer: Potomac Indexing, LLC
Artist: April Milne
Cover Designer: Anna Ishchenko

Distributed to the book trade worldwide by Springer Science+Business Media, LLC., 233 Spring Street, 6th Floor, New York, NY 10013. Phone 1-800-SPRINGER, fax (201) 348-4505, e-mail orders-ny@springer-sbm.com, or visit www.springeronline.com.

For information on translations, please e-mail rights@apress.com, or visit www.apress.com.

Apress and friends of ED books may be purchased in bulk for academic, corporate, or promotional use. eBook versions and licenses are also available for most titles. For more information, reference our Special Bulk Sales–eBook Licensing web page at www.apress.com/info/bulksales.

The information in this book is distributed on an "as is" basis, without warranty. Although every precaution has been taken in the preparation of this work, neither the author(s) nor Apress shall have any liability to any person or entity with respect to any loss or damage caused or alleged to be caused directly or indirectly by the information contained in this work.

The source code for this book is available to readers at www.apress.com. You will need to answer questions pertaining to this book in order to successfully download the code.

For the LEGO MINDSTORMS team, past and present…

Contents at a Glance

Contents

About the Author

 **James Floyd Kelly** is a freelance writer living in Atlanta, Georgia, with degrees in English and Industrial Engineering. He has written books on a variety of subjects including netbooks, free software, building your own computer, and LEGO robotics. He is editor-in-chief of the world's most popular LEGO NXT robotics blog, thenxtstep.com, which continues to draw an estimated 50,000+ readers monthly, and is a regular contributor to the LEGO MINDSTORMS development team. He is also the author of Build Your Own CNC Machine, the first book to include step-by-step instructions for building your very own computer controlled cutting and milling machine. When not writing, he and his wife enjoy time with their two sons.

About the Technical Reviewer

 **Fay Rhodes** is a member of the LEGO MINDSTORMS Community Partners and has authored two books of NXT animals—*LEGO MINDSTORMS NXT Zoo!* and *Robots Alive! Endangered Species*. She also contributed to the LEGO MINDSTORMS NXT idea Book. Fay comes to the NXT from the perspective of the artist, and has a particular interest in helping teachers use the NXT creatively with their students.

Acknowledgments

Writing books is fun. I really mean that. And part of the enjoyment of my job comes from my "co-workers." While I work from home (or a coffee shop), I still get to interact with a great group of people over at Apress. I say over, but that's not completely true as they're all spread across the globe in different cities and countries. You can read the names of all the people involved in getting this book polished and out the door a few pages back, but I'd like to make sure that Jonathan Gennick and Laurin Becker know just how much I appreciate their feedback and hard work on this book. I really hope to get to work with them again in the future.

I also want to thank Fay Rhodes for her help as the Technical Editor of the book. She found my errors and made sure I got them fixed. And many thanks to the readers of The NXT Step blog who pointed out errors in the first edition and made suggestions for this second edition.

Finally, thanks go to my wife, Ashley, as always... for her support.

Introduction

Welcome to the second edition of LEGO MINDSTORMS NXT-G Programming Guide. Since the release of the first edition in 2007, the LEGO MINDSTORMS robotics kit has exploded in popularity and continues to find its way into the hands of newcomers. The first NXT robotics kit was released in late 2006 to rave reviews, and NXT-G, the graphical software used to program robots, was a huge hit.

By following along with some built-in tutorials, users of the new robotics kit were given the basics of the software and set free to design and create some of the strangest, silliest, useful, and/or most unique robots you'd ever imagine. But programming with the NXT-G software wasn't easy for everyone to understand – some took to it immediately and others struggled to understand basic concepts.

I wrote the first edition using simple language, a familiar tone, and short chapters to try and not overwhelm those new to programming with NXT-G. I avoided technical jargon where I could and introduced readers to my version of pseudo code that I felt would help new NXT-G programmers better understand how to formulate an idea and turn it into a real NXT-G program. The feedback I received from the book was overwhelming, especially from teachers and parents who found themselves also needing to learn NXT-G to work and enjoy robot building and programming with their students or children.

In late 2009 a new version of the NXT robotics kit was release – NXT 2.0. And with the new kit came an update to the NXT-G software. Luckily, the majority of the software looked and worked just like the 1.0 version released back in 2006. There were new features and tools, yes, but the basics of how NXT-G works and looks stayed the same. Students, teachers, and parents, familiar with NXT-G 1.0, would have very little difficulty figuring out NXT-G 2.0. But what about those completely new to the NXT robotics kit?

It's my hope that LEGO MINDSTORMS NXT-G Programming Guide Second Edition will help not only those new to the NXT robotics kit but also help update those familiar with the 1.0 kit (and software) with the changes and updates found in NXT-G 2.0. Errors in the first edition have been fixed, new material has been added, and over 25 new exercises have been provided (along with solutions) for readers to take what they've learned and put their skills to the test. I've also added the building instructions for a robot that can be used throughout the book when testing programs. (A big thanks to Chris Smith for providing the images used in Appendix B.)

I hope you find the book easy and enjoyable to read… and then I hope you'll go and build and program some amazing robots that will astound your friends, family, schoolmates, co-workers, and anyone else that has the fortune to view your creations.

■ ■ ■

CHAPTER 1

Robots and Programs

If you are already familiar with the subject of robots and the concept of programming, feel free to skip ahead to the more in-depth chapters that start with Chapter 14. But, if you are just starting out with your LEGO Mindstorms NXT robotics kit and are asking yourself questions such as, "How is a robot different from a toaster?" or "Just what is this thing called programming?" then you're in the right place. If terms like *conditional statements*, *nested loops*, and *variables* make your head spin, don't worry—they make my head spin, too.

There is simply no reason that learning to use the Mindstorms NXT robotics kit should cause stress. It's supposed to be fun, right? Building robots and making them do what you want them to do shouldn't cause headaches. I don't like headaches, and I certainly don't want to give you one, so sit back and let me show you a less stressful method for getting the most out of NXT.

What Is a Robot?

I'm going to keep this short—I promise. What is a robot? There are numerous definitions. One definition is a human-shaped mechanical device that mimics human actions. Another definition is an electronic machine that functions independently, without human control. And, there are many more. There truly doesn't seem to be one official definition.

For the purpose of this book, I'm going to give you my definition. Here goes: *A robot is a device that is built to independently perform actions and interact with its surroundings.*

In a nutshell, a robot should be able to move and react all on its own. If you are controlling its actions, it's just a remote-controlled toy, right? But if your device can do things like examine its surroundings, respond to obstacles such as chairs or walls, pick out a red ball from a mix of colored balls, and hundreds of other activities without help from its human creator, then you've got a robot.

You can build a robot using all the great Mindstorms NXT components that came with your robotics kit. Your bot can have claws or hands. It can have ears to listen and eyes to see. It can walk on legs or roll on wheels. But in order for a robot to be able to do all these things on its own, you must provide it with one additional component, a program.

What Is a Program?

I know I told you that computer terminology makes my head spin, but there are some terms that cannot be avoided. The terms I want to introduce to you are easy to explain and even easier to spell, so they can't be all that bad!

When talking about the Mindstorms NXT robotics kit, I'm talking about a piece of technology. Technology almost always requires a little learning, but that shouldn't mean it has to be boring—NXT robots are cool and fun. So, let's start right off by defining one of the coolest technical terms you need to understand—*program*.

I can't really write a book about NXT programming without defining what a program is. So let's jump in with a small discussion about this word. I promise to keep it fun.

Let's take a look at a very basic robot. I call this robot SPOT and, for right now, SPOT only does one thing. He sits.

Take a look at Figure 1-1. There's SPOT doing what he does best.

Figure 1-1. My bot SPOT

Can we all agree that SPOT is a fairly boring robot? We all know that robots should do things! You could almost say that SPOT needs to be trained. That's how I'm going to define the word "program." Read the next two sentences slowly: A *program* is a set of instructions for my robot. *Programming* is what you do when you create a program.

It's not a long definition, and it certainly isn't complicated. The definition will get a little more detailed as you read more chapters, but for now, let's just start out with that very basic idea.

Programs are for Humans Too

You've encountered a lot of programs in your lifetime. Don't believe me? Let me give you an example:

Teacher: OK class, take out your math books.

[*Grumbling, the students take out their math books.*]

Teacher: I want everyone to turn to page 55.

[*With more grumbling, everyone turns to page 55.*]

Teacher: Everyone read through to page 65.

[Loud grumbling]

The teacher just gave a program to follow: take out your book, turn to a specific page, and read a specified number of pages. The students are told what page to begin reading. They are also told what page to stop reading. The teacher could have added a little more complexity to the instructions by telling the students to skip page 60 and solve the problem on page 62. My point is that there is an order to the instructions and some decision making involved. It is up to the student to determine, for example, when he or she has reached page 65 and to stop reading. Here's one more example:

Step 1: Place the widget firmly against the whatsit.

Step 2: Snap the special wonder-whatchamacallit into the widget.

Step 3: Flip the whatsit over, and bend the thingamajig to the left.

Those are steps I found in an instruction manual—a program for me to follow. If I follow the steps, my whatsit should work perfectly (my whatchamacallit still isn't working!).

Programs are Merely Instructions

A simple program is just a set of instructions (written, spoken, or maybe provided in some other method) that needs to be followed. I certainly don't want to call you a robot, but in a way, we all can frequently act like robots. When we follow a set of instructions, we are running a program! (Another word you might sometimes hear used instead of run is execute: "I told SPOT to *run* his SLEEP program" is the same as "I told SPOT to *execute* his SLEEP program.")

In the previous example, the teacher could have easily handed out a weekly reading assignment sheet like the following:

Monday: Read pages 1–20.

Tuesday: Read pages 21–40.

Wednesday: Read pages 41–60.

Thursday: Read pages 61–80.

Friday: Read pages 81–100.

Now, when the students arrive to class, all the teacher has to say is "Students, it's time for today's reading assignment." It is now up to the students to consult the reading assignment sheet (I always lost mine), open their books, and start reading. The program is the reading assignment sheet and the teacher has the students *run* or *execute* the program.

Let's go back to SPOT. He's just sitting there. How boring. Let's pretend for a moment that SPOT has ears, and I can give him some instructions. I'll start off by giving SPOT some basic movements:

Me: SPOT, move forward.

[*SPOT starts to roll forward.*]

Me: SPOT, stop.

[SPOT stops rolling.]

I've just given SPOT two very simple programs to follow. What? Two programs? Yes, the first program is "Move forward." The second program is "Stop." The simplest programs can be just one step!

The Challenge of Programming

So far, my programs in this chapter have been simple, trivial. You've probably understood them just fine. You're human though and you have a brain. Robots aren't so lucky, and that leads to one of the chief challenges of programming: the need to be specific.

Here's an example. Let's combine the two steps from the previous program into just one step.

Me: SPOT, move forward and stop.

[SPOT just sits there.]

What happened? Well, think about someone telling you to "move forward and stop." How far forward will you move? When will you stop? You're smart, but robots are not. Robots must be told exactly what to do. In this example, SPOT did exactly as he was told. SPOT moved forward and stopped. The reason you didn't see him move is because the moment he started spinning his motors, he stopped.

In the first example, I waited until SPOT began to roll before telling him to stop, so he had time to actually move. In the second example, I combined the instructions into one program (move forward and stop) without telling SPOT how far or maybe how long (in time) to move forward. So let's try it again:

Me: SPOT, move forward for 5 seconds and stop.

[SPOT moves forward for 5 seconds and then stops.]

Here is another example. Suppose I provide SPOT with the following program:

Me: SPOT, spin 180 degrees and then move forward two feet.

Believe it or not, even though this program sounds very specific in its instructions, it's still going to cause confusion with SPOT. Why? Well, let's look at the first part of the program—spin 180 degrees. Should SPOT rotate 180 degrees to the left or right? Believe it or not, it matters to a robot! Remember, a robot wants very specific instructions, so I should change this to "spin 180 degrees clockwise" or "spin 180 degrees to your right."

There's also a slight problem with the second part of the program. For me to tell SPOT to move forward two feet, I need to have defined "forward" and "backward" for SPOT. Most of us tend to think of a robot as having a face or a front and back, and that's fine. For SPOT (see Figure 1-1) his "eyes" are facing forward. His motors can rotate clockwise and counter-clockwise to move him around. When I'm programming SPOT, I need to make certain that when he is told to move forward that his motors will rotate in such a way as to propel him in the direction he is facing. I'll get into this in more detail later in the book, but for now just understand that SPOT is easily confused.

What I've figured out is that SPOT really isn't the problem. I've just discovered that when I tell SPOT to do things, I've got to be *very* specific.

Let's pretend for a moment that SPOT is good at is reading my handwriting. Let me give you another example of how specific I need to be when telling SPOT to execute a program, but this time, instead of telling him what to do, I simply take out a piece of paper and write down the following: SPOT, move forward 3 inches; turn left 90 degrees; move backward 2 inches; spin 360 degrees, and stop.

Next, I give the piece of paper to SPOT, and he reads it. He moves forward 3 inches, turns left 90 degrees, moves backward 2 inches, spins 360 degrees, and, finally, stops.

If your NXT robot is like mine, though, it probably doesn't have the ability to listen to voice commands or read a sheet of paper.

If your robot can't hear you or read your handwriting, how exactly do you tell it what to do? Easy! You're going to use programming software. There are other names such as programming suite or graphical programming environment, or blah, blah, blah—for now, let's just use programming software, OK?

You're in luck. Your Mindstorms NXT robotics kit comes with programming software called NXT-G (the *G* is for Graphical, meaning programs are not written instructions such as my previous handwritten steps for SPOT).

■ **Note** There are a lot of ways to program. Just as different people speak different languages, robots (and computers and other technical stuff) can speak different languages. Some examples of human languages are English, Spanish, French, German, and Italian. For your NXT robots, there are a variety of languages, too. I speak English, because that is the language I learned to speak in school. Your NXT Brick comes from the factory understanding one language: NXT-G.

I also speak Spanish. But it's not my native language. Your NXT Brick can learn to speak other languages, too, but its native language is NXT-G. Most people won't learn another language until they understand their native language well. That's what you need to do—learn NXT-G well so you can talk to your robot (by giving it a program).

NXT-G

NXT-G is the tool you will use to tell your robots what to do. NXT-G allows you to create programs that can be *uploaded* (installed) to your NXT robot. These programs can be instructions as simple as "move forward 2 inches and stop" or as advanced as you can imagine! NXT robots can be built with a variety of motors and sensors. But without a good program, your robot won't know what to do: Do I spin my motors? What do I do with this Touch sensor? Without programming, you'll have one confused robot on your hands.

NXT-G is installed on a computer (there are Windows and Macintosh versions) and exists as software. I'm not going to be covering the basics of using the software, so you'll need to refer to the

LEGO Mindstorms NXT User Guide that came with your NXT kit for installation instructions and steps on how to perform basic steps such as creating new programs, saving programs, and other items.

You will create and save your programs (just like you save a drawing or an essay on your computer) and then connect your NXT robot to the computer. When your NXT robot is connected, you will be able to upload one or more programs to your robot and run (execute) them.

The Wonderful Confusing World of NXT and NXT-G Versions

NXT-G is the programming software of choice for the NXT robotics kit. Unfortunately, users are currently faced with a confusing assortment of NXT-G versions. Let me try and clear it up a bit.

Right now, there are two varieties of the Mindstorms NXT-G robotics kit. The first is what is typically referred to as the Retail version. This is the version of the robotics kit that you purchase from stores or directly from LEGO (www.lego.com). The second variety is typically referred to as the Education version. This version of the robotics kit is purchased directly from LEGO Education (legoeducation.us).

First, you need to be aware that the Retail and Education versions of the robotics kit come with different inventories. They have a lot of parts in common (such as motors, sensors, and the Brick—the brains of the NXT) but they also have some differences. To make it even more confusing, the first Retail version (released in 2006) doesn't have Version 1.0 on the box, but the second Retail version (released in 2009) does have "2.0" on the box. Currently, there is only one version of the Education kit.

To make things even more confusing, there are two versions of NXT-G for both the Retail and Education kits. For retail kits, there is version 1.0 and version 2.0 of NXT-G. For education kits, there is also a version 1.0 and version 2.0 but, believe it or not, the Education versions (both 1.0 and 2.0) of the software are slightly different than their respective retail versions! It's crazy!

However, don't stress about this. I estimate that 90 percent or more of each version of the NXT-G programming software is identical. I'll do my best in this book to point out when something is different between versions, but overall you're going to find that most of the functionality of the software remains the same from version to version.

If you're not sure which version you have, take a look at Figures 1-2 to 1-4. Figure 1-2 shows the 1.0 retail version (with the Robo Center); Figure 1-3 shows the education version (1.0 and 2.0 look identical with Robo Educator but there are some slight differences); and, Figure 1-4 shows the 2.0 retail version (with completely different Robo Center robot projects). Again, don't stress too much over the version you own. There are differences, but for the purposes of this book, over 90 percent of the tools are identical.

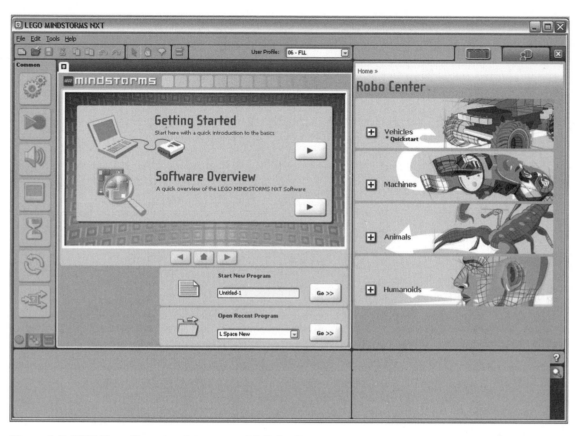

Figure 1-2. NXT-G retail version 1.0 comes with Robo Center.

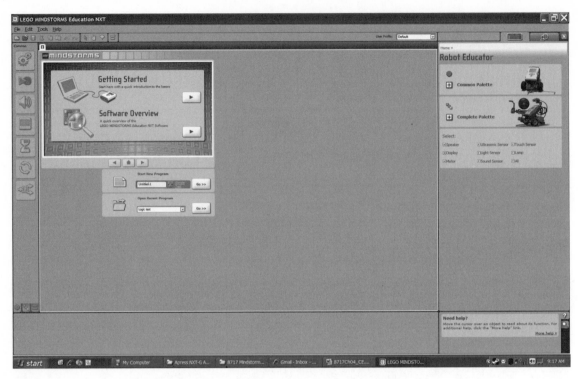

Figure 1-3. NXT-G education versions 1.0 and 2.0 comes with Robo Educator.

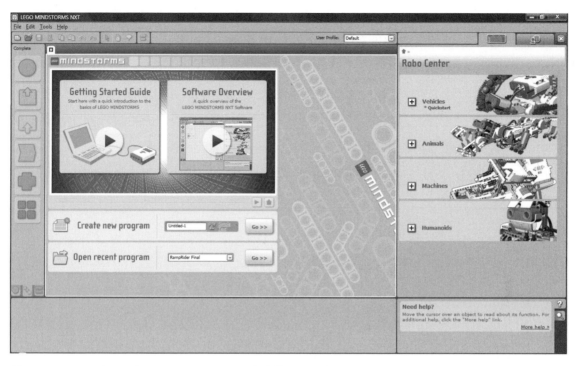

Figure 1-4. *NXT-G retail version 2.0 comes with different Robo Center projects.*

The NXT-G Programming Software is fun to use; feel free to play around with it. The best part about NXT-G is that much of it is extremely easy to figure out on your own. You'll find sample programs as well as some exercises for you to try on your own in most of the upcoming chapters. If you're ready to start learning how to create some awesome programs and get some hands-on training, turn to Chapter 2. The chapter is going to help you figure out what you want your robot to do. Go and experiment a little with NXT-G. I'll see you in Chapter 2.

CHAPTER 2

■ ■ ■

Program Structure

I don't really like using technical terms like "program structure," but it is a very useful concept that will benefit you as you begin to program your robots. The word structure implies some sort of organization or plan, doesn't it? By the time you finish this chapter, you should understand the importance of program structure to you and your robots.

What Do I Mean by Structure?

In Chapter 1, I gave you some examples of real-world programs. Would the following example have made any sense?

> Teacher: Class, open your books to page 55.
>
> [*The class looks confused.*]
>
> Teacher: Class, I want you to get out your math books.
>
> [*Giving the teacher confused looks, the students get out their books.*]

How can you read page 55 if you haven't yet been told which book to open? You might answer, "Yes, but I'm in math class, and the teacher said turn to page 55. So I'm sure the teacher means my math book!"

That's true. As a human, you are able to figure out certain instructions on your own. But remember—robots aren't that smart! They need to be given very strict and specific instructions. And those instructions need to be given in a specific order. That order is another way of saying "program structure."

Think of a house. You can't have a second floor without a first floor to build on top of, right? And you can't install a roof before you pour the concrete floor and build some walls. There's an order to how things are done when you build a house. The same goes for programming a robot.

Planning Your Program's Structure

Let's get out SPOT for another example. He's still doing his one and only trick—sit. You're not quite ready to upload an NXT-G program yet, but let's do some preplanning at this stage. I want you to use something that computer programmers call *pseudo-code*. What is pseudo-code? Well, the definition of "pseudo" is fake (as in pretend, simulated, virtual—get the idea?); it's not real. And "code" is simply another word for program. Put it all together and one way of looking at pseudo-code is this: fake program.

Our fake program isn't going to be written using NXT-G. The best way I can tell you to start creating a fake program is to pretend that SPOT has ears and tell SPOT what you want him to do. Let's try writing some pseudo-code using a numbered list:

1. SPOT, move forward until your Touch sensor is pressed and released. Then, stop.

2. OK, SPOT, I want you to turn left 90 degrees.

3. Now, I want you to give a loud Beep!

4. Good job, SPOT. Now move backward until your Light sensor detects something black. Then, stop.

5. Now, SPOT, do a little dance.

That's pseudo-code? Well, it's a form of pseudo-code. Remember how I told you there are different programming languages? People write pseudo-code differently, too. The point I want you to understand is that before you can really program your robot using NXT-G, you need to have an idea of exactly what your robot will be doing. The easiest way to do this is to simply write down, in simple language, instructions for your robot. That's the beginning of a good structure for the future NXT-G program.

When you write pseudo-code, you are accomplishing three things:

•   You are gaining a better understanding of the tasks your robot will perform.

•   You are looking at the world from the robot's point of view which is important when programming.

•   You are creating an ordered set of instructions (structure) for your robot to follow.

You will use this pseudo-code to assist you when you begin to create your program with NXT-G. One final thing I want to mention about pseudo-code is that each instruction you give the robot should be as simple as possible. Take a look at the next two examples and tell me which one has the simpler instructions:

•   *Example 1*: SPOT, move forward about 10 inches; turn left 90 degrees, and start moving forward; then start looking for a black object with your Ultrasonic sensor, because I want you to stop when you find a black object; then turn right 90 degrees, and move backward 2 feet, OK?

•   *Example 2*:

1. SPOT, move forward 10 inches and stop.

2. Now turn left 90 degrees.

3. Starting moving forward, and turn on your Ultrasonic sensor.

4. Stop when you find a black object.

5. Turn right 90 degrees and stop.

6. Now move backwards 2 feet and stop.

Which example is less complicated to read? If you said Example 2, you are right. Let's be honest—some humans would be confused if you gave them the instructions in Example 1! When writing pseudo-code, break down your instructions into short and simple statements for your robot. This will make it easier for you to convert your pseudo-code to an actual NXT-G program.

Moving Into Real Code

Are you wondering how you convert pseudo-code to a real NXT-G program? Let me give you a small preview of what's to come in the chapters ahead.

Take a look back at my original pseudo-code for SPOT and read step 4, "Now move backward until your Light sensor detects something black. Then, stop."

If I am programming in NXT-G and am familiar with all the tools it contains, I would realize that there are tools (called *blocks*) that match up to my pseudo-code. Why are they called blocks? Take a look at Figure 2-1.

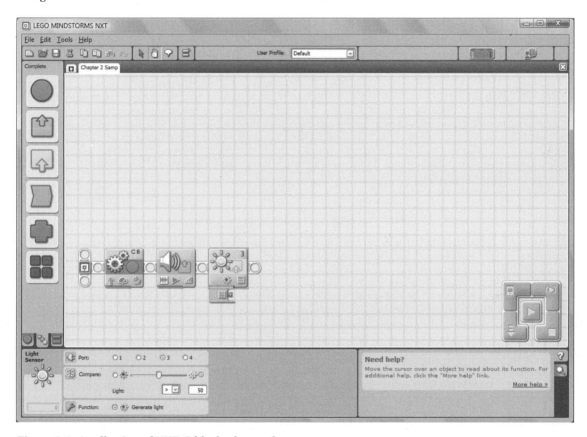

Figure 2-1. *A collection of NXT-G blocks that make up a program*

See those three squares located in the center of the NXT-G software screen in Figure 2-1? Those are blocks! The block on the left (with gears) is the MOVE block. The block in the middle (with the little speaker icon) is the SOUND block. And the block on the right is the SENSOR block—its icon tells me that it's the Light sensor block. Don't worry, you'll learn about all these blocks and more in future chapters (the SOUND block is covered in chapter 6 and the sensors are covered in Chapter 9), but for now I just wanted you to understand what a block is and what it looks like.

When I want SPOT to move backward, he's going to use his motors, right? Well, I'll be using something called a MOVE block. The MOVE block will allow me to program my robot to spin the motors (and wheels) in reverse, so SPOT moves backward.

I only want SPOT to back up until his Light sensor detects the color black. To do this, I'll use something called a SENSOR block to monitor the Light sensor. The SENSOR block will be programmed to look for the color black.

Finally, I want SPOT to stop when the SENSOR block detects the color black. For this, I can use another MOVE block that tells the motors to stop spinning.

You will use these blocks and many more to properly program your robot to follow your instructions. This book will teach you about all the different NXT-G blocks, so you'll know which ones to use when converting your pseudo-code to an NXT-G program.

If you can remember one thing from this chapter, it should be this: Programming your robot will be much easier if you take the time to write down the pseudo-code. If it helps, pretend your robot has ears, and tell it what you want it to do. Write down these instructions, and keep them short and simple.

Exercises

Now, I want to give you some practice in writing pseudo code. It won't take long, but it will require a partner. Ask a friend or teacher or parent to help you with the following two exercises. (Possible solutions to the exercises in the book can be found at the end of each chapter.) If possible, switch roles with your partner for both exercises. This will help you write pseudo code as well as see how easy (or hard) it is to follow instructions.

Exercise 2-1. Move One Object Nearer to Another

Place two objects on a table (such as a pencil and a book). Space the objects with approximately two feet between them and label the object on the left Object 1 and label the object on the right Object 2. Next, have your partner sit in front of the table, with one object to his left and the other object to his right. Write down a bit of pseudo-code and give it to your partner that will instruct him or her (while seated) to pick up Object 1 and move it to a location near Object 2. Then have your partner pick up Object 2 and move it to the approximate original location of Object 1.

Exercise 2-2. Place Objects at Corners

Ask your partner to stand in one corner of a room (any corner is fine and call it Starting Point). Give your partner two objects labeled Object 1 and Object 2. Write pseudo-code that instructs your partner to move along the wall to his right and place Object 2 on the floor at the first corner he encounters. Have your partner continue moving to the next corner (not back to the Starting Point) where he will place Object 1 on the floor. Have your partner reverse direction and return to the Starting Point.

Were there any parts of your pseudo-code that confused your partner (or vice versa)? If so, don't worry. The goal here is to understand that as you program your robots, you'll always want to strive to provide as much detail as possible. The more details, the more likely it will be that your robot succeeds in its endeavors.

What's Next?

In the next chapter, you're going to write some pseudo-code and actually convert it to an NXT-G program. The key to writing excellent NXT-G programs is understanding how the NXT-G programming blocks work. When you know how the blocks work, you'll know which blocks to use when converting your pseudo-code.

Chapter 3 is going to demonstrate the DISPLAY block, a very useful block that gives your robot the ability to write things to its LCD screen for others to read.

Exercise Solutions

There is no single hard-and-fast solution to each of the exercises in this chapter. Many solutions are possible. I present two such possible solutions here. Your own solutions may be different in some details, but overall they should be similar to the ones presented here.

Exercise 2-1

Following is one possible solution to the task of instructing your partner to move one object next to another:

1. *Partner*: Pick up Object 1 to your left.

2. *Partner*: Place Object 1 to the right of Object 2.

3. *Partner*: Pick up Object 2 on your right.

4. *Partner*: Place Object 2 in the approximate original location of Object 1.

Exercise 2-2

Following is a series of steps that should result in your partner dropping one object at each of two corners. Your own solution may vary, but it should be similar to that presented here.

1. *Partner*: Walk along the wall to your right and stop at the first corner you encounter.

2. *Partner*: Place Object 2 on the floor.

3. *Partner*: Without returning to the Starting Point, walk along the wall to the next corner and stop.

4. *Partner*: Place Object 1 on the floor.

5. *Partner*: Reverse your direction and, following the walls, return to the Starting Point.

CHAPTER 3

∎∎∎

Hello World!

There is a tradition in the world of programming for the first program you write to display the words "Hello World!" on the screen. In keeping with tradition, I'm going to show you how to create a simple version of this program for SPOT. This will allow me to demonstrate one of the simplest blocks included with the NXT software—the DISPLAY block. Once you've taken care of tradition, I'll show you the rest of the DISPLAY block's features.

Programming the DISPLAY Block

In Chapter 2, I explained to you the concept of pseudo-code. Let me now give some pseudo-code to SPOT:

SPOT, I'd like you to display the words "Hello World!" on your LCD screen.

Pseudo-code doesn't get much simpler than this. All I want SPOT to do for now is put the words "Hello World!" on his LCD screen. To convert this pseudo-code to an NXT-G program, I'm going to use the DISPLAY block.

Let's start by launching the NXT software and entering **HelloWorld** in the Create New Program text box (see Figure 3-1). Click the Go button, and the HelloWorld program is open and ready.

∎ **Note** Many of the figures used in this book show screens from version 1.0 of the NXT-G retail version of the software. In some instances, the figures are from version 2.0 of the retail software. If you're like me, you're going to have a hard time spotting the differences. In most cases, the workspace, buttons, menus, and other tools are identical between versions. Where the differences are substantial, I'll include images from both versions. In either case, when something is specific to either version 1.0 or version 2.0, I'll let you know. In most cases, however, the differences are so minor that you shouldn't have any difficulty understanding the figures, no matter which version of the software you are using.

Figure 3-1. *Start a new program called HelloWorld*

Figure 3-2 shows the new program opened (see the tab called HelloWorld in the upper left corner?) and ready for you to start dropping NXT-G blocks. The word "Start" appears on the work space beam, telling you where your first programming block will be placed.

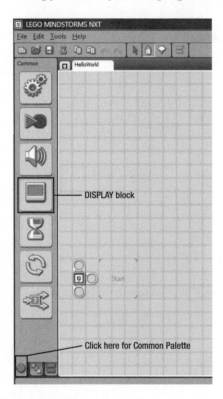

Figure 3-2. *The HelloWorld program is open and ready for the DISPLAY block.*

Are you ready for this? I want you to click the DISPLAY block on the Common Palette and hold down the mouse button. Drag and drop the block on the beam where it says "Start" (see Figure 3-3).

■ **Note** If you don't see the Common Palette along the left side of the screen, click on the green dot indicated in Figure 3-2.

Figure 3-3. *The DISPLAY block*

Anytime you drop a block on the work space, the block's configuration panel will be displayed in the lower left corner of the screen. The configuration panel is where you will be doing most of the programming work for your robots. The configuration panel is similar to a car's dashboard. In a car, you can tune to a specific radio station, turn on the windshield wipers, and even find out the car's speed from the speedometer. The configuration panel allows you to turn on and off certain things as well as receive feedback. For example, you can use the DISPLAY block's configuration panel to choose what to put on the LCD screen, but the DISPLAY block can also receive input from items outside your control, just like your car can display a warning light on the dashboard when you need to check the oil or fill up on gasoline. Figure 3-4 shows the configuration panel for the DISPLAY block you just dropped on to the work space. To see the configuration panel for any block that you've dropped into your program, simply click that block using the Pointer tool, and an aqua-colored band will appear around the block that is selected.

■ **Note** If you select multiple blocks, no configuration panel will be displayed.

Figure 3-4. *Configuration panel for the DISPLAY block*

Now, to have SPOT's LCD screen display the words "Hello World!", make sure you've first selected the DISPLAY block (click it with the Pointer tool).

As you can see in Figure 3-4, by default, the DISPLAY block's Action section has a drop-down menu with the Image option selected (there are four options: Image, Text, Drawing, or Reset). Click the drop-down menu, and select Text from the options listed. You will now see a text box with the words "Mindstorms NXT" inside. Change the text to **Hello World!**, and you'll see the same text displayed in the Position section's preview box on the right side of the configuration panel (see Figure 3-5).

Figure 3-5. The "Hello World!" text is displayed in the preview box.

Now, using the File menu, select Save, and use the Browse button to choose a location to save the file on your computer. Click the Save button when you are finished. After saving, connect SPOT to your computer, and upload the HelloWorld program. (If you're not familiar with how to upload a program, consult the Help documentation. Ideally, however, you should have worked through all the Robo Center or Robo Educator projects to familiarize yourself with this function.)

■ **Note** For the remaining chapters in the book, you'll need to remember to save your programs. I won't keep bugging you with instructions to save your programs and upload them to your robots, OK? Just get in a habit of saving often.

Waiting for the Results

After the program is uploaded, select it from the File section, and press the orange button (also called the Enter button) on the Brick to run the program.

Did you see it? The program probably ran so quickly that you didn't even see the text displayed! Why does this happen? Well, when the program runs it is supposed to write "Hello World!" to the LCD screen and then end. And that's exactly what happened—the text displays, and the program ends. This happens *so fast* that you don't even get to see the text displayed. The good news is that this is very easy to fix, so let me update the pseudo-code before I continue:

SPOT, I'd like you to display the words "Hello World" on your LCD screen for 10 seconds.

There are numerous ways to keep the text on the screen until you have a chance to read it, but I'm only going to show you one method in this chapter. You'll discover other methods as you continue with the book.

To fix this problem, I'd like you to move the mouse pointer over the WAIT block icon on the Common Palette. When you do this, a collection of WAIT blocks will appear on a fly-out menu, as shown in Figure 3-6.

Figure 3-6. Adding a WAIT block will allow you to view the "Hello World!" text.

The WAIT block does exactly what it says—it waits. As you can see in Figure 3-6, there are many different types of WAIT blocks, but the one I'm interested in right now is the WAIT block that allows me to specify how many seconds to wait. That would be the TIME WAIT block (the block that is circled on the fly-out menu in Figure 3-6).

■ **Note** For users of the 1.0 version of NXT-G, you won't see the WAIT icon to the far right in Figure 3-6. That WAIT block is for the Color sensor that is included with the 2.0 Retail set.

Select the icon for the WAIT TIME block, and place it immediately after the DISPLAY block. In the configuration panel for the WAIT TIME block, select a reasonable time for the text to be displayed—my pseudo-code asked SPOT to wait for 10 seconds, so that is what I will configure (see Figure 3-7).

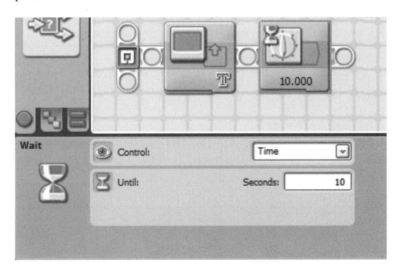

Figure 3-7. Configure the WAIT TIME block for 10 seconds.

Now run the program. You should see the text "Hello World!" display on the LCD screen for 10 seconds before the program ends.

Doing More with DISPLAY

You're probably thinking what I'm thinking, "That wasn't that exciting." But remember this: with programming, you have to start somewhere. And, in a few simple steps, you've now figured out how to add text to the LCD screen for any robot you build in the future. Now, let's look at some of the other things you can do with the DISPLAY block.

■ **Note** Every program block has its own unique settings, so each configuration panel is different. Sections for the DISPLAY block, for example, include Action, Display, File, Text, Type, and Position. Sometimes, a section will not be visible until other options are selected. Don't let this worry you; I'll be going over all the unique items for each block throughout the book.

The Display section only has one configurable item—a Clear checkbox. When this box is checked (and the block is executed in a program), the Brick's LCD screen will be cleared of any text or images that are currently on the screen. After the screen is cleared, the DISPLAY block will put what you configured on the screen.

If you leave the box unchecked, any text or graphics you configure the DISPLAY block to put on the LCD will display on the screen along with whatever is currently displayed, instead of replacing it.

This is useful when you want text to appear on multiple lines; you can use multiple DISPLAY blocks to keep adding text to make sentences and even paragraphs. Without clearing the screen, you can create your own simple images using the Drawing option in the Action section, which I'll explain next.

With the Action section, you have four options in the drop-down menu: Image, Text, Drawing, and Reset. By default, the drop-down menu is set to Image for a new DISPLAY block placed on the work space.

When you select Image in the drop-down menu, the File section is displayed; this section gives you access to a collection of small built-in pictures that can be displayed on the LCD screen (see Figure 3-8).

■ **Note** Version 2.0 of the Retail software now comes with an Image Editor that allows you to make your own images! I'll cover this feature in Appendix C.

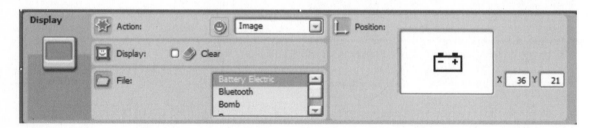

Figure 3-8. Choose an image from the File section to place on the LCD.

By clicking and holding the image in the preview pane on the right side of the configuration panel, you can drag the image around the small pane and place it wherever you wish. You can also use the X and Y coordinates to type in numbers that will place the image at a location of your choosing (see Appendix A for a brief explanation of the X/Y coordinate system if you're unfamiliar with it). You can use this ability to move the image around the preview pane to place multiple images (which require using additional DISPLAY blocks) on the LCD screen.

The next option in the Action drop-down menu is Text. You've already used this in the previous "Hello World!" example, but I'd like to add that you also have the ability to drag the text around the preview pane and place it in a particular location. The LCD screen is broken into eight horizontal lines;

you can use the small drop-down box next to the Preview pane to choose a number between 1 and 8 to define the line where text is placed.

The third option in the Action drop-down menu is Drawing (see Figure 3-9). You can choose to draw a line or a circle or to place a single point on the LCD screen, so your artistic talents will be somewhat limited. To create a detailed drawing, you would have to place dozens or more DISPLAY blocks one after the other, and the combination of lines, circles, and points would create the image. A better solution (for owners of the 2.0 retail software) is to use the built-in Image Editor that I cover in Appendix C. But the Drawing options are available to 1.0 and 2.0 software owners and are useful for drawing boxes around other text on the screen, so keep that in mind.

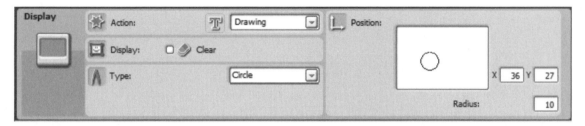

Figure 3-9. The Drawing option can be used to place points, lines, and circles.

To use the Drawing tool, select Point, Line, or Circle from the Type section (this section only appears if you have selected Drawing in the Action drop-down menu). For the point, you can drag it around the Preview pane and place it anywhere. You can also use the X and Y coordinates to place the point more accurately.

For owners of the 1.0 version of the software, if you choose the Line, the end point of the Line is at position 10,10 (in the lower left corner). Click anywhere in the Preview pane to draw a line from that point to the place where you clicked. You can change the end point (10,10) by entering new coordinates in the X and Y boxes. You can also type in X and Y coordinates for the other end of the line for more accurate control over it.

For 2.0 owners, the Line tool works similarly. A line is added automatically—simply click anywhere in the Preview pane and the line will be redrawn with one of its ends terminating on the spot you clicked. Likewise, you can use the X and Y boxes to manually select a starting point for the line as well as use the End Point X and Y boxes to manually enter an ending point for the line.

Finally, for the circle, you have the option of changing the radius of the circle by typing the number in the Radius text box. Drag the circle around the Preview pane to place it properly. Use the X and Y boxes to manually enter the center point of the circle.

The final option in the Action drop-down menu, Reset, is useful when you would like to clear the LCD screen of any items. The default NXT screen (which shows the name of the program currently running) will appear on the LCD screen.

Understanding Data Hubs

Before closing out this chapter on the DISPLAY block, I want to cover one additional item briefly: data hubs (this topic will be covered in more detail in Chapter 7). Most programming blocks come with what's called a "data hub." Take a look at Figure 3-10.

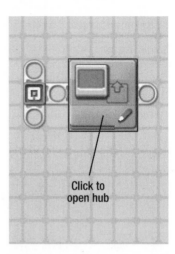

Figure 3-10. Click on the DISPLAY block here and the data hub will drop down.

If you click the bottom-left edge of a block, this section will drop down and reveal the data hub (see Figure 3-11). Click the section again, and the data hub will close. It might take some practice to find the correct place to click, so try it a few times until you get used to opening and closing the data hub.

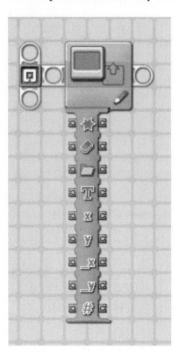

Figure 3-11. The DISPLAY block's data hub can be used for more advanced programming.

What is this data hub? The data hub allows you to draw *data wires* from one block to another using *data plugs*. Data wires and plugs will be covered in much more detail in Chapter 7, but for now, all you really need to know is that wires can connect blocks to share data. Data plugs are places on the block where you will connect wires. So there will be a data plug on one block with a wire going out and another data plug on a different block with a wire coming in. Data wires can carry information such as text, numbers, and other values. Remember all those items you could configure in the DISPLAY block? Well, items such as the text displayed or the radius of a circle can all be configured without using the configuration panel. Instead, you can draw data wires from one block's plugs into plugs on another block. I'll cover this topic in more detail later in the book (in Chapter 7), but right now, I just want you to take a look at Figure 3-12, so I can give you a preview of what's to come.

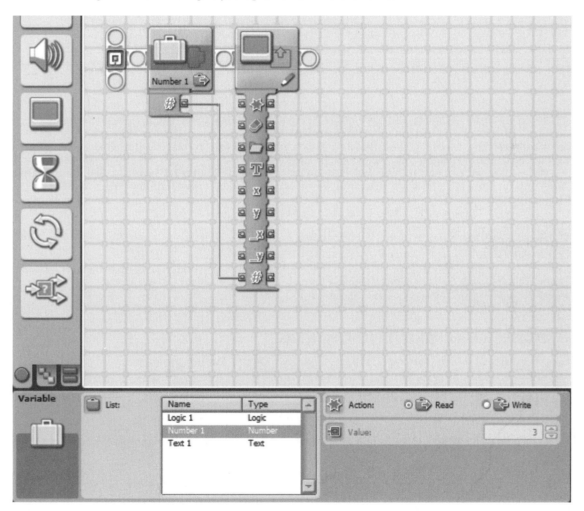

Figure 3-12. An example of one DISPLAY block plug providing data to another block.

In Figure 3-12, I've placed a VARIABLE block in front of the DISPLAY block. I cover the VARIABLE block in Chapter 18, but for now, all you really need to know is that this type of block can hold text, a number, or what's called a logic value (either True or False). In this example, I've configured the VARIABLE block to hold a number: 3.

Now, here's where it gets fun. Remember that when you draw a circle you can specify the radius of the circle in the configuration panel? Well, this VARIABLE block has only one plug in its data hub. For this block, it's holding the value of 3. I click that plug and draw a line into the last plug of the DISPLAY block's data hub. That last plug corresponds to the radius of a drawn circle (hover your mouse pointer over a plug, and it will tell you what it is). When I drag the wire *out* of the VARIABLE block plug and *into* the DISPLAY block plug, the line becomes solid yellow, and I know I've correctly configured the DISPLAY block.

■ **Note** Plugs on the left side of a block's data hub are known as *input plugs*. Plugs on the right side of the block's data hub are called *output plugs*.

If the line is dotted, it tells me I've incorrectly connected two plugs. This can happen for many reasons. For example, if I had put text into the VARIABLE block and dragged the wire into the DISPLAY block's Radius plug, I would get a dotted line. This happens because the Radius plug expects a number value to be coming out of the VARIABLE block, not text.

As I mentioned earlier, I'll cover data plugs in more detail in Chapter 7. Before you begin using these data wires for more advanced programming, however, you need to understand the basics of the programming blocks.

Exercises

Now it's time to get some more practice with the DISPLAY and WAIT TIME blocks that you learned about in this chapter. Below are two exercises for creating new NXT-G programs for SPOT. (If you get stuck, the answers are at the end of this chapter.)

Exercise 3-1. Display Your Own Text

For this exercise, I'd like you to modify the HelloWorld program. For this program, I want you to enter one line of text near the top of the LCD screen, a picture (your choice) below the text, and have both items displayed for 25 seconds before the program ends.

■ **Tip** Keeping both the text and the picture on the screen at the same time requires a special option to be deselected.

Exercise 3-2: Draw a Rectangle

Use four DISPLAY blocks to manually draw a rectangle (or make it more challenging and draw a square) to the LCD screen. After a side of the square is drawn, have the robot pause for 5 seconds before drawing the next side. When the square is completed, have the robot pause for 10 seconds before the program ends.

■ **Tip** Read Appendix A for help with the coordinate system and the starting and end points of each line.

What's Next

Spot needs to get moving! It's a little dull just watching him sit on the floor, so let's continue learning about blocks in Chapter 4 by giving him somewhere to go. You'll learn all about doing this with the MOVE block.

Exercise Solutions

Following are some possible exercise solutions. Remember, your solutions may be somewhat different. Results are what matter. Very often, there is more than one way to get to the same end result.

Exercise 3-1

Figure 3-13 shows the program for one possible solution. Figure 3-13 also shows the configuration panel for the first of the three program blocks. Figures 3-14 and 3-15 show the panels for the other two blocks. Notice that the second DISPLAY block (from the left) has its Clear box unchecked (Figure 3-14). Unchecking that box will keep the words "I did it!" on the LCD screen while the image is also displayed. If the Clear box remains checked, the text will be erased and only the image will be displayed.

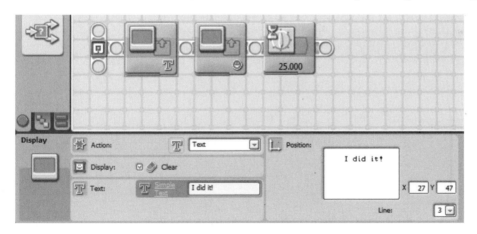

Figure 3-13. Program's blocks and configuration panel for first DISPLAY block.

Figure 3-14. Configuration panel for second DISPLAY block.

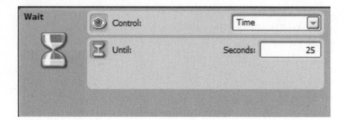

Figure 3-15. Configuration panel for WAIT TIME block.

Exercise 3-2

Figures 3-16 through 3-23 show the eight configuration panels for the eight blocks used in the program I wrote as my own solution to Exercise 3-2. Figure 3-16 shows the panel for the first block. Figures 3-17 through 3-23 show the panels for subsequent blocks.

    Notice that the first three WAIT TIME blocks (Figures 3-17, 3-19, 3-21) are all configured for 5 seconds; only the last WAIT TIME block (Figure 3-23) is set for 10 seconds. Do you see how the coordinates are manually entered to make the lines all match up perfectly? Try to modify the coordinates to draw a perfect square. Also, remember that the Clear checkbox must be unchecked for the last three DISPLAY blocks (but not the first).

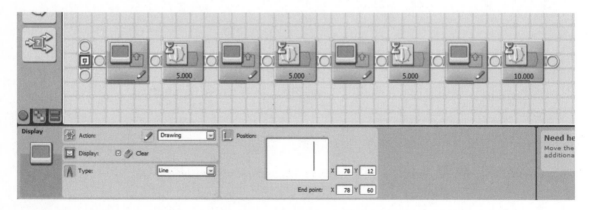

Figure 3-16. The program for Exercise 4 and the first DISPLAY block's configuration panel.

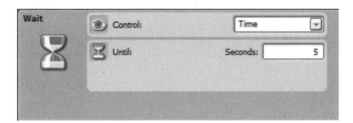

Figure 3-17. *Configuration panel for the first WAIT TIME block.*

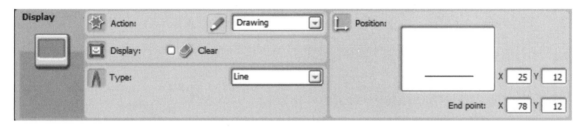

Figure 3-18. *Configuration panel for the second DISPLAY block.*

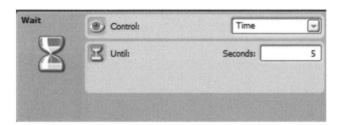

Figure 3-19. *Configuration panel for the second WAIT TIME block.*

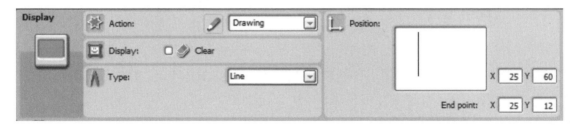

Figure 3-20. *Configuration panel for the third DISPLAY block.*

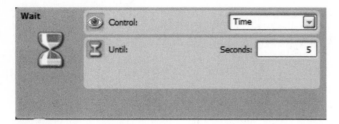

Figure 3-21. Configuration panel for the third WAIT TIME block.

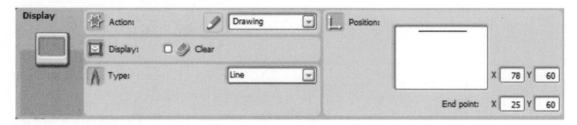

Figure 3-22. Configuration panel for the fourth DISPLAY block.

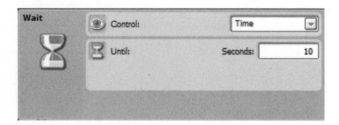

Figure 3-23. Configuration panel for the final WAIT TIME block.

CHAPTER 4

■■■

Get Movin'

I would say that the MOVE block is probably one of the most important blocks when it comes to programming a robot. Without the MOVE block, you can still build robots, but they won't be able to do much. They can sit on a desk or table (just like SPOT), but they're not going to be very exciting to watch. Any robot that you design that uses one or more motors will use the MOVE block.

So, let's go over this very important block and see what it can do.

The MOVE block

Open your Mindstorms NXT software, and drag and drop a MOVE block from the Common Palette onto the beam. The configuration panel will appear in the lower left corner of the screen (see Figure 4-1).

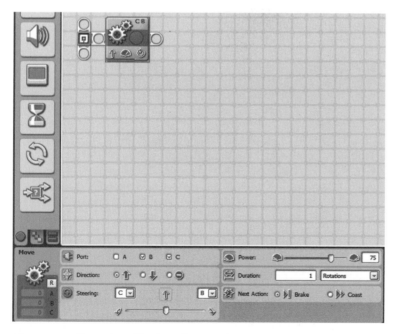

Figure 4-1. The MOVE block and its configuration panel

Your Brick has three ports for motors: Port A, Port B, and Port C. You must plug motors into these ports in order for them to work properly. Motors have numerous options including how fast they spin (Power) and how long or far they spin (Duration). By default, a MOVE block is configured to control Port B and Port C on the Brick; this is indicated by the two boxes that are checked for Port B and Port C in Figure 4-1. The other defaults include a Power setting of 75 and a Duration of 1 Rotation, and the Next Action is set to Brake. The Steering control has a small bar that can be dragged left or right. By default, it is midway between the selected motors (B and C) so there will be no tendency to turn in either direction.

Moving Forward and Backward

Before I move on, I want to bring to your attention the subject of motor spin direction. Take a look at Figure 4-2. It shows a motor in two different orientations.

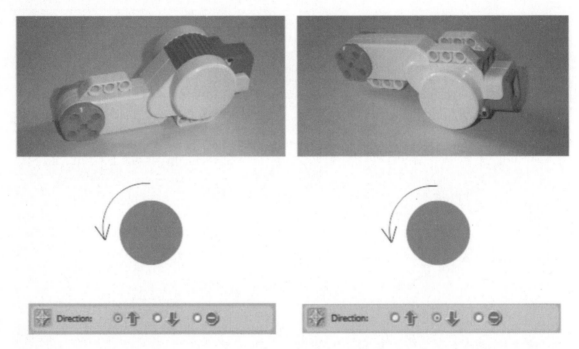

Figure 4-2. A MOVE block can configure a motor to spin in two different directions (note the direction settings for each).

All motors can spin forward and backward. But you need to be careful when describing a motor as "spinning forward" or "spinning backward," because the orientation of the motor also needs to be described. When you program, you have to take into consideration the orientation of the motor.

In Figure 4-2, the motor on the left has the up arrow selected in the Direction section on the MOVE block configuration panel. This up arrow corresponds to FORWARD, and this motor spins in the direction shown, counterclockwise. Now, if I flip this motor over (like the motor on the right side of Figure 4-2) but don't change the Direction arrow selection, the motor will spin in the opposite direction (clockwise). I have to change the Direction arrow to down (or REVERSE) to make the motor spin counterclockwise when it's positioned like the motor on the right. The good news, however, is that if you build a robot and program it to roll forward but it instead rolls backwards, it's so easy to fix. Just select the MOVE block in question and select the other Direction setting to fix the robot's movement direction.

Be sure to keep this in mind when building and programming your bots. Depending on whether you want your robot to move forward or backward, you'll have to select the proper Direction arrow (up or down) based on how the motors are attached to the robot.

Okay, now let's go over the rest of the MOVE block configuration panel.

First, I'll cover the ports. The MOVE block can control Ports A, B, and C and any motors attached to those ports. There is no rule for the way in which you connect motors to ports, but I would recommend that you decide on a "standard" method for connecting motors and stick with it for all robots you build.

As an example, look at Figure 4-3. When I build a robot I always connect the motor on the left side of the Brick (with the Brick's sensor ports on the bottom and motor ports on top) to Port B and the motor on the right side of the Brick to Port C. I always use Port A for my third motor. If I build a robot that doesn't need a third motor, Port A is always left open.

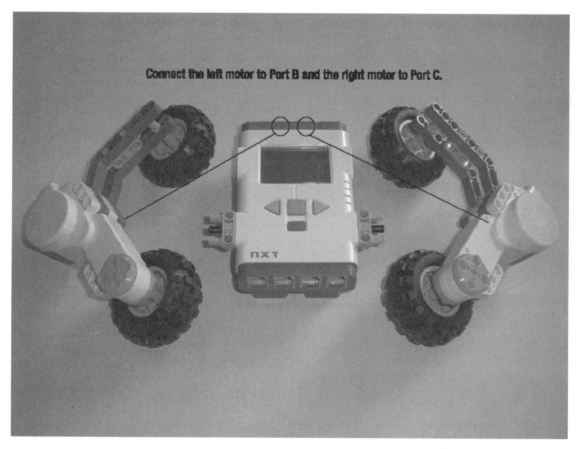

Figure 4-3. *Pick a method for connecting your motors to your ports, and try to always use it.*

When you connect a motor to a port, you must make certain to check the box for that Port in the MOVE block's configuration panel (see Figure 4-4). In Figure 4-4, you'll also notice that the motor ports you select (in this example, Ports B and C) are listed on the MOVE block in the upper right corner. This can be helpful for troubleshooting and to remind you which motors will be used.

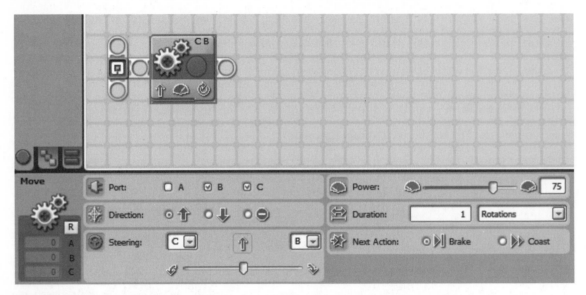

Figure 4-4. Use the MOVE block's configuration panel to select motor ports.

I've made a certain mistake more than once, and I'm sure you're likely to encounter it at some point. When you select a MOVE block and place it on the screen, ports B and C are selected by default. When programming a single motor—motor B, for example—it's very easy to forget to uncheck the box for motor C. Then, when you run upload the program to your robot and run it, all of a sudden it's doing some very strange things. Always remember to check your MOVE blocks and make certain that the ports that are selected are the motors you wish to be controlled by that particular block.

Stopping

I've already mentioned the Direction control using the up and down arrows (or FORWARD and REVERSE). The other option shown in Figure 4-5 is STOP. If you select the STOP option, check the Port boxes for the motor(s) you want to stop.

Figure 4-5. Select the STOP option in the MOVE configuration panel to stop selected motors.

Keep in mind that the Stop option is not permanent for your program. It simply stops whatever motors are being controlled at the moment. If the next block is another MOVE block that starts motor B spinning, then motor B will spin. The Stop action does not override any additional MOVE blocks that come later in the program.

Steering

The next item to discuss is steering. Figure 4-6 shows the Steering section that is available if you have selected either FORWARD or REVERSE for the Direction and have two motor ports checked.

■ **Note** If you select all three motor ports in the Port section of the configuration panel, the Steering control is turned off.

Figure 4-6. The MOVE block's Steering control in the configuration panel

The Steering control can be very useful if you know how to use it. Depending on its setting, you can configure a robot to move in a small or large circle or just spin in place.

If you have two motors configured for your robot's movement (Ports B and C, for example), you can make your robot spin in place by dragging the Steering control all the way to the left or right (the direction you drag the control will determine if the robot spins clockwise or counterclockwise). Try it! Drag the slider all to the way to the left. Save your program, upload it to your robot, and run the program. Which direction did the robot spin? Now let's change it. Drag the slider all the way to the right. Save, upload, and run the program again. Did the robot spin in the opposite direction?

You can also program your robot to drive in a circle; the size of the circle depends on how far you drag the Steering control left or right: dragging it closer to either the far right or far left will make the circle smaller. You'll have to play around with the Steering control to get the size of the circle just the way you want it. Go ahead and try this, too. Drag the Steering slider to the left but not all the way. Upload the program, and run it. Did the robot move in a small or large circle? Try it again, but this time, move the Steering slider to a different location before you upload and run the program. Did the robot move in a smaller or larger circle?

Power Settings

Next on the configuration panel is the Power section (see Figure 4-7). The Power setting range is 0 to100. You can type a value into the Power text box or drag the sliding bar to the right (to decrease power) or to the left (to increase power).

Figure 4-7. The MOVE block's Power setting has a range of 0 to 100.

Most uses of the Power setting will involve increasing or decreasing the spin speed of a motor. But there is one additional consideration, and that is lifting or pushing strength. If your robot is lifting a heavy object, for example, you might need to set the Power setting to a higher value. The motor will not spin as fast as it would if there were no resistance, but you may find that you need that extra power for the motor to successfully lift the object. The same goes for pushing. To push an object, your robot might need a higher Power setting than it will if it's not pushing anything. Surface conditions also affect power; climbing a hill will take more power and possibly slow the robot. Likewise, going down a hill won't take as much power. Also, whether a surface is smooth or rough can affect power; for example, you need more power to move over carpet than wood flooring. This is one of those settings where you'll just have to experiment. Change the Power setting, and play around with the Steering slider. See how fast or slow you can program your robot to make a circle. This will give you a better understanding of how the Power setting will affect your future bots.

Do keep in mind, too, that the Power setting will also affect the life of your batteries. Speed comes at the sacrifice of battery power. When testing your robots, I recommend setting your MOVE block power values down to 20, 30, or 40 to conserve battery power. If you find this isn't enough power during testing, bump it up. But if you want your batteries to last longer, use a lower Power setting whenever possible.

Duration Settings

The Duration section of the configuration panel offers the most control of the MOVE block. There are four options in the Duration drop-down menu: Unlimited, Degrees, Rotations, and Seconds (see Figure 4-8).

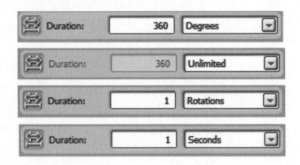

Figure 4-8. *There are four options for the Duration section of a MOVE block.*

From the Duration section, you can choose to have your motors spin forever by clicking the drop-down menu and choosing Unlimited. When the Duration is set to Unlimited, a single MOVE block will continue to spin its motors until the program ends or until you stop it. (There are other ways to stop a MOVE block such as using a LOOP block; I'll cover the LOOP block in Chapter 11.)

If you set the MOVE block Duration to Degrees, you must enter a value in the text box for the number of degrees for the motor(s) to spin. The value must be 0 or greater; it cannot be negative, but this limitation is simple to fix. If you wish for your motor to spin –90 degrees, for example, you simply type **90** in the text box and change the MOVE block Direction to its opposite setting (if it's set to spin FORWARD, just change it to REVERSE). If you've experimented with other programming environments, this may be unusual; it's possible you may have learned to use negative numbers to represent counterclockwise spinning of motors. Don't worry; you'll get used to the NXT-G method of simply changing the motor spin direction in the configuration panel. Just experiment with this concept and it will start to make sense. Remember that your robot can spin a positive number of degrees, but you have to tell it whether to spin clockwise or counterclockwise by using the FORWARD or REVERSE directional controls.

If the Duration is set to Rotations, the same rules apply. You cannot enter a negative value for rotations, but any value of 0 and higher is acceptable. In order to spin the motor(s), a negative number of rotations, just change the Direction to its opposite setting (FORWARD or REVERSE). One thing you *can* do with Rotations is use fractional or decimal values. For example, you could configure a motor to spin 2.35 rotations or 50.9 rotations.

You may be wondering why you would ever want to configure a motor to spin 2.35 rotations. Well, I'll be covering that in this book's appendix when I show you how to program MOVE blocks for specific distances. For now, just keep in mind that your bots have the ability to move very small distances or very large distances with good accuracy, and it all depends on your ability to figure out exactly how many degrees or rotations to spin the motors (feel free to skip ahead to the appendix if you just can't wait).

The last option in the Duration section is Seconds. When you choose this option, you must specify the number of seconds for the MOVE block to spin a motor (or motors). For obvious reasons, you can't configure it for a negative value (say, –5 seconds). Just type in the number of seconds you want the motor(s) to spin, and you're finished. Like rotations, you can also specify fractional times such as 3.5 seconds.

Braking and Coasting

Now, take a look at Figure 4-9, which shows the last option you can configure for the MOVE block—the Next Action section. There are two options: Brake and Coast. If you select the Brake option, any motors connected to the ports you've configured will be stopped *fast* when the Duration you set expires (for example, after 10 seconds). Braking is useful if you need your robot to stop quickly and accurately at a specific point. However, keep in mind that this takes battery power.

Figure 4-9. You can configure motors to brake or coast.

But what if you're not concerned about your robot stopping accurately? Then choose the Coast option. When you choose this option, any motors connected to the ports you've configured will stop receiving power, but the robot's momentum may carry it a little further; that's why it's labeled Coast— your robot will be coasting for a little while. You definitely want to try this out! So let's do that with some pseudo-code: SPOT, move forward 10 rotations at a Power of 75 and then Brake.

The MOVE block I've configured for SPOT is shown in Figure 4-10. Notice that I've configured Duration for 10 Rotations and Power at 75, and I've selected the Brake option. SPOT is also using Ports B and C for its motors, and I want it to travel in a straight line, so I've left the Steering control alone.

Figure 4-10. The braking pseudo-code has been converted to a NXT-G program for SPOT.

Now, when I upload and run this program, SPOT rapidly moves forward 10 rotations (about 6 feet) and comes to a quick stop.

Let's try a different test: SPOT, move backward 720 degrees at a Power of 100, and then Coast.

This time, I want SPOT to move in reverse, and I want the motors in Ports B and C to spin for 720 degrees. I want him to move *very fast*, so I've set the Power setting to 100. I don't need him to stop at a specific point, so I'll let him coast to a stop. See Figure 4-11 for the block programming of the pseudo-code.

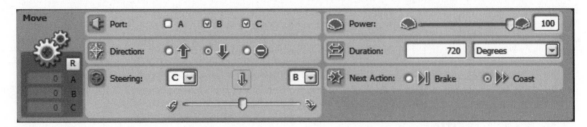

Figure 4-11. A new coasting program for SPOT

After I uploaded and ran this program, I watched as SPOT moved even faster in reverse for 720 degrees (about 15 inches). But this time, he didn't stop right away; he continued to roll for a few more inches, because I programmed him to coast to a stop.

Now, it's your turn. Using what you've learned in this chapter, create some different programs for your robot.

When you're finished, I have another test for you to run: Program your robot to move forward for 10 rotations at a Power setting of 50, and set it to Brake. Place a piece of tape on the floor, and make this your robot's starting position. Now, run the program, and mark its stopping position with tape as well.

Next, run the same program, but change the Brake option to Coast. How far did it go beyond the previous stopping position?

Finally, reduce the Power setting a little bit, and run the program again (with the Coast option). How far did it go beyond the stopping position this time?

Keep reducing the Power setting and running the program until the robot stops at the original stopping position.

Why am I asking you to do this? Recall that I told you that the Brake option uses up battery power. This test shows you that you can save battery power by reducing the Power setting and keeping the Coast option. Running tests like this will help you to figure out how best to program your robot to save battery power and to correctly perform its programmed actions!

Exercises

Before finishing up this chapter, I have a couple of exercises for you that will give you some experience using the MOVE block along with the previous blocks you've learned about (WAIT and DISPLAY). Try to create the programs yourself; if you find you need help, I'll put two possible solutions at the end of the chapter.

Exercise 4-1. Drive in a Circle

Program your robot to roll forward in a circular pattern (to the left or right) using rotations for the Duration option. Try to get the robot to stop when it's reached its original starting point. When the robot stops, have it display "I'm Home!" on the LCD screen for 10 seconds before the program ends.

Exercise 4-2: Make an "S"

Program your robot to roll forward in an S-shape pattern; have it first make a counterclockwise turn and then change direction and make a clockwise turn. The curves of the S can be as large or as short as you like.

What's Next?

That's it for the MOVE block. Feel free to play around with the MOVE block until you're comfortable with it. Then, continue on to Chapter 5, where I cover the RECORD/PLAY block.

Exercise Solutions

Following are two possible solutions to the exercises. Remember that my solutions may vary somewhat from your own. It's the end result that matters. If your program produces the result you're after, then you've succeeded.

Exercise 4-1

Figures 4-12 through 4-14 show the program and the three configuration panels for the three blocks used in this program. Notice that the MOVE block has its steering control dragged slightly to the right but not all the way; when I uploaded this to my robot, it caused the robot to move in a counterclockwise direction. You'll need to experiment with the number of rotations; the distance you've dragged the steering control to the right or left will affect the number of rotations required to return to the starting point. The DISPLAY and WAIT TIME configuration panels are also shown.

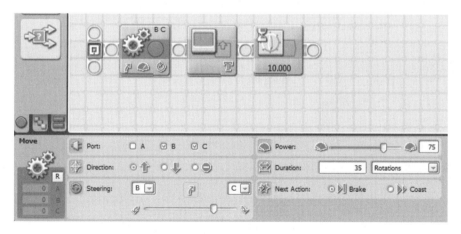

Figure 4-12. The complete program and the MOVE block configuration panel

Figure 4-13. The DISPLAY block configuration panel

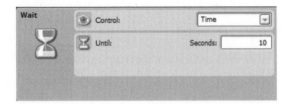

Figure 4-14. The WAIT TIME block configuration panel

Exercise 4-2

Figures 4-15 and 4-16 show the program and the two configuration panels for the two blocks used in this program. Notice that the first MOVE block has its steering control dragged slightly to the right with a Duration setting of 3 rotations. This will have the robot rolling forward in a counterclockwise direction. After 3 rotations of the motors, the second MOVE block will have the robot roll forward for 3 rotations, but this time the steering control is dragged to the left slightly. This will have the robot rolling forward in a clockwise direction, finishing the S-shaped path.

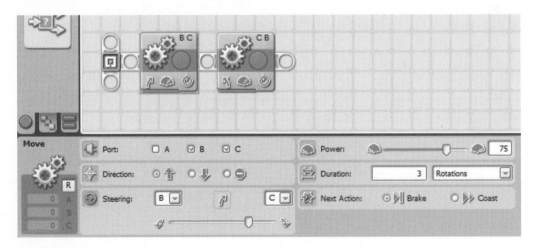

Figure 4-15. The complete program and the first MOVE block's configuration panel

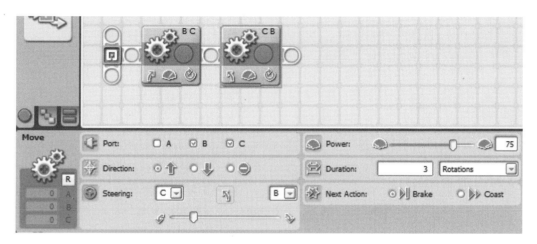

Figure 4-16. *The second MOVE block's configuration panel*

CHAPTER 5

■ ■ ■

Record and Playback

One nice feature of the NXT-G programming language is the RECORD/PLAY block. With this block, you can record the movements of your bot's motors to a file that is stored on the Brick. This file can be used to later play back the bot's movement.

For this chapter, we'll use SPOT again. But this time, I'm going to add one additional motor (motor A) to make SPOT do something silly, like spin an arm or a sensor around. Feel free to do what you like. My SPOT has motor B (in Port B) spinning the left wheel of my robot and motor C (in Port C) spinning the right wheel. I have motor A (in Port A) spinning a small propeller (like an airplane) on the front of the robot (see Figure 5-1).

Figure 5-1. SPOT with his new propeller

The RECORD/PLAY Block

I'm ready to record some basic movement. If you've built your own version of SPOT, follow along.

The RECORD/PLAY block is located on the Common Palette directly below the MOVE block. Drag and drop a RECORD/PLAY block on the beam (see Figure 5-2).

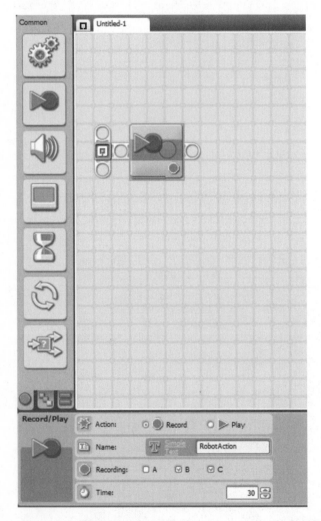

Figure 5-2. Start recording a bot's movements with the RECORD/PLAY block.

I know it seems like common sense, but I still need to say it: we cannot play back SPOT's recorded movements until we've actually recorded some. So the first thing we need to do is configure the RECORD/PLAY block to record SPOT's movements. To do this, in the block's Action section, select the Record option as shown in Figure 5-3. This is the default setting when you drop a RECORD/PLAY block onto the workspace.

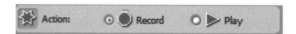

Figure 5-3. First, choose the Record option in the Action section.

Next, we need to specify a name for the recorded movement. As an example, I want SPOT to move forward two feet (motors B and C will be spinning forward) and turn left. I then want motor A to spin the propeller a few times. I'm going to type the words **Takeoff** in the Name text box, shown in Figure 5-4, but you can type whatever description you like that will help you remember the purpose of the recorded movement.

Figure 5-4. Give your recorded movement a unique name.

The name you type in the Name text box is the name of a file that will be stored on the Brick. This file must be stored on the Brick in order for you to later play back the movement, so try to make the name memorable and easy to understand.

Now, look at Figure 5-5. The Recording section of the configuration panel is where you will specify which ports should be monitored. In my example, motors B and C will move my robot around, and motor A will spin the propeller. So I want to select all the ports. If you are not using one of the motor ports, you don't need to select it. You won't get an error if you select a motor port and don't use it, however.

Figure 5-5. Configure the motor ports to monitor and record.

The last item you will need to configure is the amount of time (in seconds) you wish to record your bot's movements (see Figure 5-6). You can type in the number of seconds you want to record or click the up and down arrows with your mouse to select the number in the Time section.

Figure 5-6. Enter the number of seconds to record in the Time section.

You can record anywhere from one second up into the hundreds of minutes. Is this realistic? Not really. Your NXT Brick has a limited amount of memory, and you'll find that you are limited to a few minutes at most. And even recording a few minutes of movement will probably not leave much memory for your actual program. You'll have to play around with the Time section to test its limits.

Recording Movement

Once you've got your RECORD/PLAY block configured, save the program, and upload it to your NXT bot. Place the robot at its starting position, and press the Run button for your new program. *Using your hands,* guide the robot through the movements you wish your robot to perform.

For my example, I simply push the robot forward two feet and stop. I then turn the robot to the left and stop. Next, I spin the little propeller on the front of the robot five or six times, and I'm finished.

I suggest that you time your movements as you're doing them. If you come close to the number of seconds you configured, you can simply leave the recording time alone. If you didn't have enough time, go back and add the right number of seconds to your program, save it, and run it again to record the complete movements. Most importantly, if you originally configured *too much time*, reduce the number of seconds you entered in the Time section; because the recording process will continue to run until the time is over, the file stored on the Brick will be larger than it needs to be.

Replaying Movement

Okay, so you've successfully recorded your bot's movements, and there is a file stored on the Brick with the name you gave it in the Name section (you can verify this by connecting your Brick to your computer and checking its memory contents). Now, let me show you how to play back the file.

It's so easy, you're going to laugh. Create a new program, and drop in a RECORD/PLAY block. This time, however, select the Play option in the Action section (see Figure 5-7).

■ **Note** If you have your NXT Brick connected to your computer via the USB cable, any files stored on the NXT that you created using the RECORD/PLAY block will appear in the File section seen in Figure 5-7. Rather than type the name of the file, you can select it from the list. If you do not have your NXT Brick connected, you will need to remember the name of the file and type it in the Name section.

Figure 5-7. Configure your robot to play back the recorded movement.

The only other section that can be configured now is the Name section. Type the name of the file that contains the recorded movements in the Name section (see Figure 5-8). For my example, I've typed **Takeoff**, the name I gave the file that moves the robot forward two feet, turns it left, and then spins the propeller a few times.

Figure 5-8. *Enter the name of the file you created during the Record process.*

Next, you need to save the new program and upload it to your Brick. Before you run the program, place your robot in the original starting position (or wherever you like), and press the Run button to run the program. The robot will begin to move and will match the movements you recorded earlier. That's it for the RECORD/PLAY block.

Having Fun with Record/Play

Here are some ideas for using the RECORD/PLAY block:

- A fun use for it is to record your robot doing some sort of dance (for ten to twenty seconds) and save it to a file called Dance. If you keep the Dance file on your Brick, you can drop in a RECORD/PLAY block anywhere in your program and have your robot do the little dance (you can drop it in multiple times, too).

- Teams could use this block when giving a presentation. The robot might have interesting parts and mechanisms that you wish to focus attention on, and the RECORD/PLAY block could be used to let the audience view these more easily. Configure the times properly, and you can synchronize it to a speech given on the robot and its different components.

Exercises

Now, let's try some exercises using what we know. If you need solutions to the following exercises, I've placed them at the end of this chapter.

Exercise 5-1: Record a Cha-cha-cha Movement

Record your robot performing a short (3–4 seconds) cha-cha-cha movement—just wiggling back and forth in short movements. Have the file saved as "ChaChaCha" on the Brick.

Exercise 5-2: Roll Forwards and Backwards First

Program your robot to roll forwards a few inches and then backwards a few inches using MOVE blocks… and then do a cha-cha-cha movement. Have your robot perform this set of actions one more time.

What's Next?

Chapter 6 will show you how to give your robot the ability to talk and make some noise! While this isn't a requirement for your robot, adding sound makes a robot much more interesting. There's even a way to add your own sounds and music to the NXT (for NXT 2.0 owners)! I'll show you how all this is done next.

Possible Solutions to Exercises

Below are the solutions for the exercises I gave you earlier. Keep in mind that you can modify these exercises and try new things—it's a great way to learn.

Exercise 7

Figure 5-9 contains the program and the single configuration panel used in this program. Be sure to write down the name you used for the file as you'll need it for Exercise 8. Save this program and upload it to your robot. Run the program and perform the back and forth movements for no more than five seconds.

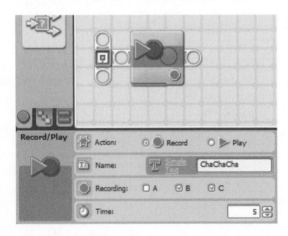

Figure 5-9. *A single RECORD/PLAY block is required to record a movement.*

Exercise 8

Figures 5-10 through 5-15 contain the program and the configuration panels for the blocks used in this program. Note that although the MOVE blocks look similar, the only change between the first and second MOVE blocks is the Direction setting (and the same goes for the third and fourth MOVE blocks). This instructs the robot to roll forward one rotation and then roll backwards one rotation… and then do the cha-cha-cha movement. The last three blocks are simply repeats of the first three.

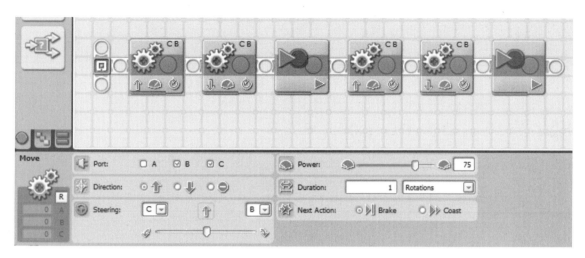

Figure 5-10. The complete program and the first MOVE block's configuration panel

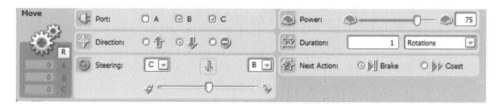

Figure 5-11. The second MOVE block's configuration panel

Figure 5-12. The first RECORD/PLAY block's configuration panel

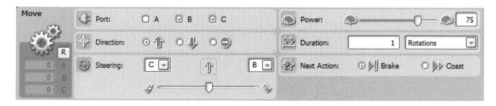

Figure 5-13. The third MOVE block's configuration panel

49

Figure 5-14. The fourth MOVE block's configuration panel

Figure 5-15. The final RECORD/PLAY block's configuration panel

CHAPTER 6

■ ■ ■

Make Some Noise!

Sound can be used to give a bot more personality. Think about how boring R2-D2 would be without all the chirps and whistles. Well, you can give your bot plenty to say by using the SOUND block. Sound isn't limited to just giving your bots character, though. Sounds can be useful as a way to judge your bot's progress through a maze, for example, with the bot programmed to issue specific sounds when it makes a left or encounters a dead end. And if you find that the sound you need for your robot doesn't exist— well, users of NXT-G 2.0 will find a new feature that allows them to record and use custom sounds using the SOUND block! Read on for all the details on the SOUND block.

The SOUND Block

When you drop in the SOUND block on the beam, you are given access to the configuration panel shown in Figure 6-1.

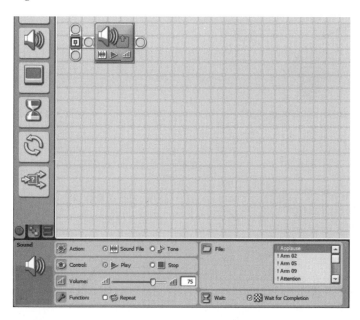

Figure 6-1. The SOUND block's configuration panel

Action Settings

The first section I want to cover is the Action section. You have two options: Sound File or Tone.

Sound File

Select the Sound File option, and take a look at Figure 6-2. See the section called File? Clicking the Sound File option opens the File section; the File section contains a large collection of prerecorded sounds that your bot can play through the Brick's speaker. Click one of the sound files, and if your computer has speakers, you will hear the sound file play. There are over 100 unique sound files that you can select from the list.

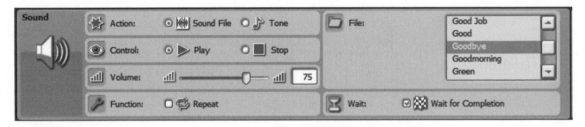

Figure 6-2. The Sound File option allows you to select a sound from the File section.

■ **Note** If you are using NXT-G 2.0, I'll show you later in the chapter how to use the built-in Sound Editor that allows you to modify existing sounds or create your own! If you follow the instructions carefully, any new sounds you add will appear in the File listing in Figure 6-2.

Tone

Now, select the other option, Tone. Notice that the File section changes to a section called Note (see Figure 6-3).

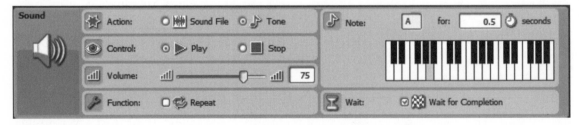

Figure 6-3. The Tone option allows you to specify tones from the Note section.

Note Settings

The Note section provides you with a few options. The easiest option is to simply click one of the piano keys. You will hear the tone played if your computer has speakers attached. Notice that when you click on a key, the note you click is displayed in the text box above the keys in the form of a letter: A, B, C, D, E, F, or G (with sharps for the black keys).

The other option available in the Note section is the ability to specify how long the note will play. Type a number in the text box for the number of seconds to play the note.

That covers the Action section; the remaining sections for the SOUND block (Control, Volume, Function, and Wait) are the same regardless of whether you choose the Sound File or Tone option. Now, let me explain each of these remaining sections.

Control Settings

The second section on the SOUND block is Control. This section has two options: Play and Stop (see Figure 6-4).

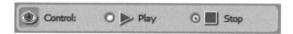

Figure 6-4. The Control section of the SOUND block

The Play option is simple. Select it, and any sound file or tone you selected in the Action section will play. Not too difficult, right?

The Stop option requires a little more explanation. To do this, I need to jump ahead to the Function section (see Figure 6-5).

Figure 6-5. The Function section of the SOUND block

Function Settings

The Function section has only one option: Repeat. If the box is checked, the Sound File or Tone will continue to play until your program ends, or until another SOUND block is reached with the Stop option selected in the Control section. If the box is unchecked, the sound file or tone will play only *one* time.

So, you can see that the Stop option is useful *only* when you have another SOUND block that is continually playing.

Volume Settings

OK, now for the Volume section. You can see in Figure 6-6 that the Volume control can be changed either by using the slider or by typing a value (0 to 100) in the text box. You will have to experiment with the Volume control to determine what works best for your robots, but keep in mind that loud sounds will use up more battery power than sounds played at a lower volume.

Figure 6-6. *The Volume section of the SOUND block*

Wait Settings

The last section in the SOUND block is the Wait section (see Figure 6-7). When you have selected a sound file or tone to play and the Repeat box (in the Function section) is not checked, the Wait for Completion checkbox is available.

Figure 6-7. *The Wait section of the SOUND block*

If you place a check in the Wait for Completion box, the Sound File or Tone you choose will play completely before any further programming blocks are executed. Let me give you an example using pseudo-code: SPOT, play me a C note for ten seconds and then move forward five rotations.

Now, here's how I will convert the pseudo-code into a NXT-G program. First, I drop in a SOUND block and configure it to play a C note for ten seconds (see Figure 6-8). I'm going to leave the Wait for Completion box unchecked and set the Volume to 75.

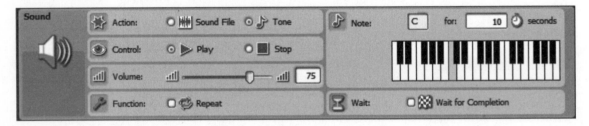

Figure 6-8. *SPOT will first play a C note for ten seconds.*

Next, I'm going to drop in a MOVE block (see Figure 6-9). I'll configure this MOVE block to spin motor B and motor C FORWARD for five rotations and then Brake. I'm also going to set Power at 50.

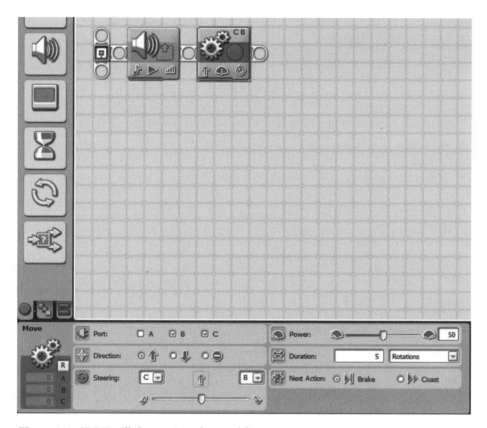

Figure 6-9. SPOT will then MOVE forward five rotations.

Next, I save the program, upload it to SPOT, and run it. Go ahead and create and run this same program on your bot. What happens?

Well, I pressed the Run button and the C note started to play. But before the C note stopped, motors B and C started spinning. What happened?

Go back to Figure 6-8, and notice that the Wait For Completion box is unchecked. This means that when the SOUND block starts playing, the program will continue to the MOVE block that spins the motors. But that's not what I wanted SPOT to do. Take a look again at the pseudo-code: SPOT, play a C note for ten seconds and *then* move forward five rotations.

I wanted SPOT to play the C note for ten seconds before moving forward. To do this, I simply need to go back to my SOUND block and check the Wait for Completion box. This will tell SPOT to wait until the SOUND block is finished (ten seconds) before continuing with the program. So, I make this change (see Figure 6-10) and run the program again.

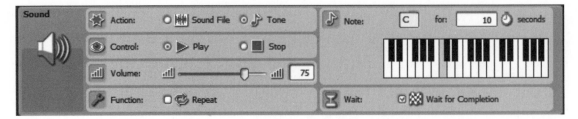

Figure 6-10. Making one change to the SOUND block will fix the problem.

This time, SPOT does exactly what I wanted him to do. He plays the C note for ten seconds, and when the SOUND block is finished, motors B and C spin, and SPOT moves forward five rotations. Perfect!

Now you can add sound files and tones to your robots to give them more personality. But before we finish this chapter, let me also tell you that sounds can be used when testing your robots. For example, in a complex program you can drop in a SOUND block to let you know when the robot has reached a certain portion of the program. Let's say you want to know when your robot has reached the part of a program where it has to decide between turning left and turning right. You could place a SOUND block directly in front of the MOVE blocks, and program a sound to play when turning left and a different sound for turning right. After you've tested and verified the program is working properly, you can remove the SOUND blocks and run the program normally. In this example, SOUND blocks give you an idea of where a robot's program is currently executing by giving you an audible alert, which is very useful for troubleshooting and testing.

Custom Sounds

NXT-G comes with over 100 pre-programmed sounds from which to select, but maybe you're wishing for a unique sound that's not in the list? If so, and you're running NXT-G 2.0, you are in luck! The newest version of NXT-G comes with a built-in tool called Sound Editor, which will allow you to create your own sounds for use with your robots—up to five seconds in length. Click on the Tools menu and select Sound Editor and the new tool will open, as shown in Figure 6-11.

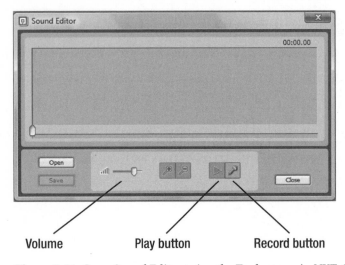

Figure 6-11. Open Sound Editor using the Tools menu in NXT-G.

You must connect an external microphone to your computer or laptop if it does not have one already built in. Press the Record button and begin recording your voice or other sound effect. Keep in mind that your final sound will be limited to five seconds, but you can record as long as you like; you'll be required to edit it down before saving the file. Press the Record button again to stop the recording process.

Figure 6-12 shows that I've recorded myself saying, "That looks dangerous!" I've recorded it over and over so I can find the one that sounds best. I can use the Play button to listen to my recording.

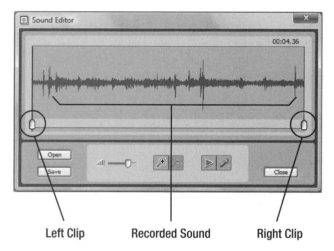

Figure 6-12. *A recorded sound appears as a waveform in the center of the screen.*

You next use the Left Clip and Right Clip bars indicated in Figure 6-13 to edit down your recorded sound to a five-second clip. If the sound wave between the two clip bars is red in color, the sound file is still too long. Continue to drag the left and right clip bars until the sound wave turns green.

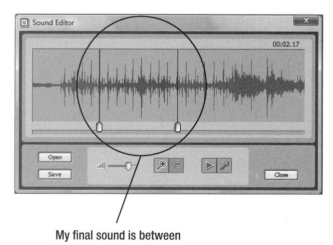

Figure 6-13. *Reduce the length of your sound using the clip bars.*

Now all that's left is to save your sound file so you can use it. Click on the Save button and a window will appear, like the one in Figure 6-14. If you wish to use the sound with your robot, don't make any changes to the file's location; the default path provided will save the file and allow you to select it from within a SOUND block.

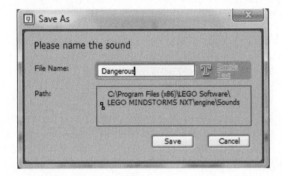

Figure 6-14. *Give your sound file a name save it to your computer.*

Give your sound a short but easy-to-remember name and click the Save button. I've named mine "Dangerous." Let's now see if I can use it. I've dragged a SOUND block into the program, shown in Figure 6-15, and selected the File option. As you can see in Figure 6-15, the sound Dangerous appears in the list.

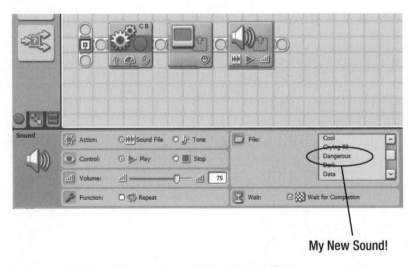

Figure 6-15. *Search for your sound file in the File listing.*

There are a few more things you can do with the Sound Editor. You can click the Open button and open an existing sound file (either one of the pre-configured sounds or one of your own) and perform more editing on it by using the left and right clip bars to increase or decrease its length. You can use the Volume slider to pre-configure the volume of your new sound as well as use the Zoom-in (and Zoom-out) button to fine-tune your sound recording and minimize its length. Experiment with the buttons a bit and you'll see how easy the Sound Editor is to use.

▦ **Note** You should know that all sounds saved to your computer using the Sound Editor are stored as files with an .RSO file extension. This means you can go out on the Internet and search for sound effects saved in the .RSO format that other NXT owners have created and are sharing; if you find one you like, save it to your hard drive, open Sound Editor, click the Open button, browse to the location of the sound file, and use the controls to edit it as needed.

Exercises

That's it for the SOUND block, but I want to leave you with a couple of easy exercises to give you some hands-on practice with this new block. You can find my solutions at the end of the chapter.

Exercise 6-1

Write a program for your robot that will have it spin in circles at the same time that it plays one sound file over and over. Set a limit for the MOVE block so it will stop after 20 rotations and the program will end.

Exercise 6-2

Program your robot to roll forward two rotations and stop before yelling "one!" Have it do this two more times as it counts "two!" and "three!"

What's Next?

Now, before we investigate any new blocks, I want to go over the different ways your robots receive input—this includes motors, sensors, timers, and the buttons on the Brick. The rest of the blocks that we'll be covering later in the book will all depend, in some manner, on your understanding of how sensors, motors, and buttons are used to send and receive signals. A good understanding of Chapter 7 will help you to create some really powerful and interesting programs for your robots, so let's keep moving forward.

Possible Solutions to Exercises

Following are a couple of possible solutions to the exercises. Remember, your solutions may not exactly match my own.

Exercise 6-1

Figures 6-16 and 6-17 show the program and the two configuration panels used in my solution to Exercise 6-1. Notice that the SOUND file is set to loop so it plays over and over. Since the Wait for

Completion box is disabled, after the SOUND file starts to play, the MOVE block will immediately start the robot spinning. After 15–20 rotations, the program will terminate.

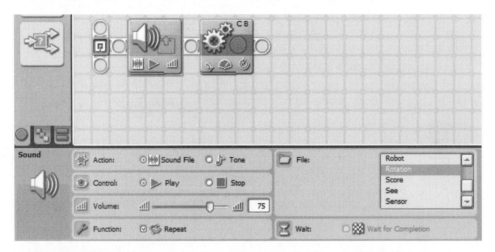

Figure 6-16. *The complete program and the SOUND block's configuration panel*

Figure 6-17. *The MOVE block's configuration panel*

Exercise 6-2

Figures 6-18 through 6-23 show the program and the six configuration panels used in my solution. In all three SOUND blocks I have left the Wait for Completion box checked; this will keep a MOVE block from starting until after its matching SOUND block has executed.

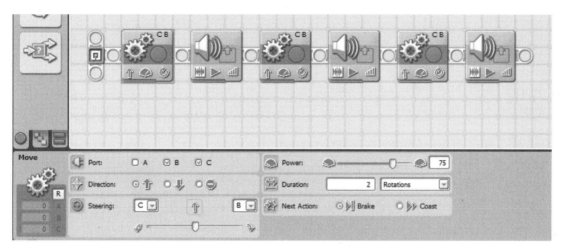

Figure 6-18. *The complete program and the first MOVE block's configuration panel*

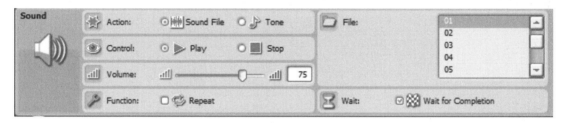

Figure 6-19. *The first SOUND block's configuration panel*

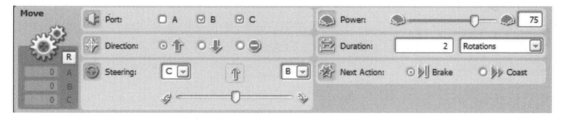

Figure 6-20. *The second MOVE block's configuration panel*

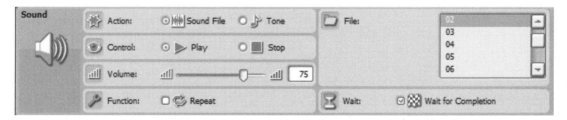

Figure 6-21. *The second SOUND block's configuration panel*

Figure 6-22. The third MOVE block's configuration panel

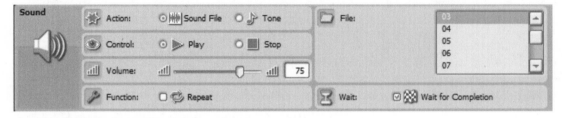

Figure 6-23. The third SOUND block's configuration panel

■ ■ ■

CHAPTER 7

Wired!

Some of the questions I hear the most are related to data hubs and wires—and for good reason! A block's data hub can be confusing, especially when a block has numerous options on the hub. And wires can be just as difficult to figure out.

In this chapter, I want to take a short break from learning about any new NXT-G programming blocks and give you some background and tips on how to use data hubs and wires. I'll also be using some of the NXT-G blocks you've already learned about, so you'll be able to see how these crazy things called wires actually work. I hope that any confusion you have will be cleared up by the end of this chapter.

The Problem

To help you understand hubs and wires, let me start with a fake programming block called the COLOR block. This block is shown in Figure 7-1.

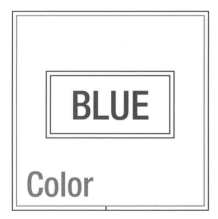

Figure 7-1. The COLOR block

This imaginary block is one of the simplest blocks you'll ever encounter. It can hold one color. This block holds Blue. It will always hold Blue and nothing else. There is no way to change the color. There's even worse news—the block has no way of sharing this color with a robot. Think of the solid wall surrounding the block as keeping information from coming into the block or leaving the block. It's a very boring and useless block.

A Simple Solution

What would make my color block useful to us? Well, first, it would be nice to be able to change the color. My favorite color is green, so I'd at least like to change the block to a Green block. I might not be able to do anything else with the block at this point, but at least it will contain my favorite color! To do this, I need a way to access the wall surrounding the block.

One of the things the block in Figure 7-1 lacks is a way to get inside the block and change Blue to Green. What's so great about creating the COLOR block is that I can change it whenever I like (because it's a fake block). The first thing I'm going to do is attach a very small color keyboard to the block so I can change the color. This color keyboard is a strange type of keyboard, though; it will only let me type colors. If I try to type in "Jim" or "five," the keyboard will buzz to let me know that it's not going to cooperate. Take a look at the updated COLOR block in Figure 7-2.

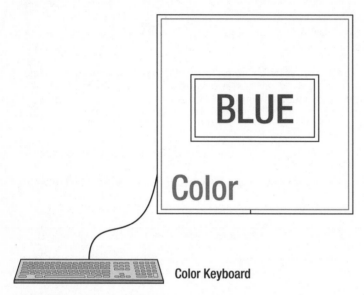

Figure 7-2. *I've added a fake color keyboard, so I can change the Blue block to a Green block.*

Perfect! Now I can type Green. Later, if I want to change to Yellow or Red, I can simply type the new color, and the block will change.

Now I've changed the color, and I have a Green block. Other than looking at it, there's really not much I can do with it. Just like I added a small keyboard to the block, I think I'll now connect a small, fake color screen to the block that will take whatever color is stored inside and display it. This screen is just like my weird keyboard; it will only display a color. (If I had a "direction screen" and I connected it to the block, it wouldn't know what to do with a color. But if I connected it to a DIRECTION block that holds North, East, West, or South, then it would definitely work!)

Figure 7-3 shows my new color screen connected to the Green block.

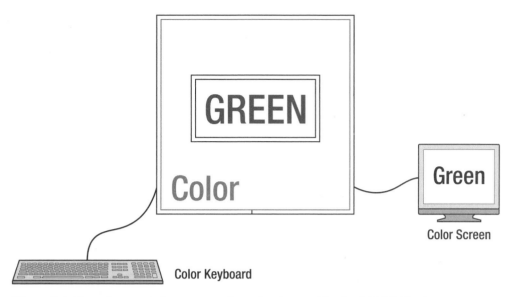

Figure 7-3. *The color screen lets me see what color is stored in the COLOR block.*

So, let's review how this works: the COLOR block can hold only one color, not a number or a day or a name.

Next, the COLOR block has a color keyboard attached. I can change the color the COLOR block holds but only by using this special keyboard, and this keyboard will let me type in *only* colors.

Finally, I've attached a color screen to the COLOR block. This special screen will display only colors and nothing else, not names or types of food.

If I detach the color keyboard, can I still display the color inside? Yes, but only if I keep the color screen attached.

If I detach the color screen, can I still change the color inside the block? Yes, again, but only if I keep the color keyboard attached.

Let me give you another way to describe this COLOR block:

- The COLOR block will accept a color as input from the keyboard.

- The COLOR block will also provide a color as output to the screen.

There are some programming words for you in that description: input and output. When thinking about blocks, always remember that any information that is provided to a block is *input*. Any information that the block can give out (share) can be considered *output*.

The NXT-G Solution

Now, let's look at a block with a few more options. Take a look at the fake CUP block in Figure 7-4.

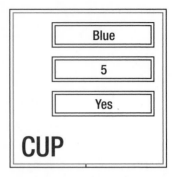

Figure 7-4. The CUP block is a little more complex.

The CUP block can hold three pieces of information: the cup's Color, its Height in inches, and a Yes answer if the cup is empty or a No answer if the cup is not empty. Now, here's where it gets fun.

Take a look at Figure 7-5. The COLOR block has an easier way for me to provide input to the block and to receive output from the block. It's called a *hub*.

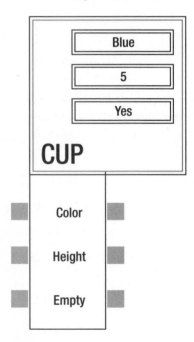

Figure 7-5. The CUP block has a hub for connecting things.

You can see in the figure that there are three input ports (also called plugs) on the left side of the hub and three output ports on the right side. These are where I will plug in keyboards, screens, and other items.

I'd like to take a moment and show you a few hubs from real NXT-G blocks. Figure 7-6 shows three blocks with their hubs expanded. (Normally an NXT-G block has its hub closed.)

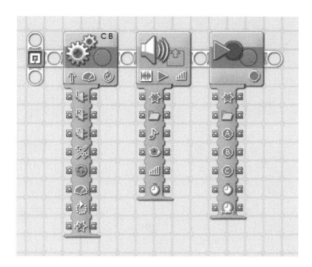

Figure 7-6. *Data hubs for the MOVE, SOUND, and RECORD/PLAY blocks*

■ **Note** Most NXT-G blocks have data hubs but not all. Each of those little square plugs you see running down the left side of a hub is an input data port. The small square plugs running down the right side are output data ports. Some blocks have more data ports than others, but the ports all work the same; they are simply a way to send data into a block and receive data out of a block. I'll cover many of the data ports later in the chapters specific to certain blocks, but for now I just wanted you to see what they look like for the blocks you've already read about in earlier chapters.

Now, let's return to our COLOR block and CUP block examples and work with the input and output data ports a bit.

Just like the COLOR block, the CUP block is very picky about what types of devices are connected to it. For the Color input plug, I can only connect something that supplies a color. We already know that a color keyboard will work. I could connect a color keyboard and change the color of the cup from Blue to Green. But there's a better way!

Remember that COLOR block we played around with earlier? Well, it has a data hub, too; it was just hidden inside the block. If I click on the lower left edge of the COLOR block, the COLOR block's hub will pop down; this is shown in Figure 7-7.

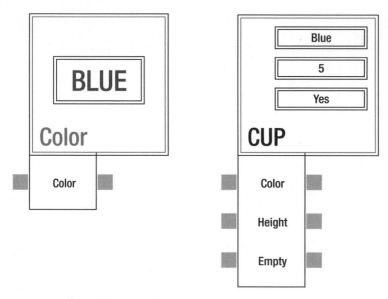

Figure 7-7. *The COLOR block also has a hub.*

The input plug on the left side of the COLOR block is where I can plug in a color keyboard to change the color inside the block. The output plug on the right can be connected to a color screen, but, in truth, it can be connected to any *input* plug that can accept a color. Notice the CUP block has an input plug that will accept a color! So instead of connecting a color keyboard to the CUP block, I can use a simple wire to connect the output plug on the COLOR block to the input plug on the CUP block (see Figure 7-8).

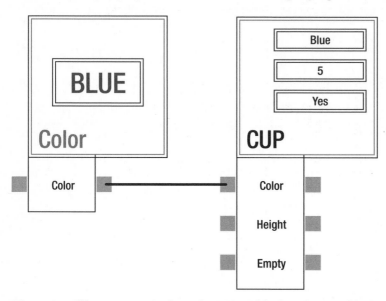

Figure 7-8. *I'll connect a wire from the COLOR block to the CUP block.*

I can also connect a numeric keyboard that can only be used to type in a number for the cup's height in inches. If I try to type in anything besides a number, the keyboard won't work. I'll also connect a logic keyboard to the Empty input plug. A logic keyboard is a very special keyboard—it can only be used to provide Yes or No answers (not Maybe or Sometimes—only Yes or No).

An Example

What I would like to do with the CUP block is to connect it to a screen that will display one of two things (but not both):

- Fill the [Color] cup with [Height] inches of water.

- The [Color] cup is not empty.

To do this, I can use a screen to display the color and height that are provided by the CUP block (Figure 7-9 shows my setup so far).

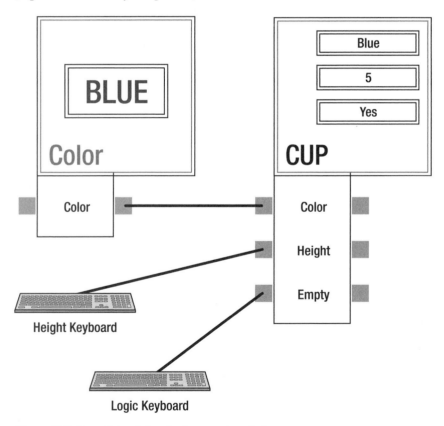

Figure 7-9. Everything is hooked up and ready to use.

But before I display the color and height, I need another special block that can examine the contents of the cup and determine if it is empty or not empty. Now, all I need to do is reveal my new EXAMINE block, shown in Figure 7-10.

The EXAMINE block can perform a nice trick. It takes a Yes or No answer (logic) and, depending on the answer, performs action 1 or action 2. Action 1 will occur if the answer is Yes (the cup is empty); action 2 will occur if the answer is No (for more information on logic, feel free to jump ahead to Chapter 8).

I can use this block to examine the contents of the CUP block. It will first look at the data plug labeled Empty. If the data the Empty data plug provides is Yes, the EXAMINE block will use the "EXAMINE = Yes" screen. If the data is No, the block will use the "EXAMINE = No" screen.

Figure 7-10 shows that when this program is run, the screen will display "Fill the Blue cup with 5 inches of water." It does this because the EXAMINE block receives the Yes data from the CUP block. It then performs the actions required for a Yes answer.

If I go back and change the Color to Yellow and the Height of the cup to three (using a color keyboard and height keyboard), this information will be passed from the CUP block to the EXAMINE block. If I change the logic answer from Yes to No using the logic keyboard, the EXAMINE block will receive the No data from the CUP block and perform the action required for a No answer: the screen displays "The Yellow cup is not empty."

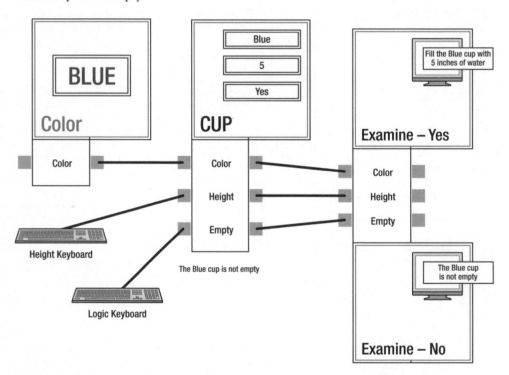

Figure 7-10. *The new EXAMINE block*

There are many more fake blocks that I could create, but I hope you're starting to understand how blocks can receive input data and provide output data. Both types of data (input and output) can be provided by you (by typing information in or selecting options in a configuration panel), or the data can be provided by other blocks using wires.

Types of Data

You'll be happy to hear this bit of information: I've created a bunch of fake blocks that can accept color and height. I could go further and create a *bunch* of fake types of input. But you're fortunate, because LEGO has better judgment than I sometimes have. When it comes to NXT-G, you only need to know about three types of data:

- *Text:* Letters, words, sentences, and even numbers can be considered text.

- *Number:* Numbers can be positive or negative, and sometimes they are limited to integers (only numbers like -3, 0, 4, 8, or 10 and no numbers with decimal points like 4.3 or 8.5).

- *Logic:* This can be Yes or No (another way to say it is True or False).

▥ **Note** For number data, some blocks have a range. For example, the MOVE block's Power setting can only be in the range of 0 to 100. If you connect a wire to the MOVE block's Power input data plug and it receives a value greater than 100, that value will automatically be reduced to 100. Just be aware that the fact that a block can receive a number value doesn't mean that value will be accepted.

When you are programming, the only data that can be passed to and from a block are text, numbers, and logic types (Yes/No or True/False)—only these three! And just as your CUP block wouldn't let you use a logic keyboard to type in the color, a block's input and output data plugs will be very picky about the types of data they accept. The good news is that if you ever drag a wire from one plug to an incompatible plug (if you try to drag a wire from a Text plug to a Logic plug, for example), the wire will be *broken*. By that, I mean that the wire will become a dashed gray line, indicating that you made a mistake. You can see this in Figure 7-11.

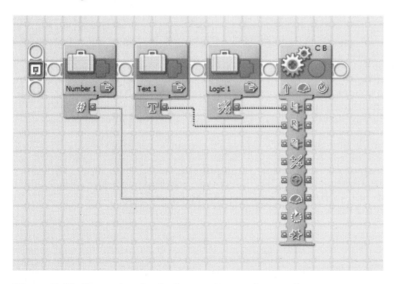

Figure 7-11. Data wires for logic, number, and text values

Variables

Notice that the third block from the left in Figure 7-11—called a VARIABLE block and covered in Chapter 18—has a dotted gray line. It's trying to send a Yes or No signal to the MOVE block's port that controls the left motor. That input data port is looking for a number (specifically, a value of 1, 2, or 3 where 1 equals Motor A, 2 equals Motor B, and 3 equals Motor C).

Likewise, the second block from the left (also a VARIABLE block) is trying to send text to the port that controls the right motor. This, too, will fail, as that input port is looking for a value of 1, 2, or 3.

Only the first block from the left, the VARIABLE block set to provide a number, has a solid yellow line. This is because it's connected to the MOVE block's data input port for the Power value. The Power input data port can receive a value from 0 to 100 (anything over 100 is reduced to 100 and anything less than 0 is converted to 0). Because I've connected the first VARIABLE block's output data port to the Power input data port, the line appears solid and is properly connected.

Now, if you correctly connected a wire, the wire will have a color. This color depends on the type of data being sent over the wire:

- The wire is yellow for the Number data type.

- The wire is orange for the Text data type.

- The wire is green for the Logic data type.

- If the wire is gray (and dashed), the wire is broken and will not work.

It takes practice to drag and connect wires from plug to plug. Sometimes, the wires will do strange things and go off in strange directions. You'll just have to play around with them until you figure out how to control them properly.

A Real NXT-G Block

Now it's time to get back to real NXT-G blocks. You'll see in the figures I provide that many times I'll have a block's data hub opened. If you hover the mouse pointer over a data plug, it will show you the name of the data plug (something like Empty or Height in my examples).

For some of the plugs (or ports—use whichever you prefer), it's fairly easy to figure out what type of data type they use (the Number plug requires the, duh, Number data type). Others aren't so easy to figure out. You can either check the help documentation, which provides a detailed description of a block's data hub plugs along with the types of data they accept, *or* you can just experiment and drag some wires to it; the color of the wire will tell you if you're correct, or a gray wire will tell you to try again.

My last bit of good news is that you cannot ruin a program with incorrect wires! If you connect a wire that's incompatible, just click the input end of the wire (a wire always has an input end and an output end), and the wire will disappear. No worries!

This is a *lot* of information to absorb, and you've only scratched the surface of what wires can do for you. But there's *power* in wires! Wires can save you time by allowing you to use existing data over and over again; wires can be split, meaning you can split one wire and provide two different blocks with the same data! The splitting occurs automatically when NXT-G detects you are dragging a wire from a data plug that already has a wire attached. You can see an example of this in Figure 7-12. Drag a wire from an output data port that's already providing input to a plug and the wire will automatically split.

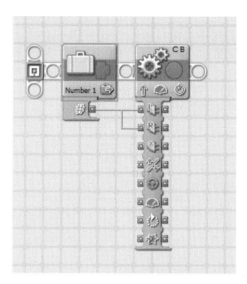

Figure 7-12. Data wires can be split and provide the same data to more than one port.

You also need to know that the help documentation contains a complete description of every data port, including a picture of each data port, what type of data it can send and receive and any limitations that exist (such as a range of numbers or length of text). Figure 7-13 shows a snippet of the Help documentation for the MOVE block and its eight data ports.

	Plug	Data Type	Possible Range	What the Values Mean	This Plug is Ignored When...
	Left Motor	Number	1 - 3	1 = A, 2 = B, 3 = C	
	Right Motor	Number	1 - 3	1 = A, 2 = B, 3 = C	
	Other Motor	Number	1 - 3	1 = A, 2 = B, 3 = C	
	Direction	Logic	True/False	True = Forwards, False = Backwards	
	Steering	Number	-100 - 100	< 0 = Steer towards left motor, > 0 = Steer towards right motor	
	Power	Number	0 - 100		
	Duration	Number	0 - 2147483647	Depends on Duration Type: Degrees/Rotations = Degrees, Seconds = Seconds	Duration Type = Unlimited
	Next Action	Logic	True/False	True = Brake, False = Coast	Duration Type = Unlimited. Steering not equal to zero (this may only be temporary. pending firmware fix for this not to be ignored)

Figure 7-13. Consult the Help documentation to discover the type of data a port can accept.

Wires can also go in the other direction, so you can send an output wire from the end of your program all the way back to an input plug at the start of your program! Keep your eyes open throughout this book to learn some new ways to use wires. Experiment on your own, and you'll discover even more uses for wires.

There aren't any exercises for this chapter, so just take some time and try your hand at dragging wires around on the screen. If you drag enough wires around, you'll also likely see how wires will automatically try to space themselves on the screen and around other wires. And don't worry—you're going to get a lot of chances in later chapters to use wires in actual programs.

What's Next?

Up next in Chapter 8 is a short discussion on a method robots use for making decisions, using Yes and No answers. It's going to cover the LOGIC block that I briefly mentioned earlier in this chapter. The LOGIC block is useful because so many of the NXT-G electronics (motors and sensors) are able to have their NXT-G blocks send Yes and No signals to and from other blocks. LOGIC blocks give your robot the ability to make decisions based on multiple inputs, and that's just one step to making your robots fully autonomous and able to function on their own.

■ ■ ■

CHAPTER 8

True or False?

What is the difference between the following two questions?

- What color is the sky?
- Is the sky blue?

Well, there are a *lot* of differences: the first question has five words and the second one has four words, for example. My real point in asking these two questions is to point out that the first question is open-ended; the sky could be blue, or gray, or any number of answers. The second question, however, has only two possible answers: Yes or No.

When it comes to programming your robots, you need to understand that many times your robots can only *provide* you with those two answers: Yes or No. At other times, your robots can *understand* only a Yes or No answer. Understanding how to take a Yes/No answer and use it to properly program your bots is the focus of this short chapter.

One or the Other

Let's have a question/answer session with SPOT:

Me: SPOT, what color is the box in front of you?

[SPOT sits there and gives no response.]

Me: SPOT, what is the position of your Touch sensor button?

[SPOT still sits there and gives no response.]

Hmmm . . . SPOT doesn't seem to be too responsive today. I seem to remember, however, that SPOT prefers Yes/No questions, so let me try this again:

Me: SPOT, is the color of the box in front of you blue?

SPOT: Yes *[appears on the LCD screen]*.

Me: SPOT, is your Touch sensor button pressed?

SPOT: No *[appears on the LCD screen]*.

OK, now we're getting somewhere. SPOT does prefer to communicate with me using Yes or No answers. Another way of saying this is that SPOT prefers to communicate using *logical responses;* a logical response is simply Yes or No.

■ **Note** Some computers and robots use True or False, but it's all the same: Yes = True and No = False. Some computers and robots even use 1 or 0 as a logical response, where 1= True and 0 = False. There's even another method: On or Off! In that case, On = True and Off = False. But for the purposes of this chapter and programming, let's stick with either Yes/No or True/False.

Sensors: Yes or No

Let's have another conversation with SPOT:

Me: SPOT, is your Ultrasonic sensor detecting an object six inches in front of you?

SPOT: True.

Me: SPOT, is your Right button being pressed?

SPOT: False.

Apparently, SPOT's sensors have the ability to return a logical response to SPOT that he can pass along to me. SPOT listens to his sensors' conditions and responds with True or False.

What does all this have to do with programming, though? Here's your answer: your NXT robots can send and receive logical responses to and from the sensors, motors, buttons, and other items. As an example, take a look at Figure 8-1.

What you are looking at in Figure 8-1 is the TOUCH SENSOR block and its configuration panel. Notice also that the TOUCH SENSOR block has its data hub visible (see Chapter 7 for a discussion of data hubs and Chapter 9 for a more detailed discussion of the sensors). If you are seeing only one data output plug on the data hub, click the data hub again to expand it to its full size.

On the data hub, you'll see some small input and output data plugs. If you hover the mouse pointer over the third plug from the top, the words "Yes/No" will appear. What this tells you is that this data plug can provide output (using a data wire) in the form of a Logic data type.

But how do you know if the output will be Yes or No? How do you know what it means when a sensor returns one answer or the other? Simple—the answer is based on what you are monitoring with the sensor.

In Figure 8-1, notice that the Touch sensor's Action section has the Pressed option selected. This means that if the Touch sensor's button is pressed down (and not released) the Yes/No Logic plug will provide a Yes answer. If the button is not pressed, the Yes/No Logic plug will provide a No answer.

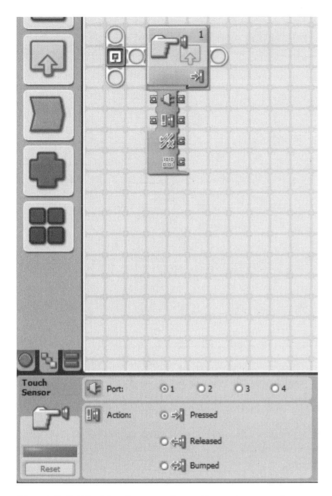

Figure 8-1. The Touch sensor's configuration panel

Variables and the Logic Type

Think back to Chapter 7; I told you that when you connect two blocks with a wire, the input and output data plugs *must* be carrying the same data type. In this case, if you wish to connect a wire from the Yes/No data plug, it must be going into a block that has a Logic data type input plug. As an example, take a look at the new block in Figure 8-2.

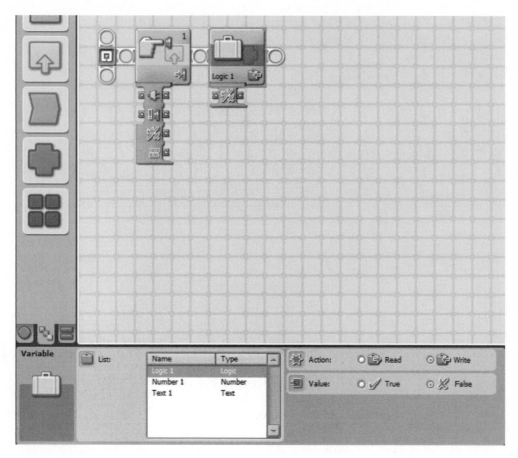

Figure 8-2. I've dropped a VARIABLE block on the beam.

This new block is a VARIABLE block. I cover this block in more detail in Chapter 18, but for now all you need to know about the VARIABLE block is that it can hold one of the three data types: Logic, Number, or Text. In Figure 8-2, I've configured the VARIABLE block to hold a Logic value. I've also opened the data hub, so you can see that it has a Yes/No input data plug. All that I need to do is connect it to the TOUCH SENSOR block with a wire (see Figure 8-3).

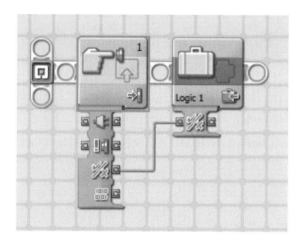

Figure 8-3. Connecting two blocks with a wire

When connecting blocks in a program using data wires, always keep in mind that a data wire will work *only* if it is connected to input and output plugs that expect the same data type (Logic, Number, or Text). I also need to point out that many blocks hold either a True or False value as a default setting. For example, the VARIABLE block in Figure 8-2 is configured to hold a default value of False. But you could easily change this to True (I've got more examples, later in the book, where you'll configure True/False values).

The Logic data type can be found in many blocks, especially the sensor blocks (see Figure 8-4). The sensor blocks all have a data plug that provides a Yes/No response. These plugs are designated by a check mark and an "X," which symbolize the Yes/No response.

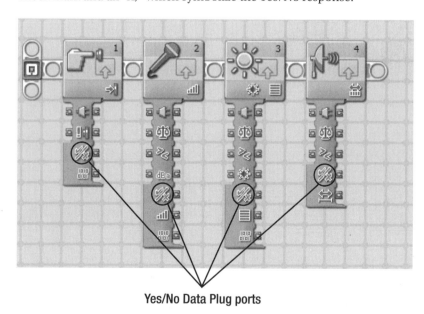

Yes/No Data Plug ports

Figure 8-4. These four sensors (Touch, Sound, Light, and Ultrasonic) all have Logic data plugs.

■ **Note** The Sound sensor is not included with the NXT 2.0 robotics kit. It has been replaced with an extra Touch sensor. Likewise, the NXT 2.0 kit does not come with the Light sensor but it does come with the Color sensor, which can be also be configured to work as a Light sensor.

Where the Logic data type really comes in handy, however, is with the LOOP and SWITCH blocks (these are covered in Chapters 11 and 12, respectively). Logic data types are very useful when programming a bot to make decisions on its own, and the LOOP and SWITCH blocks can both use a Yes/No response (as input) to give your robot more complex behaviors and control of itself. The bot can examine a sensor, motor, or other type of input and, based on the Yes/No response, make further decisions about what it does next.

Using Logic to Configure Settings

Before we leave this chapter, let's take a look at a few more examples of NXT-G blocks that use the Yes/No Logic data type. Keep in mind that many blocks use a Yes or No answer to control actions. In these cases, a Yes or No answer isn't so much an affirmative or negative response as it is simply a way for a block to distinguish between two actions. Here's a perfect example of this situation. Figure 8-5 shows a MOVE block's data hub.

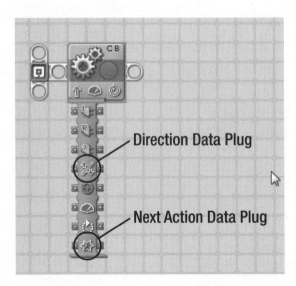

Figure 8-5. The MOVE block has two data ports that use the Logic data type.

For the MOVE block, you can configure the direction (forward or backward) using the configuration panel; you simply click the Up or Down arrow in the Direction section to assign a spin direction. But the direction of spin can also be controlled by sending a Yes or No signal to the Direction Data Plug (see Figure 8-5). A Yes signal is interpreted as Forward and a No signal is interpreted as Backward. The same concept works for the Next Action section—you can use a Yes signal to indicate that the robot should brake when the spin action is completed or a No signal to tell the robot to coast!

How might you use this? I've created a small program in Figure 8-6. It has the Touch sensor mentioned earlier in this chapter. You'll learn all about this sensor in Chapter 9, but for now focus on the Touch sensor's data hub. I've dragged a wire from its Yes/No output plug into the MOVE block's Direction input plug.

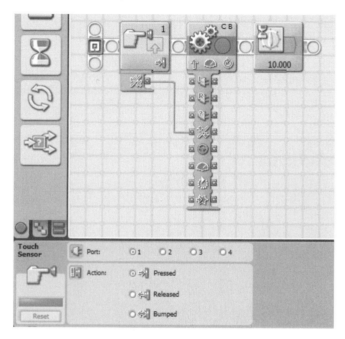

Figure 8-6. This program uses the Touch sensor to control the motors' spin direction.

This program doesn't do much other than spin the motors forward or backward for ten seconds, depending on whether the Touch sensor button is pressed. When I run the program, if I hold down the Touch sensor button the motors will spin in the forward direction for ten seconds before the program ends. You can see in the Touch sensor configuration panel in Figure 8-6 that I could have changed the Action to Released by selecting that option. If I had done this, what do you think would happen if I pressed the button when I started the program?

Think about it for second—if the Action the Touch sensor is testing for is set to "Released," then when the button is pressed, it is not released, right? That means the Touch sensor will send a No signal (or False) to the MOVE block. A No signal means the motors will spin backwards!

You'll learn all about the various sensors and how they work in the next chapter. Once you've got a good grasp of their functions and how their data hubs work, you'll be able to use wires to send Yes and No signals to other blocks and give your robots some amazing decision-making abilities. Your robots will be able to interact with objects, avoid walls, detect light or dark rooms, and much more. And many of these abilities hinge on your robot being able to use Yes and No logic responses to make decisions.

Exercise 11

Before we move on to Chapter 9, I've got an exercise for you that should help you better understand how to interpret a Yes/No signal and determine what it will do. If you get stumped, I've provided the answer at the end of this chapter.

Figure 8-7 shows a small program I've created and the four configuration panels for the four NXT-G blocks. Examine it and determine what actions the robot will take given the following situation:

- Touch sensor button is NOT pressed
- Light sensor detects the room's lights are turned on

Look carefully, as the settings are a little tricky!

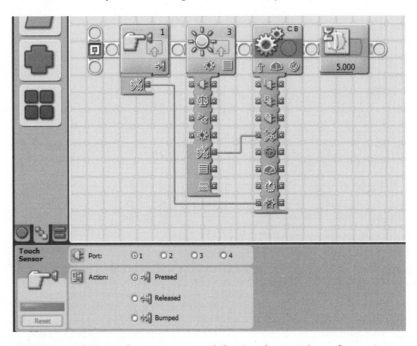

Figure 8-7. The complete program and the Touch sensor's configuration panel

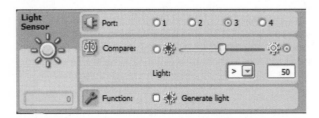

Figure 8-8. The Light sensor's configuration panel

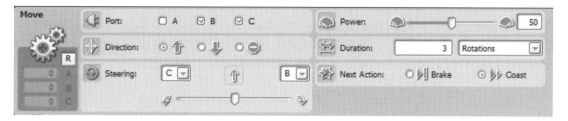

Figure 8-9. The MOVE block's configuration panel

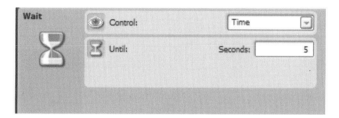

Figure 8-10. The WAIT TIME block's configuration panel

What's Next?

And that's it for this short chapter on logic. As I said, you'll get a more detailed description of how to use the Logic data type with the LOOP and SWITCH blocks in Chapters 11 and 12. Now let's change direction in Chapter 9 and take a look at some more items that can be used to communicate with the NXT Brick: sensors, buttons, and timers.

Exercise Solution

Let's go over each block before deciding what will happen when the program is executed. First, the Touch sensor block is configured to send a Yes signal to the MOVE block's Next Action input port (in Figure 8-7) if the button is Pressed. Next, the Light sensor is configured to send a Yes signal to the MOVE block's Direction input port (also seen in Figure 8-7) if the room's lights are turned on. (Without going into too much detail, I've set the sensor to detect a light reading of 50 or greater (see Figure 8-8); the Light sensor detects the light level in the room and assigns a value between 0 and 100. If the lights are on and bright enough, the reading will usually be around 70–80, meaning the Light sensor will detect a light value greater than 50 and send a Yes (or True) signal to the MOVE block.)

Now, examine the MOVE block's configuration panel in Figure 8-9. I've configured the MOVE block to spin motors B and C forward and to Coast when done. (The WAIT TIME block will allow the motors to complete their action before waiting for five seconds and stopping the program).

So, if the Touch sensor button is pressed (a YES signal), the MOVE block's Next Action input data plug will receive it. A Yes signal tells the motors to Brake. But didn't I use the configuration panel to set the motors to Coast? Yes, but the configuration panel's setting will always be ignored if a wire is used to receive a signal. So, the Yes signal will override the Coast configuration panel setting and have the robot brake instead.

What about the Light sensor? Well, it's sending a Yes signal to the Direction input data plug, which corresponds to a Forward setting. I had already configured the MOVE block for a Forward direction (see Figure 8-9) so this setting will not be changed.

So, when the program runs, the motors will spin for three rotations (at a Power setting of 50) and then the motors will brake. The robot will sit for five seconds and then the program will end.

CHAPTER 9

Feedback

Your LEGO Mindstorms NXT kit comes with a collection of motors and sensors. And the NXT Brick has three built-in timers plus the buttons on the Brick. Would it surprise you to learn that all of these items are able to provide some sort of feedback to the NXT Brick? The sensors are a little obvious; a sensor is designed to respond to external conditions such as light, touch, color, or sound and report this information to the Brick. But what about motors? And how can a timer be used as input or feedback to the Brick? All these questions have answers, and this chapter provides them. It's a little longer than most chapters, but you'll find this information very useful for giving your robot the ability to monitor external conditions (as well as time) and make decisions on its own.

What's Your Condition?

Let's start with the word *condition*. A traffic light has three conditions: red, yellow, and green. A light switch has two conditions: on and off. Just using these two simple examples, I can give you some pseudo-code for SPOT:

Me: SPOT, move forward until the traffic light turns red.

Me: SPOT, display the words "Light On" on your LCD screen until the light switch is off.

In both these examples, I'm assuming that SPOT has eyes and can see the traffic light or light switch. If SPOT doesn't have eyes, then I would need a way for the traffic light or light switch to provide their conditions to SPOT. The traffic light and light switch could then provide feedback, or input, to SPOT.

Asking a traffic light to provide input isn't realistic, but your NXT robots do have the ability to receive feedback from items such as the sensors. So I can change the pseudo-code for SPOT:

Me: SPOT, move forward until the Light sensor reports a value of 20.

Me: SPOT, display the word "Hello" until the Touch sensor reports that it has been pressed and released (also known as bumped).

Me: SPOT, play a C note when the Ultrasonic sensor detects an object six inches in front of you.

The motors, too, can provide feedback:

Me: SPOT, spin motor A until motor B reports that it has spun ten degrees.

Me: SPOT, display "5 rotations" when motor C has rotated five times.

I mentioned that the Brick has three built-in timers plus three buttons that can be used, so I could also write the following pseudo-code:

Me: SPOT, when 20 seconds have elapsed, turn 90 degrees.

Me: SPOT, play a B note if I press the left button and a C note if I press the right button.

Okay, so you can see that the sensors, motors, buttons, and timers can provide input to the Brick to control other actions (MOVE, SOUND, and other blocks). You program your robot to perform specific actions based on the conditions of these items. Just like you know a light switch has two conditions, on and off, you need to know the various conditions that the sensors, buttons, timers, and motors possess and can report to the Brick.

So, for the rest of this chapter, I'm going to explain the settings for these items, so you'll know how to configure them properly. Future blocks that we'll cover, including the WAIT, LOOP, and SWITCH blocks, will depend on your understanding of how to properly configure the conditions.

The method I'm going to use to do this is fairly simple: I'll describe each item (sensor, motor, button, and so on) and provide a description of the settings that can be modified within the item's configuration panel. Please note that I am also providing information on the so-called *legacy* items: the previous version of Mindstorms (Robotics Invention System, or RIS) included motors, sensors, and a lamp. These RIS items can be used with NXT robots but require special converter cables to connect to the NXT Brick. I call them "legacy" because they come from the older Mindstorms system, but they are still very useful and fully compatible with the NXT system.

■ **Note** Right now, only the education version of the NXT kit comes with software support for the legacy/RCX items. If you are running the retail version, you may download NXT programming blocks for the RCX motors and sensors by visiting http://mindstorms.lego.com/Support/Updates/. Click on the Patches option along the left side of the screen and download the files from the Legacy Block section for your specific language (English, German, French, Japanese, and Dutch are the only options currently available).

Configuring the Sensors

Let's start with the sensors—NXT Touch, RIS Touch, NXT Sound, NXT Light, RIS Light, NXT Ultrasonic, NXT Rotation, RIS Rotation, NXT Color, and RIS Temperature—which have some interesting rules to abide by.

First, sensors detect a change in a condition. The condition could be a change in light level, a change from seeing a blue ball to a red ball, a change in volume (sound), or maybe a change in position (movement). The sensor is simply "watching" the changes in its condition. The Light sensor, for example, can detect changes in the level of lighting in the room. The Ultrasonic sensor is detecting changes in distance from an object or wall in front of it.

Second, sensor programming blocks can respond *only* to one condition at a time. When you drop a sensor block into an NXT-G program, it has to be configured to test one condition. A single Light sensor, for example, cannot be configured to respond to whether the light in a room is below 80 *and* greater than 50. In order to test both conditions, you would need to use two Light sensor blocks in your program.

In Chapter 8, we learned how logic values can be sent and received between NXT-G blocks using data plugs. Well, sensors can provide a Logic type response, True or False, depending on the conditions that their respective configuration panels are programmed to detect. Think of our traffic light for a moment. Let's assume that every car has special traffic light sensors mounted on top. These light sensors are programmed to examine the conditions of the traffic light. Cars will move while the light is green and stop when the light is red. If the light is yellow, the car will slow down.

■ **Note** There are many more types of information a sensor can provide. For example, a Light sensor can provide a numeric value related to the light level in a room. The Sound sensor can provide a decibel level. This type of information is all provided using the data plugs found on a sensor block's data hub. I'll talk about this later in the book, but this chapter is mainly concerned with the ability of sensors and motors to provide Yes or No (True or False) signals to other blocks.

These traffic light sensors, then, can detect one of three possible conditions: green, yellow, or red. An NXT sensor can check only *one* condition, so if this were an NXT traffic light sensor, each car would require three traffic light sensors:

- If the first traffic light sensor detects green, the car should keep moving.

- If the second traffic light sensor detects yellow, the car should start slowing down.

- If the third traffic light sensor detects red, the car should stop.

Notice that *only* one condition can be true at any given time; the light cannot be green and red at the same time. So when the sensor detecting green is triggered, yellow and red cannot be triggered. Therefore, we can examine a sensor's Logic data type for a True/False response to the condition the sensor is configured to monitor.

Let's take a look now at the sensors.

NXT Touch Sensor

The NXT Touch sensor's configuration panel is shown in Figure 9-1.

Figure 9-1. The NXT Touch sensor's configuration panel

In the Port section, select the port where the NXT Touch sensor has been connected. The default port for the Touch sensor is Port 1.

In the Action section, you can select Pressed, Released, or Bumped. Remember that Bumped means quickly pressing and releasing the button—less than .5 seconds for the entire press-and-release action.

The NXT Touch sensor's data hub is shown in Figure 9-2. Remember that you can hover your mouse pointer over a data plug to obtain the plug's name.

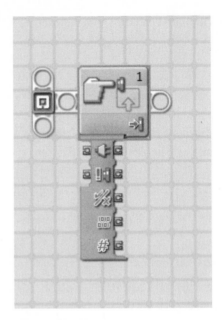

Figure 9-2. The NXT Touch sensor's data hub

The port number can be configured using the Port data plug and a Number data type wire with an input value of 1, 2, 3, or 4. This value can also be used as output by dragging a data wire out of the output Port data plug.

The Action data plug can use a Number data type with an input value of 0 for Pressed, 1 for Released, or 2 for Bumped.

The Yes/No data plug can provide an output value of True or False. It can send and receive a Logic data type.

The Raw Value data plug can provide an output Number value with a range of 0–1024.

The Logical Number data plug provides a 1 for pressed and a 0 for released. Instead of a logic value, however, this data is a Number data type.

■ **Note** The NXT-G 1.0 version of the software does not contain the Logical Number data plug. This comes only with the 2.0 version of the software. It's always good to know which version of NXT-G you are using, but if you find a data plug described in this book that you don't see on your own data hub, it's likely that you're running version 1.0 of the software.

For the remaining blocks in this chapter, I will not be describing the blocks' data hubs—only the blocks' configuration panels (I simply wanted to show you that the sensor blocks can use their data hubs for even more options than just sending and receiving logic data signals). Many data plugs are identical from block to block, so you'll likely find that learning just a few of them will allow you to recognize all of them. But if you're not familiar with any of the data hubs at this point, click the Help menu, and select the "Contents and Index" option to view the Help files. Along the left side of the screen, select the name of a programming block (see Figure 9-3). Details for the block's data hub can be found at the bottom of that block's Help documentation (also shown in Figure 9-3). You can always consult this Help documentation to determine the data types for the various data plugs (Number, Logic, or Text).

This chart shows the different characteristics of the plugs on the Touch Sensor block's data hub:

	Plug	Data Type	Possible Range	What the Values Mean	This Plug is Ignored When...
	Port	Number	1 - 4	1 = Port 1, 2 = Port 2, 3 = Port 3, 4 = Port 4	
	Action	Number	0 - 2	0 = Pressed 1 = Released 2 = Bumped	
	Yes / No	Logic	True/False	Result of comparison	
	Raw Value	Number	0 - 1024	Raw (unscaled) value read from sensor	
	Logical Number	Number	0 - 1	0 = Released 1 = Pressed	

Figure 9-3. Data hub details for the Touch sensor are described.

RIS Touch Sensor

The legacy RIS Touch sensor's configuration panel is shown in Figure 9-4.

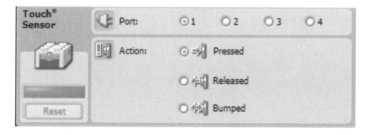

Figure 9-4. The RIS Touch sensor's configuration panel

In the Port section, select the port where the RIS Touch sensor has been connected. The default port for the Touch sensor is Port 1.

In the Action section, you can select Pressed, Released, or Bumped.

NXT Sound Sensor

The NXT Sound sensor's configuration panel is shown in Figure 9-5.

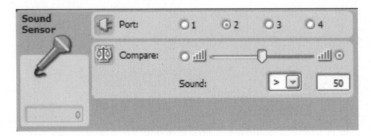

Figure 9-5. The NXT Sound sensor's configuration panel

In the Port section, select the port where the NXT Sound sensor has been connected. The default port for the Sound sensor is Port 2.

In the Compare section, you must configure the sound value (0–100) as well as whether the sensor will monitor for sounds less than or greater than the configured value. You can use the drag bar to select the value or enter a numeric value in the range of 0–100 in the text box. Select the less-than option (<) or the greater-than option (>) from the drop-down menu *or* click the left or right radio button to configure this option.

NXT Light Sensor

The NXT Light sensor's configuration panel is shown in Figure 9-6.

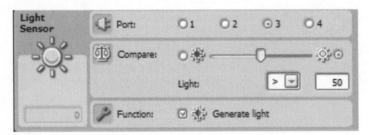

Figure 9-6. The NXT Light sensor's configuration panel

In the Port section, select the port where the NXT Light sensor has been connected. The default port for the Light sensor is Port 3.

In the Compare section, you must configure the light value (0–100) as well as whether the sensor will monitor for a light value less than or greater than the configured value. You can use the drag bar to select the value or enter a numeric value in the range of 0–100 in the text box. Select the less-than option (<) or the greater-than option (>) from the drop-down menu, or click on the left or right radio button to configure this option.

If you leave the "Generate light" box checked, the Light sensor will turn on its built-in LED to provide an artificial light source for assisting with determining light levels. If you uncheck the box, the Light sensor will detect only *ambient light levels*—that is, normal light conditions.

RIS Light Sensor

The RIS Light sensor's configuration panel is shown in Figure 9-7.

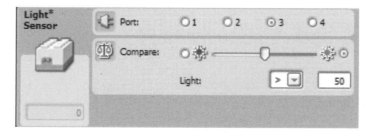

Figure 9-7. The RIS Light sensor's configuration panel

In the Port section, select the port where the RIS Light sensor has been connected. The default port for the Light sensor is Port 3.

In the Compare section, you must configure the light value (0–100) as well as whether the sensor will monitor for a light value less than or greater than the configured value. You can use the drag bar to select the value or enter a numeric value in the range of 0–100 in the text box. Select the less-than option (<) or the greater-than option (>) from the drop-down menu, or click the left or right radio button to configure this option.

NXT Ultrasonic Sensor

The NXT Ultrasonic sensor's configuration panel is shown in Figure 9-8.

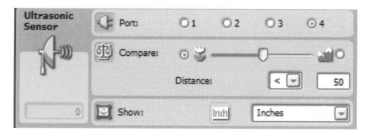

Figure 9-8. The Ultrasonic sensor's configuration panel

In the Port section, select the port where the NXT Ultrasonic sensor has been connected. The default port for the Ultrasonic sensor is Port 4.

In the Compare section, you must configure the Distance value as well as whether the sensor will monitor for a distance value less than or greater than the configured value. You can use the drag bar to select the value in the range of 0–100, or you may type a value in the text box with a lower limit of 0 but an upper value greater than 100. Using the drag bar limits you to a range of 0–100, but you are able to type in a value greater than 100. Select the less-than option (<) or the greater-than option (>) from the drop-down menu, *or* click on the left or right radio button to configure this option.

In the Show section, select either Centimeters or Inches from the drop-down menu.

NXT Rotation Sensor

The NXT Rotation sensor's configuration panel is shown in Figure 9-9. Remember that the Rotation sensor is built into the NXT motors, so don't go looking for an actual NXT Rotation sensor by itself.

Figure 9-9. The NXT Rotation sensor's configuration panel

In the Port section, select the motor port where the NXT motor (Rotation sensor) has been connected. The default port for the Rotation sensor is Port A.

In the Action section, you should select the Read option if you want the built-in rotation sensor to monitor the value (count) returned by the sensor. Select the Reset option to set the sensor count back to zero.

In the Compare section, select the motor's spin direction (Forward or Reverse) to monitor. Select Degrees or Rotations from the bottom drop-down menu, and enter a numeric value in the text box. You must also decide whether the sensor will monitor for a value less than or greater than the configured value by selecting the option in the other drop-down menu (using the Yes/No data plug, you can test for a True or False logic response based on the settings you have configured in the panel).

RIS Rotation Sensor

The RIS Rotation sensor's configuration panel is shown in Figure 9-10.

Figure 9-10. The RIS Rotation sensor's configuration panel

In the Port section, select the port where the RIS Rotation sensor has been connected. The default port for the Rotation sensor is Port A.

In the Action section, you should select the Read option if you want the built-in rotation sensor to monitor the value (count) returned by the sensor. Select the Reset option to set the sensor count back to zero.

In the Compare section, select the motor's spin direction (Forward or Reverse) to monitor. Enter a numeric value in the text box for the number of ticks you wish to monitor; there are 16 ticks in one rotation. You must also decide whether the sensor will monitor for a value less than or greater than the configured value by selecting the option in the other drop-down menu.

■ **Note** NXT-G 1.0 software users will find that the Rotation sensor block will only allow for comparisons in units of Rotation. With NXT-G 2.0, the software has been updated to allow the Rotation sensor block to also compare using units in Degrees in addition to number of rotations.

NXT Color Sensor

The NXT Color sensor is new to the NXT 2.0 kit. Its configuration panel is shown in Figure 9-11.

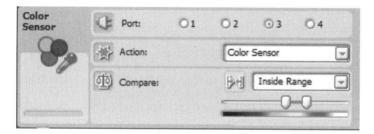

Figure 9-11. The NXT Color sensor's configuration panel

In the Port section, select the port where the Color sensor has been connected. The default port for the Color sensor is Port 3.

In the Action section, you can select the Light Sensor option, which will allow you to use the Color sensor as a Light sensor. When used as a Light sensor, the configuration panel will change to mimic the Light sensor's configuration panel, with the exception of allowing you to choose the color of the reflected light—Red, Blue, or Green.

If the Color Sensor selection is left in the Action section, click the drop-down menu for the Compare section and select either Inside Range or Outside Range. You then use the two small drag bars to define a single color or a range of colors to check. Figure 9-12 shows how I've configured the Color sensor to look for a color outside of green and red; this would mean that yellow is also ignored. (I select the Outside Range for the comparison so the Color sensor can report a True signal if a detected color falls outside that range.)

Figure 9-12. The NXT Color sensor can detect ranges of colors.

RIS Temperature Sensor

The RIS Temperature sensor's configuration panel is shown in Figure 9-13.

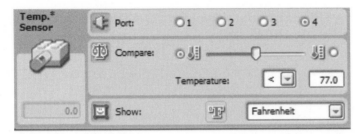

Figure 9-13. *The RIS Temperature sensor's configuration panel*

In the Port section, select the port where the RIS Temperature sensor has been connected. The default port for the Temperature sensor is Port 4.

In the Compare section, you must enter a numeric Temperature value in the text box or use the drag bar to set a value. The value for Celsius must be in the range of -20 (negative 20) to 70. The value for Fahrenheit must be in the range of -4 (negative 4) to 158. Select the less-than option (<) or the greater-than option (>) from the drop-down menu, or click on the left or right radio button to configure this option.

In the Show section, select either Fahrenheit or Celsius from the drop-down menu. The value ranges the sensor can monitor are determined by this selection.

Yes/no vs. Discrete Values

All of the configuration panels that I've described so far are used to program a condition. When that condition is met, the block is capable of sending a True (or Yes) signal to another block via a data wire. If the condition is not met, the block can be programmed, once again using a data wire, to send a False (or No) signal.

But what do you do if you wish to use a piece of data detected by a sensor that isn't a logical data type? How would you, for example, take the Intensity value of the Light sensor (0–100) and have that value control the speed of the motors? (Thus, a brightly lit room would make your robot move faster, vs. a dark room where the robot would move slowly.)

Stay tuned—I'll explain about non-true/false data later in the chapter, in the section called "Data Hub Power." There you'll see how to use both a sensor's yes/no result and its intensity value to control different aspects of your robot.

Other Input Types

There are three other methods that can be used to provide feedback to your NXT robots. These include the NXT buttons, the NXT timers, and a message received using Bluetooth technology by the NXT Brick using a RECEIVE MESSAGE programming block. I'll cover the RECEIVE MESSAGE block (and its partner, the SEND MESSAGE block) in Chapter 25, so let me close this chapter with details on the NXT buttons and timers.

Your NXT Brick has four buttons on its front: Left, Right, Enter (orange), and Cancel. The Cancel button cannot be used as input; its function is simply to cancel a running program, or if you are navigating around the on-screen LCD tools, it can be used to move back to a previous screen. That leaves the Left, Right, and Enter buttons—any program you create can use these three buttons to provide input.

Figure 9-14 shows the configuration panel for the NXT BUTTONS block.

Figure 9-14. *The NXT buttons are configured here.*

In the Button section, select the button (Enter, Left, or Right) from the drop-down menu. The default selection is the Enter button.

In the Action section, select Pressed, Released, or Bumped. These work just like the Touch sensor, by the way. Now your robot can detect the condition of any of its buttons and send a True/False signal to other blocks that can, in turn, perform more actions.

The NXT Brick also has three built-in timers. These timers begin counting the moment you press the Enter button to begin running a program. Figure 9-15 shows the TIMER block configuration panel.

Figure 9-15. *The NXT Timer configuration panel*

In the Timer section, select 1, 2, or 3 from the drop-down menu to select the timer you wish to use. The default selection is Timer 1.

In the Action section, select the Read option to obtain the current value of the timer. If you select Reset, the timer will be reset to zero when this block is executed.

The Compare section allows you to specify a value (in seconds) as a trigger that can be tested. Select either the greater-than option or the less-than option from the drop-down menu, and the TIMER block can now be used to provide a True/False Logic data type response. For example, if you configure the TIMER block for greater than ten seconds for Timer 1, the Logic data plug will provide a False response until Timer 1 exceeds ten seconds. After that, the data plug will provide a True response.

Data Hub Power

So now you know how to configure the various sensor blocks to detect conditions and provide a logic signal (True or False) using a data wire. If you've programmed your Light sensor's configuration block to detect when the light level is greater than 50, then a wire from its output Yes/No data plug that runs into a MOVE block's Yes/No data plug will have the motor spin Forward if the light level is truly greater than 50 (a Yes signal is sent over the wire) or have the motor spin Backward (if the light is less than 50, a No signal is being sent over the wire).

Just keep in mind that a True (or Yes) logic signal will be sent using the Yes/No data plug when the condition described on a configuration panel is met. When the condition is not met, a False (or No) logic signal will be sent.

But what about all those other data plugs in a sensor block? Glad you asked. Take a look at Figures 9-16 through 9-18. This shows a small program I've created for SPOT.

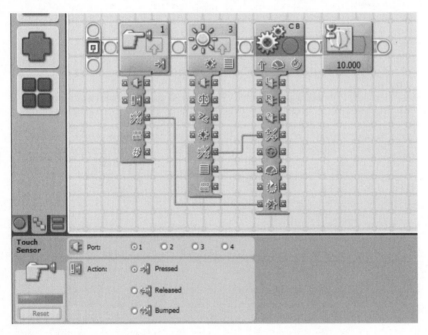

Figure 9-16. A program using data plugs for control and the configuration panel for the Touch sensor

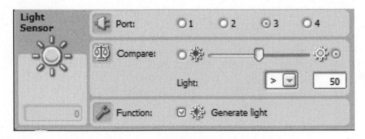

Figure 9-17. The Light sensor's configuration panel

Figure 9-18. *The MOVE block's configuration panel*

Let's walk through this program carefully. Notice first that when the program is executed the Touch sensor will send a Yes signal to the MOVE block via a wire if the button is Pressed. A Yes signal will tell the MOVE block to Brake vs. Coast. If the button isn't being pressed the moment the program is executed, the wire will carry a No signal, indicating the motors should coast when they complete their programmed action (in this case, spin for five rotations).

Next, the Light sensor is going to take a light-level reading (Intensity) on a scale of 1 to 100 and send this value to the MOVE block's Power data plug. At the same time, if it detects the light level is greater than 50, it will send a Yes signal (via a logic data wire) to the Direction data plug on the MOVE block and have the motors spin in a Forward direction (a No signal will spin the motors backward).

Here you can see how I'll control the speed (Power) of the motors by linking them to the Intensity of the light being detected by the Light sensor. In a slightly darker room (with an Intensity value greater than 0 but less than 50), the robot will not only roll slower but it will also roll backwards!

Finally, after the motors complete their movement, the program will pause for ten seconds before ending.

Are you beginning to see how each data plug in a block can be used to control other blocks? Sensors are the best for doing this because they have so many different data plugs that can supply different signals. With some experimenting, you can easily program your robots so they make left turns when the Sound sensor detects a loud CLAP!

Or maybe you'd like to have your robot run from a flashlight? Easy—just program its Light or Color sensor block to detect a bright light hitting its surface and tell the robot to roll backwards, away from the light.

With the various sensors available to you, you have the ability to give your robot some real decision-making skills. Run from a light or loud sound? Move closer and inspect? Shut down and hibernate? Detect a nearby wall? Move closer or farther away?

Your creativity and skill with using data wires is your only limit. And I haven't even covered the majority of the NXT-G blocks available to you to use in your programs! Once you know how all the blocks work, you'll have moved into the realm of real power programming and your robots will amaze.

Now, before leaving this chapter, try your hand at creating a small program that satisfies the requirement specified in Exercise 9-1.

Exercise 9-1

Create a small program that takes the Sound level (range of 0 to 100) detected when the program first executes and uses it to control the Power of the motors. The robot should also use its Ultrasonic sensor to see if anything is directly in front of it and no closer than five inches. If something is five inches or closer, it needs to roll away from the obstacle instead of closer to it. Have the robot's motors spin for a total of ten rotations.

What's Next?

This chapter showed you only how to configure a handful of blocks using the configuration panel and perform some small tricks with data wires. The real power comes with using these tricks in conjunction with other blocks, such as the LOOP, WAIT, and SWITCH blocks.

Chapter 11 will show you how to use the LOOP block to repeat certain tasks. When using a LOOP block, you can have the block *loop* forever, that is, perform the tasks over and over again until you cancel the program. Your other option is to configure the LOOP block to stop looping when a certain condition is met—for example, if the Light sensor detects a light level below 20, the Sound sensor detects a noise over level 80, or maybe a motor spins more than 20 degrees (Rotation sensor).

It's the same with the WAIT and SWITCH blocks. Both of these blocks will allow you to use what you've learned in this chapter to give your robots decision-making power.

So, read on—the WAIT block is up next in Chapter 10.

Exercise Solution

Figures 9-19 to 9-21 display the blocks and the three configuration panels used in this program. Notice that the Sound sensor is sending a Number data type value (yellow wire) to the MOVE block's Power setting and the Ultrasonic sensor is sending a Logic data type value (green wire) to the MOVE block's Direction setting.

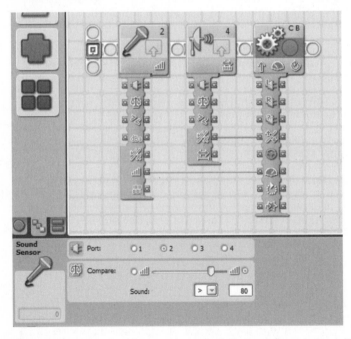

Figure 9-19. The complete program and the Sound sensor's configuration panel

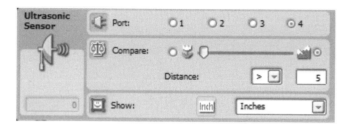

Figure 9-20. *The Ultrasonic sensor block's configuration panel*

Figure 9-21. *The MOVE block's configuration panel*

CHAPTER 10

■ ■ ■

Wait for It!

One of the most useful things your robots will be doing is waiting. Yep, you heard me right—waiting. Don't believe me? Okay, think about it this way:

- SPOT is moving toward a red line, *waiting* for the Color sensor to detect the line.

- SPOT is preparing to throw a ball at a target, *waiting* for the Touch sensor to be pressed and released.

- SPOT is rolling towards the wall, *waiting* for the Ultrasonic sensor to detect the wall.

- SPOT is sitting on the start line, *waiting* for me to push the Left button to let it race forward.

Are you beginning to see that waiting is an important part of a robot's program? Your robots will probably *always* be waiting for something to happen. It may be as simple as waiting for you to press the Enter button on the Brick or something similar to the preceding examples. All this waiting is accomplished using the WAIT block, so keep reading to figure out how to program your bots to "wait for it!"

The WAIT Block

When discussing the WAIT block, you need to understand one important concept: The WAIT block will *stop waiting when a specific condition is met. Until the condition is met, the* WAIT *block will essentially pause the program and keep it from executing any more blocks.*

It doesn't matter if you are using the Color sensor, Sound sensor, Touch sensor, Ultrasonic sensor, Light sensor, or a simple time limit. When you use a WAIT block, you must tell the WAIT block what condition must be met before the waiting ends.

So, to show you how this works, let me give SPOT some more pseudo-code:

Me: SPOT, keep moving forward until something happens.
Vague, isn't it? What does "something happens" mean? Well, it can be anything:

- Until five seconds have passed

- Until the Sound sensor detects a loud noise

- Until the Ultrasonic sensor detects something eight inches in front of it

- Until the Color sensor detects a blue card on the ground

Do you get the idea? I want SPOT to keep moving forward until a special condition is met. And with NXT-G, that condition can occur using data from a sensor, an NXT button, or a time limit. I'm going to go over each of these individually, so you'll see how the conditions are configured. To demonstrate different conditions, I'm going to have you first create an extremely simple program for SPOT (or your own bot).

Open the NXT-G software, and start a new program. Drop a MOVE block on the workspace, and configure it to spin motors B and C forward with an Unlimited Duration and a Power setting of 50 (see Figure 10-1).

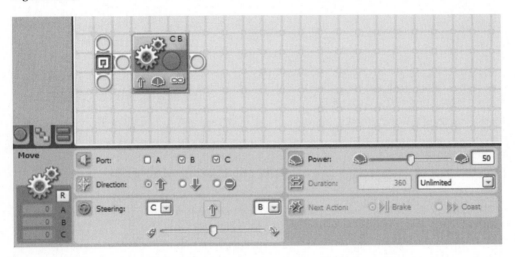

Figure 10-1. A new NXT-G program for SPOT

Now it's time to play around with different conditions that will end SPOT's forward movement. The WAIT block is our answer.

■ **Note** When I discuss the WAIT block, I'm going to put another word in front of it or behind it to tell you how I will configure it. For example, a WAIT TIME block will use time as the condition. If I want to use the Sound sensor to end the wait, I'll use a SOUND SENSOR WAIT block. OK?

The WAIT blocks are found on the Common Palette. When you move your mouse pointer over the WAIT block, a fly-out menu appears with six options (see Figure 10-2).

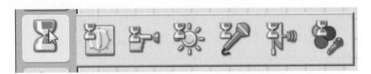

Figure 10-2. There are six WAIT blocks that can be selected.

■ **Note** If you are using the NXT-G 1.0 version of the software, you will not see the COLOR SENSOR WAIT block, the right-most icon in Figure 10-2.

Let me start with the easiest to configure—the TIME WAIT block. Figure 10-3 shows the TIME WAIT block added and its configuration panel.

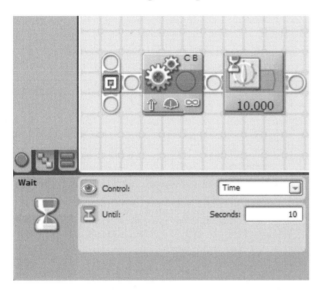

Figure 10-3. The TIME WAIT block and configuration panel

There are two items that can be configured on the TIME WAIT block. The first is a drop-down menu in the Control section. If you click this, you'll see that the WAIT block can be set to Sensor or Time. Don't change it yet, but be aware that by selecting Sensor you can change the TIME WAIT block to a SENSOR WAIT block.

The other option in the TIME WAIT block that can be configured is the Until section. You'll notice that it expects you to enter a number in the text box for the number of seconds you wish for the WAIT block to . . . wait.

Figure 10-3 shows that I've configured the TIME WAIT block for ten seconds. Go ahead and save the program, upload it to your bot, and then run it. What happens?

Did the motors run for ten seconds and then stop? If not, check to make sure you configured the TIME WAIT block for ten seconds; that's the most likely problem.

Well, that's it for the TIME WAIT sensor. Now let's take a look at some of the SENSOR WAIT blocks.

For the basic SENSOR WAIT blocks, I'm going to cover the configuration panels and the options available. I highly encourage you to practice these with the program you've just created: replace the TIME WAIT block with each of the SENSOR WAIT blocks discussed in the following sections. Configure each SENSOR WAIT block and play around with it; upload each to your bot, and see how it works.

■ **Note** The RECEIVE MESSAGE WAIT block will be covered later in the book when I discuss using Bluetooth to send and receive messages between bricks.

To get started, let me give you a shortcut for changing the type of the WAIT block. Go back to your original program with the MOVE block and the TIME WAIT block (shown in Figure 10-3). Click the TIME WAIT block to access the configuration panel. Click the Control section's drop-down menu, and choose Sensor instead of Time. When you change to Sensor, you now have a new configuration panel section (called Sensor) with another drop-down menu. Click the drop-down menu, and take a look at your options (shown in Figure 10-4).

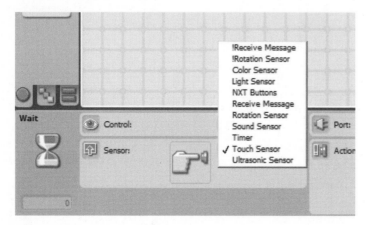

Figure 10-4. The options available to you in the Sensor section drop-down menu

■ **Note** You may not see all the options displayed in Figure 10-4 listed in the drop-down menu on your screen. Owners of the 1.0 version of the software will have a slightly different list, and if you have not installed the Legacy Blocks (see Chapter 9), these will also not be listed.

I'd like to show you most of these options and their corresponding configuration panels. Refer to Chapter 9 for details on the configuration panels for the sensors, NXT buttons, and timers.

The LIGHT SENSOR WAIT Block

Figure 10-5 shows the LIGHT SENSOR WAIT block and its configuration panel.

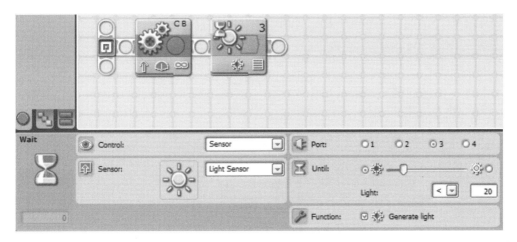

Figure 10-5. The LIGHT SENSOR WAIT block and configuration panel

In this example, the WAIT block has been configured to wait until the Light sensor detects a light level less than 20. When this occurs, the motors will stop spinning, and SPOT will stop moving forward.

The NXT BUTTONS WAIT Block

Figure 10-6 shows the NXT BUTTONS WAIT block and its configuration panel.

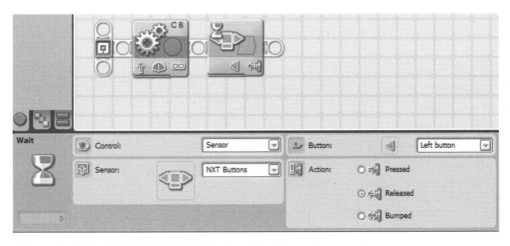

Figure 10-6. The NXT BUTTONS WAIT block and configuration panel

In this example, the WAIT block has been configured to wait until the Left button has been released. When this occurs, the motors will stop spinning, and SPOT will stop moving forward.

The ROTATION SENSOR WAIT Block

Figure 10-7 shows the ROTATION SENSOR WAIT block and its configuration panel.

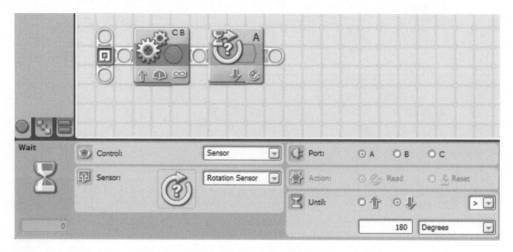

Figure 10-7. *The ROTATION SENSOR WAIT block and configuration panel*

In this example, the WAIT block has been configured to wait until motor A has spun in the Reverse direction for 180 degrees or more. When this occurs, motors B and C will stop spinning, and SPOT will stop moving forward.

The SOUND SENSOR WAIT Block

Figure 10-8 shows the SOUND SENSOR WAIT block and its configuration panel.

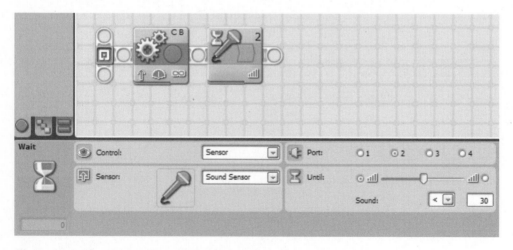

Figure 10-8. *The SOUND SENSOR WAIT block and configuration panel*

In this example, the WAIT block has been configured to wait until the Sound sensor detects a sound level below 30. When this occurs, motors B and C will stop spinning, and SPOT will stop moving forward.

The TIMER WAIT Block

Figure 10-9 shows the TIMER WAIT block and its configuration panel.

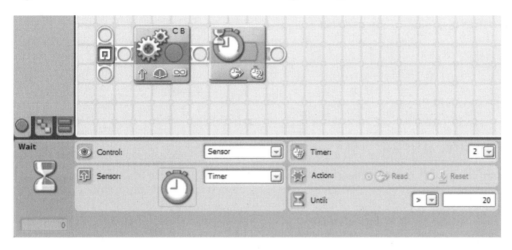

Figure 10-9. The TIMER WAIT block and configuration panel

In this example, the WAIT block has been configured to wait until Timer 2 exceeds 20 seconds. All timers start counting immediately when you run a program. So once you press the orange Enter button on the NXT Brick to run a program, this WAIT block will wait until the value read from Timer 2 equals 20 before the program continues. When this occurs, the motors will stop spinning, and SPOT will stop moving forward.

Later, you'll learn how to reset the timers, but for now, you just need to know that there are three timers—Timer 1, Timer 2, and Timer 3—and all start counting when a program starts.

The TOUCH SENSOR WAIT Block

Figure 10-10 shows the TOUCH SENSOR WAIT block and its configuration panel.

107

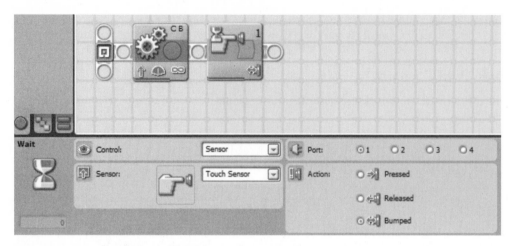

Figure 10-10. The TOUCH SENSOR WAIT block and configuration panel

In this example, the WAIT block has been configured to wait until the Touch sensor button has been Bumped (pressed and released quickly). When this occurs, motors B and C will stop spinning, and SPOT will stop moving forward.

The ULTRASONIC SENSOR WAIT Block

Figure 10-11 shows the ULTRASONIC SENSOR WAIT block and its configuration panel.

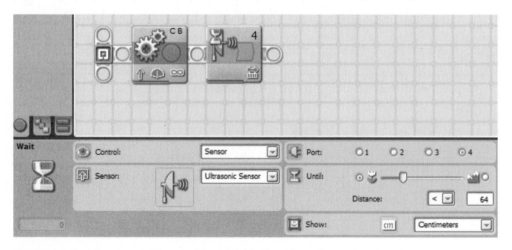

Figure 10-11. The ULTRASONIC SENSOR WAIT block and configuration panel

In this example, the WAIT block has been configured to wait until the Ultrasonic sensor detects an object (or obstacle) less than 64 centimeters in front of it. When this occurs, motors B and C will stop spinning, and SPOT will stop moving forward.

The COLOR SENSOR WAIT Block

Figure 10-12 shows the COLOR SENSOR WAIT block and its configuration panel.

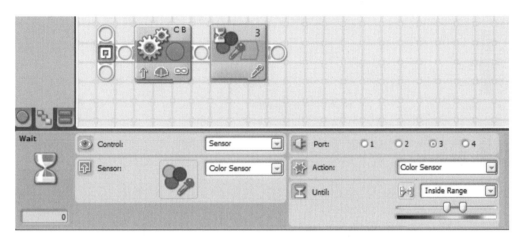

Figure 10-12. The COLOR SENSOR WAIT block and configuration panel

In this example, the COLOR SENSOR WAIT block has been configured to wait until the Color sensor detects an object (tape, piece of paper, ball, etc.) that is the color yellow. When this occurs, motors B and C will stop spinning, and SPOT will stop moving forward.

And that's it! Now you can configure your robots to wait for a variety of different conditions. You know how to use the sensors, the built-in timers, and the NXT buttons to trigger a WAIT block to stop waiting.

And now it's time for an exercise. I want to give you a scenario for SPOT where you'll need to use a variety of sensors to allow the robot to complete a very specific movement. I've provided one possible solution to the exercise at the end of the chapter.

Exercise 10-1

SPOT needs to navigate a cluttered floor. Figure 10-13 shows a bird's-eye view of a small area where SPOT will do some rolling.

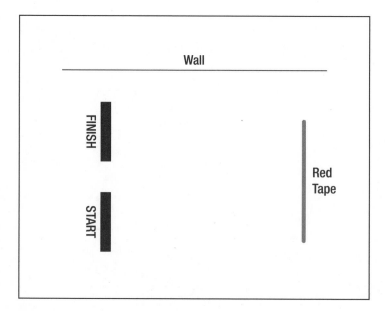

Figure 10-13. Get SPOT from the START line to the FINISH line.

Place SPOT behind the START line and pointing in the direction of some red tape that's been placed on the floor. When the program starts (by selecting the program and pressing the Enter button), have SPOT wait until the Touch sensor button is pressed and released (bumped) before beginning to roll forward. Have SPOT continue to roll forward until the Color sensor detects the red tape. When the red tape is detected, have SPOT stop, turn left (90 degrees), and then roll forward towards the wall. SPOT should continue to roll forward until the Ultrasonic sensor detects the wall is three inches in front of the robot. SPOT will then stop, turn left (90 degrees), and roll forward until it crosses the FINISH line and you press the Touch sensor button.

What's Next

Now, let me ask you a question. You know how to make your robot wait and wait and wait—but do you know how to make your robot do something else over and over again? To do this, you'll use something called a LOOP block. I'll show you how it works in Chapter 11.

Exercise Solution

Figures 10-14 through 10-21 show the complete program and configuration panels for Exercise 10-1. Keep in mind that you'll want to attach the Ultrasonic sensor so it faces forward (and can detect the wall) and the Color sensor so it faces down and can detect the tape on the floor. The Touch sensor can be placed anywhere that doesn't impede the robot's movements or other sensors. You will also need to experiment with the value for Degrees in the second and fourth MOVE blocks to get your robot to make a good 90-degree turn.

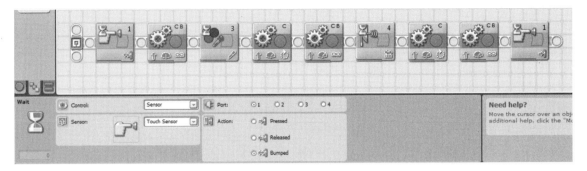

Figure 10-14. The complete program and TOUCH SENSOR WAIT block's configuration panel

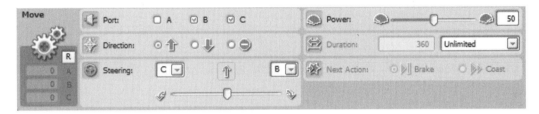

Figure 10-15. The first MOVE block's configuration panel

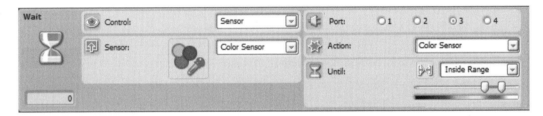

Figure 10-16. The COLOR SENSOR WAIT block's configuration panel

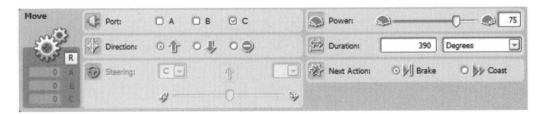

Figure 10-17. The second MOVE block's configuration panel

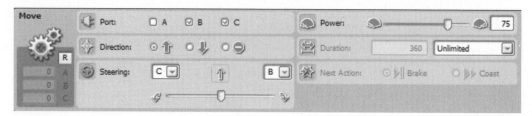

Figure 10-18. The third MOVE block's configuration panel

Figure 10-19. The ULTRASONIC SENSOR WAIT block's configuration panel

Figure 10-20. The fourth MOVE block's configuration panel

Figure 10-21. The fifth MOVE block's configuration panel

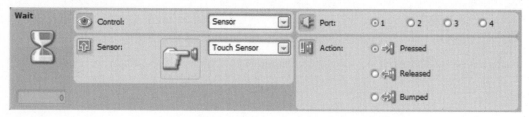

Figure 10-22. The second TOUCH SENSOR WAIT block's configuration panel

CHAPTER 11

Round and Round

At this point in the book, we're almost finished with the blocks in the Common Palette. Throughout the remainder of the book, I'll be introducing you to blocks and concepts that will allow you to build more complex programs that do more than simply tell your bots to move forward, backward, or in a circle.

Now, I'd like to take a short break to introduce you to another concept. I'll make this one fun too, I promise. Then, I'll show you a new NXT-G programming block that you'll really like.

Do It Again and Again and Again . . .

Let's go back to our friendly bot, SPOT. Once again, let's just pretend that he's got a pair of ears and can understand verbal commands. I'm going to give him a set of unusual commands:

Me: SPOT, I want you to move forward six rotations, stop, and turn right 90 degrees.

[SPOT moves forward six rotations, stops, and turns right.]

Me: SPOT, move forward six rotations, stop, and turn right 90 degrees.

[SPOT moves forward six rotations, stops, and turns right.]

Me: SPOT, move forward six rotations, stop, and turn right 90 degrees.

[SPOT moves forward six rotations, stops, and turns right.]

Me: SPOT, move forward six rotations, stop, and turn right 90 degrees.

[SPOT moves forward six rotations, stops, and turns right.]

Now, where is SPOT? That's right—he's back where he started. The path he followed was square-shaped, and he's once again waiting for my instructions.

If you were to create an NXT-G program for SPOT to make this square, you'd simply place eight MOVE blocks on the workspace (as shown in Figure 11-1) and configure each MOVE block with the same two settings, right? One MOVE block will spin motors B and C for six rotations and the next MOVE block will have SPOT make a right turn. I then repeat this pattern three more times, for a total of eight MOVE blocks.

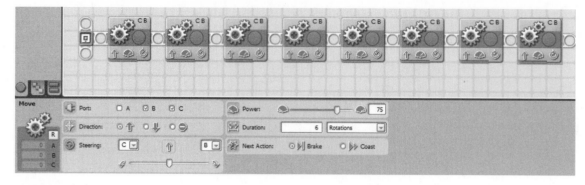

Figure 11-1. *NXT-G program for SPOT to follow a square-shaped path*

Well, it would work. But it seems like a lot of work just to make SPOT drive around in a square and return to his starting position. Is there a better way?

Let's see if we can improve the pseudo-code a bit:

Me: SPOT, I want you to move forward six rotations, stop, and turn right 90 degrees.

[SPOT moves forward six rotations, stops, and turns right.]

Me: SPOT, I want you to repeat my first set of instructions three more times.

[SPOT moves forward six rotations, stops, and turns right.]

[SPOT moves forward six rotations, stops, and turns right.]

[SPOT moves forward six rotations, stops, and turns right.]

Much better! I only had to tell him the instructions one time and ask him to do them again three more times. It takes just as long for SPOT to perform the movements, but I get to save my voice a bit!

In the pseudo-code, I gave SPOT commands, and I set a condition. You should be able to find the commands for SPOT: move, stop, turn right 90 degrees. But what is a condition? Remember, a condition is simply a rule your robot (SPOT) must follow and meet before the program can continue or end. So my rule for SPOT is "Repeat my first set of instructions three more times." I could have told him to repeat it twice or 60 times; it doesn't matter as long as SPOT knows the rule and follows it.

Instead of telling him to repeat it three times, could I have used a different condition? Sure—here are some examples:

Me: SPOT, I want you to repeat my first set of instructions until your Touch sensor is triggered.

Me: SPOT, I want you to repeat my first set of instructions until your internal timer goes over 45 seconds.

Me: SPOT, I want you to repeat my first set of instructions forever.

Another way to look at it is that I've given SPOT instructions to do over and over and over—until *something else happens.* It could be that the Touch sensor is pressed or the Color sensor detects a green line on the ground or the time reaches *infinity* (but trust me, SPOT's batteries won't last that long; eventually he'll stop)!

If SPOT keeps doing something over and over again, someone might say, "That robot is loopy!" And that's exactly right—he's *looping.* He is executing a loop!

What is a loop? In real life, a loop could be a racetrack or a long piece of string with its ends tied together—no matter how large it is, if you follow its path, you'll eventually come back to your starting position. A programming loop is very similar. It just circles back on itself, either forever or until you program an escape from the loop.

And it just so happens that the NXT-G software has a block just for this special occasion—the LOOP block (see Figure 11-2).

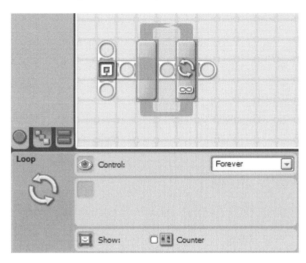

***Figure 11-2.** A new NXT-G program for SPOT to follow a square-shaped path*

The LOOP block, by itself, is very boring. By default, it is set to loop *forever;* you can see this in the Control section of the LOOP block's configuration panel.

Right now, any blocks that I drop inside the LOOP block will keep repeating, over and over. Let me give you an example.

■ **Note** When dropping a block inside a LOOP block, continue to hold down the mouse button and move the new block inside the LOOP block until the LOOP block expands.

I'm going to place a MOVE block inside the LOOP block. This MOVE block will be configured to spin the motors in Ports B and C for one rotation (see Figure 11-3).

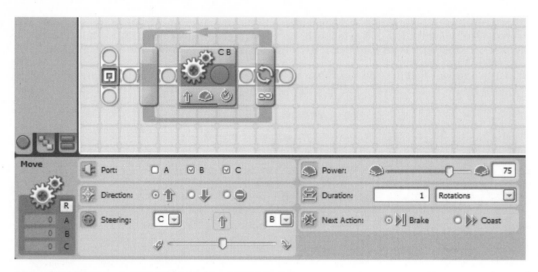

Figure 11-3. A simple MOVE block inside a LOOP block

I then save the program, upload it to SPOT, and run it. SPOT moves forward one rotation, and then there's a slight pause. Next, SPOT moves forward one more rotation, and there's another pause. This continues until I get tired of watching him, and I cancel the program.

The pause is occurring when the MOVE block finishes its action and the LOOP block checks its condition (this happens very quickly). Remember, the condition is a rule that the bot must follow. The rule for this program is for the LOOP to continue forever, so it runs again and again and again—you get the picture. That explains the short pause between rotations of SPOT's motors. SPOT is checking to see if it can end the loop; because it is set to run forever, the program jumps back to the start of the LOOP block and runs the MOVE block again.

Now let's change the condition. How would we tell SPOT to run the MOVE block four times?

Take a look at the LOOP block's configuration panel. The Control section has a drop-down menu. Go ahead and click it, and you'll see some options (shown in Figure 11-4).

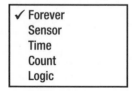

Figure 11-4. The Control section of the LOOP block

The options are Forever, Sensor, Time, Count, and Logic. Let me start with one of the easiest of the bunch: Time. Select Time from the drop-down menu in the Control section, and the configuration panel will change (see Figure 11-5).

Figure 11-5. The Control section of the LOOP block configured for Time

When you select Time as the Control, you have access to another section. The Until section is where you'll enter a time (in seconds) in the text box. This is the amount of time that any programming blocks *inside* the LOOP block will run. Earlier I mentioned that a loop will cycle forever until you program an *escape*. Well, by setting this time limit, you've provided that escape from the loop. And that escape goes by another term—*loop break*.

A *loop break* occurs when the loop stops. After the loop breaks, your program will continue with the next programming block, or it will stop if the LOOP block is the last block in your program. Easy, isn't it? The loop can break if you cancel the program, but it can also be configured to break when a specific condition is met. In one of my earlier examples, I told SPOT to stop when the Touch sensor was bumped. The Touch sensor will break the LOOP block.

I need to make one important point: if there are multiple blocks inside the LOOP block, they will *all* complete before the LOOP block breaks. So if you configure your LOOP block to run for 25 seconds and the blocks inside take 40 seconds to finish one run, the 25-second time limit will expire before the internal blocks are finished, so the LOOP block will not loop again.

What happens if the blocks inside take 15 seconds to run? Well, when the LOOP block starts, the timer begins counting down from 25. After the blocks inside have completed their first run, there are still ten seconds left on the timer. So the program jumps back to the start of the LOOP block and runs the inner blocks again. But this time, the timer will run down to zero before the blocks have completed. When the blocks have finished executing, the LOOP block checks the timer, sees that time has expired, and breaks the loop.

The other section, Show, has one option: you can either enable or disable the counter. Every time the LOOP block loops, the counter increases by one. If the box is checked, the LOOP block will provide a small data plug (see Figure 11-6). I covered data hubs and data plugs in Chapter 7, but what you need to know about this option is that you can use the data plug to provide an output Number data type. This Number value is the number of loops the LOOP block has performed. This value could be useful for more advanced programs where you wish to keep track of the number of times a LOOP block loops and use this for decision-making. For example, you might consider creating a program that uses the number value provided by the counter to increase the distance that the Ultrasonic sensor scans. Inside the loop, you could wire the counter plug to the Ultrasonic sensor's Trigger Point input data plug. Every time the loop executes, the Ultrasonic sensor will increase the distance it scans (in inches or centimeters) by a value of one.

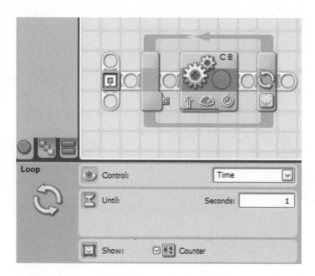

Figure 11-6. If you select the Show option, a small data plug becomes available.

Let' take a look at another easy Control option for the LOOP block—the Forever setting shown in Figure 11-7.

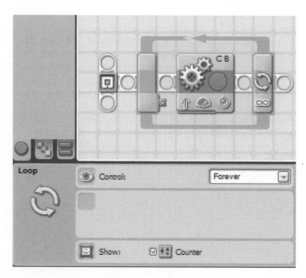

Figure 11-7. A LOOP block set to Forever

When you configure a LOOP block to run forever, that's exactly what will happen: any blocks inside the loop will run over and over again until you cancel the program or the batteries give out.

Now click the drop-down menu in the Control section, and select Sensor; next, click the drop-down menu in the Sensor section to see the drop-down menu shown in Figure 11-8.

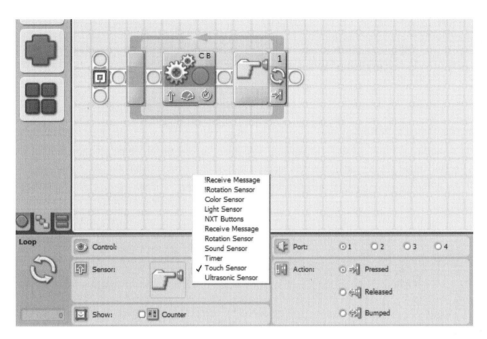

Figure 11-8. A LOOP block configured for Sensor input

As you can see, the Sensor section's drop-down menu offers,many options, including Light Sensor, NXT Buttons, Receive Message, Rotation Sensor, Sound Sensor, Timer, Touch Sensor, Color Sensor, and Ultrasonic Sensor. Most of these were covered in Chapter 9 and are easy to use. What you are doing when you select one of these options is configuring the trigger that will break the loop.

For example, in Figure 11-9, I have selected the NXT Buttons options from the Sensor section drop-down menu.

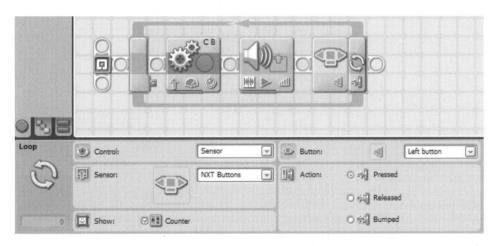

Figure 11-9. A LOOP block configured to break when the Left button is pressed

In this example, I have configured the loop to break when the Left button on the NXT Brick is pressed. Inside the loop, I have configured one MOVE block to move SPOT forward one rotation. I have also added a SOUND block that will play a short beep. Once the program is running, SPOT will move forward one rotation and beep, and he'll continue to do this until the Left button is pressed. (I'll have to chase him to press the Left button!)

■ **Note** In some situations, the break condition must occur at the exact moment that the LOOP block is checking its break condition. For example, in Figure 11-9, if I'm walking with my robot and press the Left button during the MOVE block's execution or the SOUND block's execution, the loop will not break. I must press the Left button after the robot beeps but before it begins moving again. There are ways to fix this and I'll show you how later in this chapter.

Just keep in mind that when you choose an option from the Sensor section, you are configuring a condition that *must* be met before the LOOP block will break.

Your next possible option is to break the loop with a Count. Select Count from the drop-down menu in the Control section (see Figure 11-10).

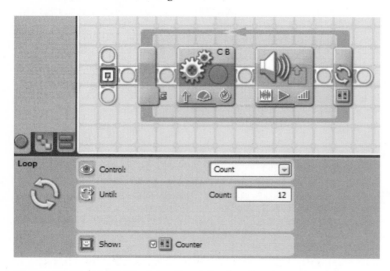

Figure 11-10. A LOOP block configured to break using a Count

When using the Count option, you must provide an integer value in the Until section's text box. You cannot use negative numbers, only zero and positive integers (1, 2, 3, and so on).

In Figure 11-10, I've configured the LOOP block to break when the Count reaches 12. When I run the program, SPOT will execute the first MOVE and SOUND blocks. When these are finished, Count goes from 0 to 1, and the loop starts again. The MOVE and SOUND blocks are executed again, and Count increases to 2. After the blocks have been executed a total of 12 times (Count = 12), the loop will break, and the program will end.

The last option available to break a loop is the Logic setting, shown in Figure 11-11.

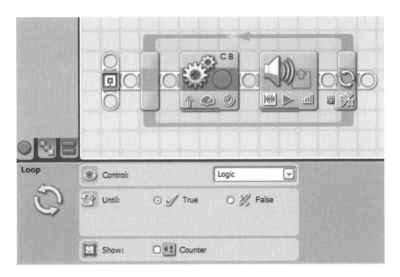

Figure 11-11. *A LOOP block configured to break using a Logic response*

In Figure 11-11, notice that when Logic is selected in the Control section drop-down menu, a small data plug appears on the LOOP block.

This data plug will accept only a Logic data wire as input. This means that the LOOP block will break when the Logic data type (True or False) you selected in the Until section is received. I'll show you an example using this option in the next section.

That's it for configuring an individual LOOP block. But there's one more thing I'd like to show you with the LOOP block: nested loops.

Nested Loops

To demonstrate this new concept, I'm going to create a simple program for SPOT that I'd like you to follow and create yourself. First, let me explain what I want SPOT to do using pseudo-code:

Me: SPOT, I want you to move forward along a circular path for 3.5 rotations and then use your speaker to beep! Do this two more times (for a total of three times), and then check to see if your Light sensor detects a Light level greater than 90. If the Light sensor is not triggered, repeat this entire process.

I can use a LOOP block to hold a MOVE block and a SOUND block that will repeat three times. This is shown in Figure 11-12.

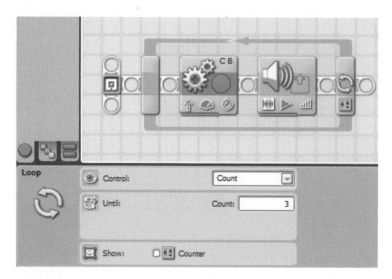

Figure 11-12. *This LOOP block contains a MOVE block and a SOUND block and will use a Count of 3.*

I've dropped a MOVE block and a SOUND block inside this LOOP block. In the Control section, you'll see that I've selected the Count option and set it to 3. The next thing I want to do is see if the Light sensor is triggered. I've added and configured the Light sensor in Figure 11-13.

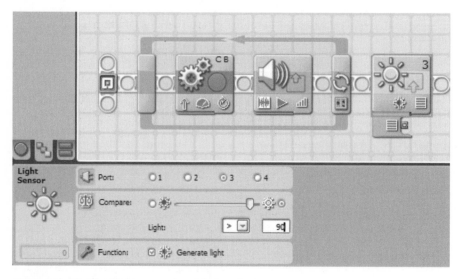

Figure 11-13. *The Light sensor is added to the program.*

But now I've got a problem. If you follow along with the program, you can see that the LOOP block will run three times: the MOVE and SOUND blocks inside it will execute three times and then the LOOP breaks. Then the Light sensor is tested. If the Light level is greater than 90, the program ends. But what if the

Light level is less than 90? How do I make the program run again? One option is to simply have SPOT run the program again. I'll have to press the Enter button on the Brick to run the program again, but this will work. It will also be very annoying. There ought to be an easier way, and there is.

Take a look at Figure 11-14, and you'll notice that the entire program I just created is now *inside* another LOOP block.

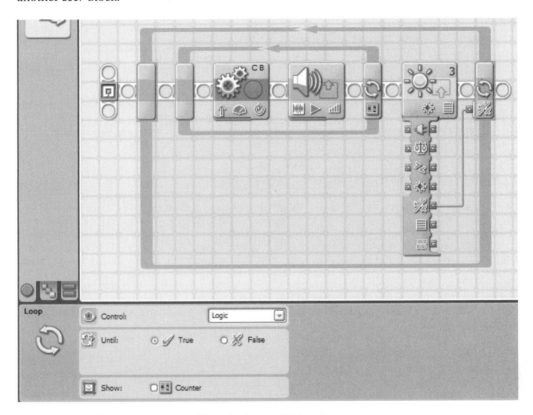

Figure 11-14. There is now a LOOP block inside a LOOP block.

This is called a *nested loop*, which just means a loop inside a loop. When the program runs, any blocks inside the outer LOOP block will run—this includes the inner LOOP block! First, the inner LOOP block will run three times (executing the MOVE and SOUND blocks inside it) and then break. Then the Light sensor will send a True/False Logic response to the outer LOOP block's data plug. If the Light sensor does not detect a light level greater than 90, the outer LOOP block will not break and will run whatever is inside it again.

Notice in Figure 11-14 that there is a data wire connecting the Light sensor to the outer LOOP block. In the Control section of the outer LOOP block, I've selected the Logic option and programmed it to wait until it receives a True response from the Light sensor block. If the Light sensor block does not detect a light level greater than 90, the Yes/No data plug sends a False signal to the outer LOOP block, causing the outer LOOP block to loop again.

For my final example, Figure 11-15 shows a complicated situation. Can you determine what will happen?

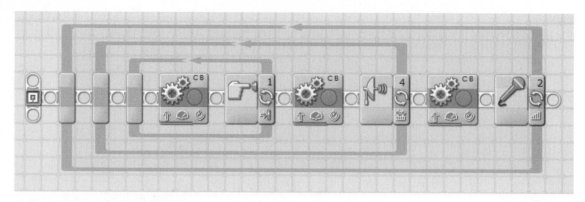

Figure 11-15. LOOP blocks everywhere

Yes, that is a loop inside a loop inside a loop—three LOOP blocks! If you examine this program carefully, you should be able to see what will happen when it is run.

First, the innermost LOOP block will begin to execute a MOVE block until the Touch sensor is triggered (in this case, bumped). Then the innermost LOOP block will break. Next, the middle LOOP block will begin executing a MOVE block until the Ultrasonic sensor is triggered. At that point, the middle LOOP block will break. Then the final, outer LOOP block will begin executing a MOVE block until the Sound sensor is triggered. Finally, when the Sound sensor is triggered, the outer LOOP block breaks, and the program ends.

The LOOP block is a very useful and powerful block; you should spend some time experimenting with all the different options. You'll use the LOOP block often when you want your robots to repeat certain blocks.

Now, I have a slightly more complicated exercise for you to examine. Earlier in the chapter I mentioned a situation where I would have to press the Left button at the exact moment when the last NXT-G block executes inside a block—otherwise the LOOP block wouldn't detect the button push and it would begin running the program again. How might we fix this?

Exercise 11-1

Take a close look at Figure 11-16. It may look a little strange to you with that extra block sitting way up above the main program. Can you see how the program works? I'm using a block that might be new to you—the VARIABLE block. I'll cover it in more detail in Chapter 14, but for now just follow along and configure the block as I describe here. After examining the program, modify it to break the loop when the Color sensor detects a red line on the floor.

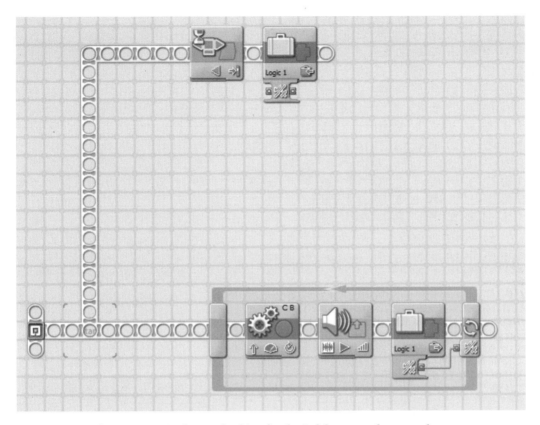

Figure 11-16. This program is always checking for the Left button to be pressed.

I created this program by adding an extra sequence beam. To do this, move your mouse pointer to the very start of the sequence beam, as shown in Figure 11-17.

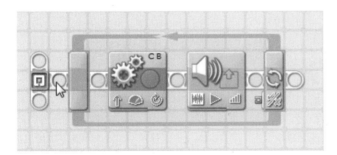

Figure 11-17. Create a new beam by starting at the beginning of the existing beam.

While holding the Shift key down, click and hold your left mouse button and drag up to where the first bend in the new beam will appear. This is shown in Figure 11-18.

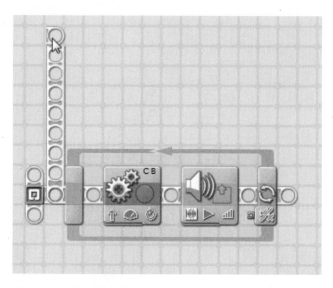

Figure 11-18. *Drag the new beam up away from the main program.*

Next, release the mouse button and drag the pointer to the right. Drag it to increase the length of the new beam that will run parallel to the main beam below it. Double-click your left mouse button to create the ending of the new beam. This is shown in Figure 11-19.

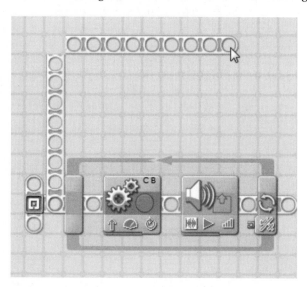

Figure 11-19. *Drag the new beam to the right and parallel to the main beam.*

Now, drop a NXT BUTTONS WAIT block onto the new beam, as shown in Figure 11-20. (Dropping additional blocks will automatically extend the new beam to the right.)

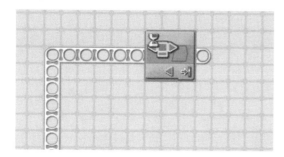

Figure 11-20. Add a `NXT BUTTONS WAIT` *block to your new beam.*

Any blocks added to your new beam will run in parallel to the blocks on the main beam. Next, add a `VARIABLE` block to the top beam and configure it as shown in Figure 11-21.

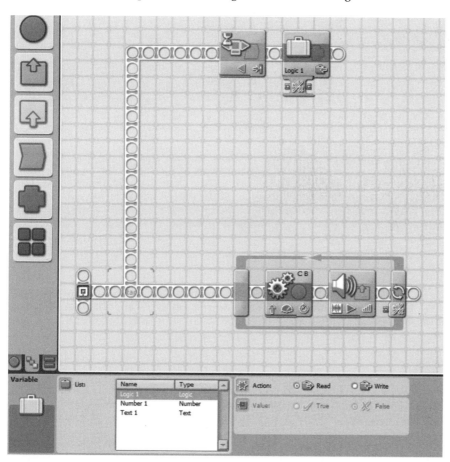

Figure 11-21. Add a `VARIABLE` *block to the top beam and configure it to Read the Logic 1 value.*

Notice that the configuration panel for the VARIABLE block has its Action setting set to Write and the Value is set to True. Also, the Logic 1 value is selected in the List box.

Finally, add another VARIABLE block inside the LOOP block. Drag a wire from its Yes/No data plug, as shown in Figure 11-22, and configure it as shown in the configuration panel.

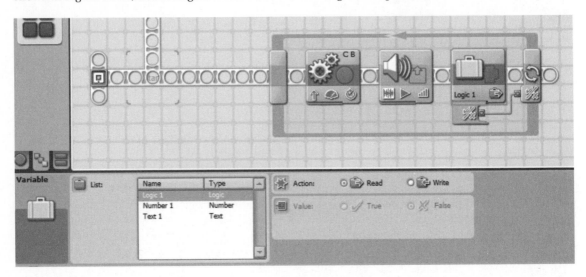

Figure 11-22. Add another VARIABLE block inside the loop and configure it to Read the Logic 1 value.

Now, when the program runs, all the blocks inside the LOOP block will execute until the VARIABLE block sends a True signal and breaks the loop. How will the VARIABLE block get a True signal? On the top beam, after the left button is pressed, the VARIABLE block after it will write a True value to the variable named Logic 1. By default, the VARIABLE block starts out holding a False value. When the left button is pressed, the Logic 1 value changes from False to True… and then when the LOOP block finishes the SOUND block, the Logic 1 value is checked in the VARIABLE block and the True value it now holds will break the loop!

What's Next?

Now you know how to have your robot repeat certain actions such as turning left and moving forward ten rotations. Up next in Chapter 12, I'm going to show you how to give your robots the ability to make choices: should SPOT turn left and move forward five rotations or turn right and move forward two rotations?

Exercise Solution

Figures 11-23 and 11-24 show the complete program and the configuration panel settings for the LOOP and COLOR SENSOR WAIT and VARIABLE blocks (you can use any settings you like for the MOVE and SOUND blocks). Notice that once again I'm using a LOOP block configured to break when it detects a logical True value stored in the VARIABLE block placed inside the loop. For the Color sensor configuration panel, I've configured it to look for the color red by dragging the left and right drag bars to surround the color red and setting the Compare setting to Inside Range. If you want to read about the VARIABLE block, feel free to skip to Chapter 14 and come back to this exercise when you're done.

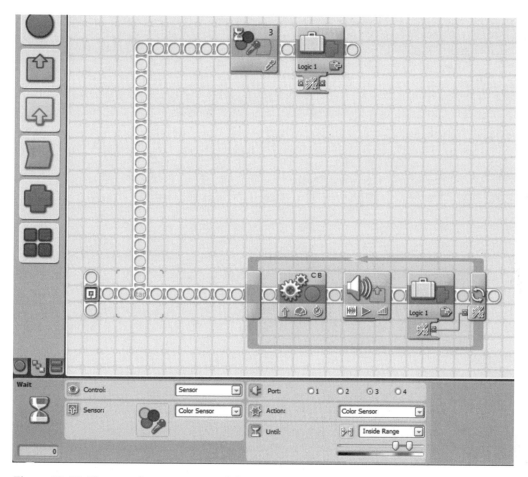

Figure 11-23. *The complete program and the COLOR SENSOR WAIT block's configuration panel*

Figure 11-24. *The LOOP block's configuration panel*

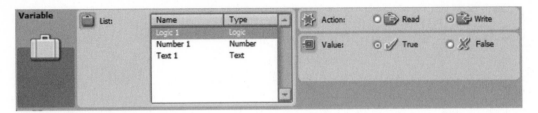

Figure 11-25. The top VARIABLE block's configuration panel

Figure 11-26. The bottom VARIABLE block's configuration panel (inside loop)

CHAPTER 12

■ ■ ■

Decisions, Decisions

This chapter covers the final block in the Common Palette. When you are finished with this chapter, you will have the ability to create some great programs for your robots and give them the ability to move, talk, listen, bump, stop, wait, and a lot more. (But there are plenty more NXT-G blocks to learn about, so don't stop reading yet!)

Let's give your robots one more talent—the ability to make choices and select from multiple possible actions. Choices are very important to your robot; with the ability to decide between two or more options, your robot can perform much more complicated actions.

Left or Right? Door One or Door Two?

Let me give SPOT some pseudo-code for his next task:

Me: SPOT, I want you to move forward three rotations and stop. If your Light sensor detects a light level over 30, turn left. Otherwise, turn right.

At this point, you already know how to program SPOT with a MOVE block that moves him forward three rotations. But how do you take the light value from the Light sensor and use it to help SPOT make a decision about turning left or right?

The answer is easy. You'll use the SWITCH block shown in Figure 12-1.

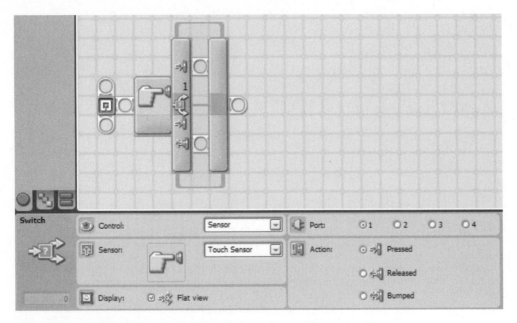

Figure 12-1. The SWITCH block lets your robots make choices.

The SWITCH block uses an input value to determine a path to take. This value can be a number, a bit of text, or a Logic value (True or False). And you're not just limited to two paths. You could configure a SWITCH block to handle the following pseudo-code:

Me: SPOT, pick a random number from 1 to 5.

Me: If the number is 1, turn left.

Me: If the number is 2, turn right.

Me: If the number is 3, spin 180 degrees.

Me: If the number is 4, spin 360 degrees.

Me: If the number is 5, keep moving forward.

In this example, I have SPOT pick a random number. This is done using the RANDOM block that you'll learn about later in Chapter 14. But for now, let's just assume for the moment that SPOT can pick his own numbers. Now, since there are five potential numbers (1, 2, 3, 4, and 5), there are five potential actions that can be taken. Throughout the remainder of this chapter, I'm also going to use the term *path* instead of *action*, because the SWITCH block will allow your robots to choose from different paths available to them.

Depending on the path a robot selects, different actions will occur. One path can have your robot moving forward, checking its Ultrasonic sensor for an object in front. Selecting a different path might send the same robot in the reverse direction, waiting for its Touch sensor to be pressed and counting the number of rotations the motors spin. That's the great thing about the SWITCH block. Each potential path choice can have unique programming blocks that give your robots even more power. (And you can add another SWITCH block to a path, creating another set of paths for your robot to choose from! It's like nesting LOOP blocks but instead you're putting a new SWITCH block into an existing SWITCH block.)

Flat and Tabbed Views

Now, before I show you how the SWITCH block works, I need to mention one special item in the SWITCH block's configuration panel. Take a look at Figure 12-2.

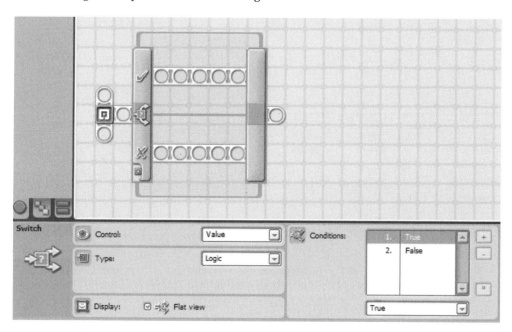

Figure 12-2. *Flat view for the SWITCH block*

When using the SWITCH block, you need to choose between Flat view and Tabbed view. When using Flat view, you need to leave the Flat view box checked (as shown in Figure 12-2). Flat view does have a limitation that you need to be aware of, however. When using it, you can program *only* two paths. Notice in Figure 12-2 that there are two paths: one labeled with a checkmark and the other with an "X". The checkmark path is also called the *default* path (more on this in a little bit). The icons for the default path and the other path will change, however, if a sensor is selected as the Control. I'll show an example of this shortly.

Now, in Figure 12-3 I've unchecked the Flat view box, and you can now see that the SWITCH block has tabs along the top edge.

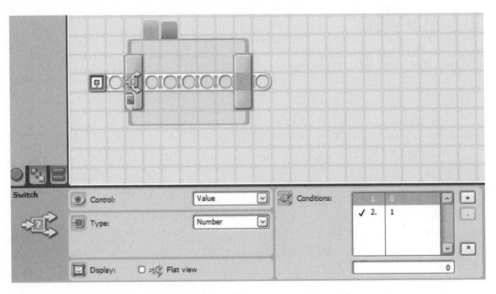

Figure 12-3. Tabbed view for the SWITCH block

With the Tabbed view, you must click a tab to see the programming blocks (if any) that have been placed inside it. This is a small price to pay for the ability to specify more than two options, however. Remember the earlier pseudo-code where SPOT picked a random number between 1 and 5? Figure 12-4 shows a SWITCH block with five tabs; each tab will now correspond to one of the potential actions I asked SPOT to perform.

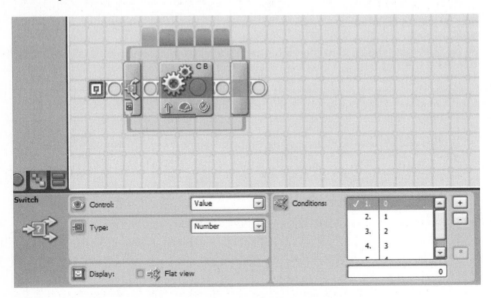

Figure 12-4. This SWITCH block has five tabs for five different paths.

Choices

Now it's time to show you how to configure the SWITCH block, so you can use it to give your robot choices.

In Figure 12-5, I've placed a single SWITCH block that is using the Flat view. This means I only have two possible paths for my robot to take. The first path (with the small flower icon) is on top and the second path (with the small mountain icon) is on the bottom.

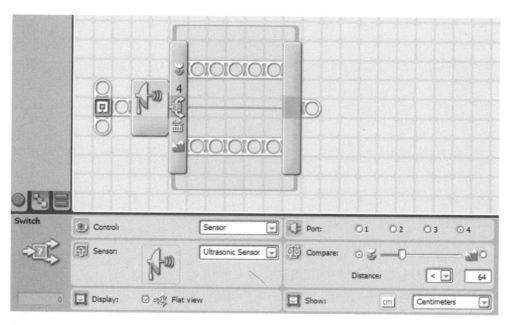

Figure 12-5. *This SWITCH block has two possible paths.*

This example also shows you the power of the SWITCH block. In the Control section, you have a pull-down menu that offers two options: Sensor and Value. Choosing the Sensor option will allow you to configure the SWITCH block to determine the correct path for your robot using the sensor and its trigger, which you select.

In this example, I've selected the Ultrasonic sensor. I've configured the Ultrasonic sensor to detect when an object or obstacle is detected less than 64 centimeters (but not equal to 64) in front of the robot. If this condition is met (True), the SWITCH block will execute any blocks found in the True path (the upper beam, with the small flower icon). If the condition is not met (False), the SWITCH block executes any blocks found in the False path (the lower beam, with the mountain icon).

For the moment, let's assume that SPOT has his Ultrasonic sensor and Sound sensor mounted. I'm going to give SPOT the following pseudo-code:

Me: SPOT, when your Ultrasonic sensor detects an object less than 64 centimeters in front, turn left if your Sound sensor detects a sound level greater than 20.

I've already shown you how to configure the first SWITCH block to use the Ultrasonic sensor. Let's assume that SPOT's Ultrasonic sensor detects an object less than 64 centimeters in front of him. This means that any blocks on the upper beam (True path) will be executed. From the pseudo-code, you know that if the first condition is met, you want SPOT to turn left only if his Sound sensor detects a sound greater than 20. How will you do this? Simple—you'll use another SWITCH block!

First, you drop another SWITCH block on the top beam and configure it, as shown in Figure 12-6.

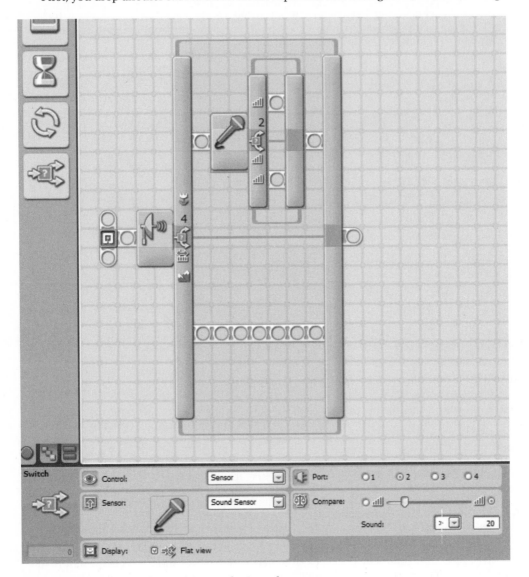

Figure 12-6. This second SWITCH uses the Sound sensor.

Next, configure the second SWITCH block to use the Sound sensor and to detect a sound greater than 20. If this happens, the True path (upper beam) in the second SWITCH block will execute any blocks found inside it. And that is where you'll place the MOVE block that allows SPOT to turn left (see Figure 12-7).

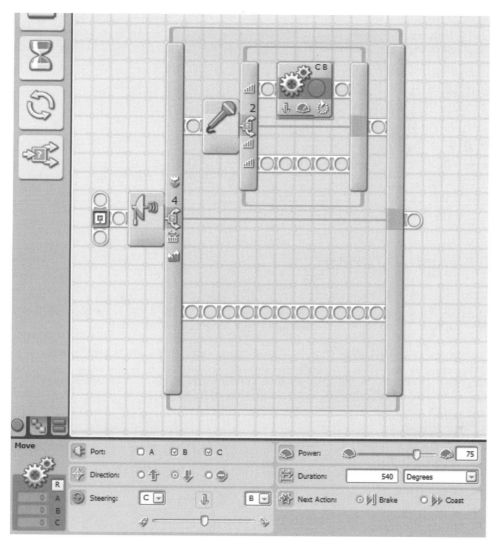

Figure 12-7. SPOT will turn left if the first and second SWITCH block conditions are met.

This is an example of embedded SWITCH blocks. You could keep going and place more SWITCH blocks inside other SWITCH blocks. This will give your robots some excellent decision-making control!

More Than Two Conditions

But what if you need to program your robot to test a greater number of conditions? Not all situations will have conditions that only have two options, right? Let's take another example for SPOT. Have a look at Figure 12-8.

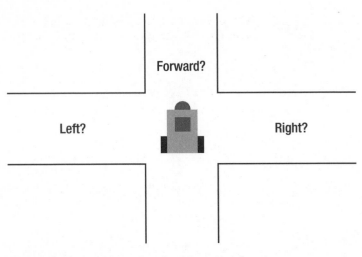

Figure 12-8. SPOT has some decisions to make.

Here's the pseudo-code:

Me: SPOT, when you come to the hallway intersection, pick a number from 1 to 3. If the number is 1, turn left. If the number is 2, turn right. And if the number is 3, move forward.

To do this bit of programming, recall you'll have to turn off the Flat view for a SWITCH block to use more than two conditions. That's the first requirement. The second requirement for configuring a SWITCH block for more than two paths is that the SWITCH block must be configured to use the Value option. This is found in the drop-down menu in the Control section and is shown in Figure 12-9.

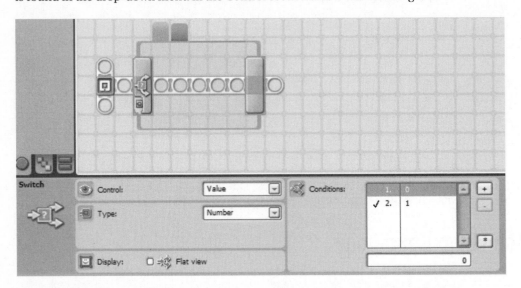

Figure 12-9. Start with a SWITCH block with Flat view turned off and using a Value.

The SWITCH block now has a small input data plug that will be used. This data plug can accept a Number data type, a Text data type, or a Logic data type, and you select the option from the drop-down menu in the Type section.

Using the pseudo-code, you can see that there are three possible conditions:

- Turn left if the number SPOT picks is 1.

- Turn right if the number SPOT picks is 2.

- If the number is 3, move forward.

For this example, I'm going to use the RANDOM block that is discussed in Chapter 14. For now, don't worry about how it works—just drag and drop a RANDOM block from the Complete Palette onto the beam, and place it in front of the SWITCH block, as shown in Figure 12-10. (If you really want to know how the RANDOM block works, just jump ahead and read Chapter 14. I'll wait for you right here.)

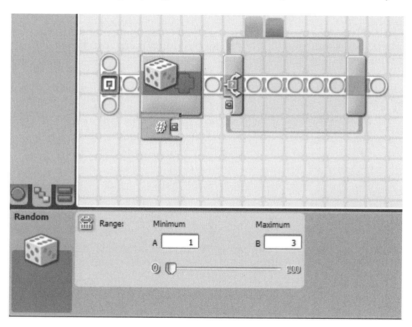

Figure 12-10. A RANDOM block will generate a value of 1, 2, or 3.

For the configuration panel of the RANDOM block, simply enter a value of 1 in the Minimum text field and a value of 3 in the Maximum text field, as shown in Figure 12-10.

Drag a data wire from the RANDOM block to the SWITCH block (see Figure 12-11).

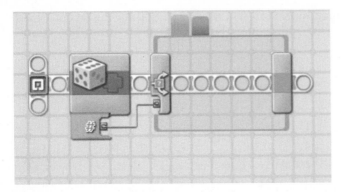

Figure 12-11. Connect the RANDOM block to the SWITCH block with a data wire.

Next, you need to configure the SWITCH block to accept more than two conditions. To do this, click the SWITCH block again (if it isn't already selected), and look at the configuration panel. On the left side of the configuration panel, you'll see the Conditions section (shown in Figure 12-12).

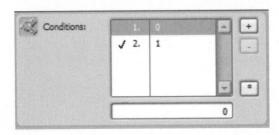

Figure 12-12. The Conditions section of the SWITCH block

Let me explain what you are looking at. This is a list consisting of path numbers. Each path number has a default value that the SWITCH block will check. In this example, you see the following:

1. 0

2. 1

The 1 and 2 on the left are the possible conditions, and these match the number of tabs you see along the top edge of the SWITCH block. The 0 and 1 values in the right column are the default Number values that the SWITCH block will use to pick a path. For example, if the Number value coming into the SWITCH block's data plug is 0, then the first condition will be selected, and any blocks found under the first tab will be executed.

But you need three conditions—one for each if the RANDOM block generates the number 1, 2, or 3. To do this, click on the small plus button (+) in Figure 12-12. It adds the third condition and automatically configures it with a default value of 2. This is seen in Figure 12-13. If you click on the new condition, you can change the default value of 2 to any number you like. You're going to need to do that shortly.

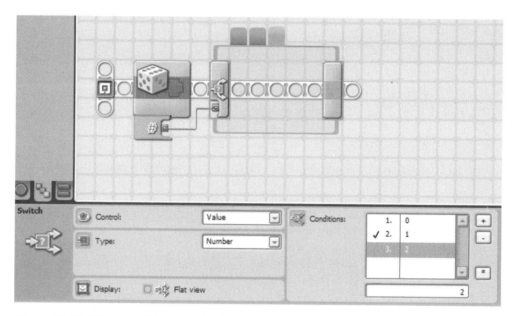

Figure 12-13. Three possible paths for the SWITCH block

Notice that there is now a new row in the Condition section:

1. 0

2. 1

3. 2

There are now three tabs on the SWITCH block. Tab 3 will have its blocks executed if the SWITCH block detects a Number value of 2.

Here you have a small problem: SPOT will pick only 1, 2, or 3. But the only options shown are 0, 1, and 2. How can you change this? If you click one of the conditions, you can change its value in the text box just below the Condition section. First, click the condition whose value you want to change (see Figure 12-14).

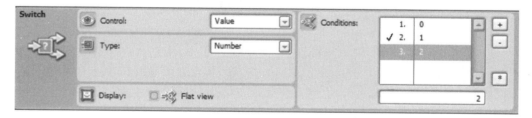

Figure 12-14. Click a Condition to change its value.

In this example, the third condition is selected, which has a default value of 2. In the box below the conditions, enter the value of 3 as seen in Figure 12-15 and press Enter.

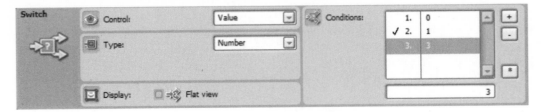

Figure 12-15. Select a condition you wish to change by clicking on it.

You'll do this for the first and second conditions also, changing their respective values to 1 and 2, as seen in Figure 12-16.

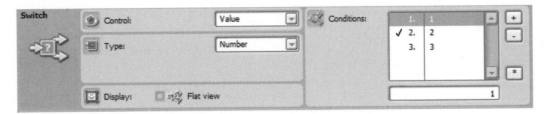

Figure 12-16. Change the Number values for all conditions.

Default Decisions

Finally, you may have noticed the checkmark next to a condition. In Figure 12-16 it is next to the second condition (indicated by the numeral 2). The checkmark indicates which condition the SWITCH block considers the default value to use and the tab (and its blocks) to select if the SWITCH block is unable to make a decision. For example, suppose I had configured the RANDOM block to select a value between 1 and 5. There are no conditions specified for what to do if a 4 or 5 is randomly selected. Suppose you wish a 4 or 5 to be treated as a value of 3. In this case, the blocks found on the third tab will be executed because you have selected condition 3 by selecting the third condition and clicking on the small asterisk button (*), as seen in Figure 12-17.

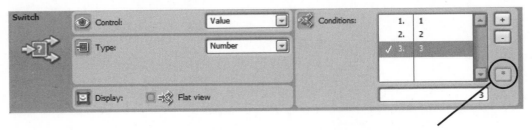

**Click here to select the
default condition**

Figure 12-17. Configure the default setting to be used by the SWITCH block.

■ **Note** When a SWITCH block is encountered, something must be done. One of the conditions must be satisfied for the program to continue running. Therefore, a default condition must be specified in most instances. You can always leave a path empty, with no NXT-G blocks on it, for one of the conditions. In cases where you have a program that should not react to a condition, provide a blank path and set that blank path as the default. Then, if a sensor or RANDOM block or other block does not trigger a suitable condition you've specified for the SWITCH block, the default condition will be chosen and no blocks executed, allowing the SWITCH block to complete and the program to continue.

■ **Caution** Please be aware that you cannot have two or more conditions with the same Number value. This is because the SWITCH block would get confused and not know which path to take. Make sense? If condition 1 has a Number value of 1 and condition 2 has a Number value of 1, which path would the SWITCH block take if the RANDOM block sends a value of 1? Fortunately, the SWITCH block is smart and will not allow you to make this mistake.

Execution!

Now that you've configured the three conditions and the default (condition 3), you can drop in a collection of MOVE blocks that will allow SPOT to turn left, turn right, or move forward.

If SPOT picks 1, then he turns left. So, you'll click the first tab (see Figure 12-18) and drop in a MOVE block that will allow SPOT to turn left.

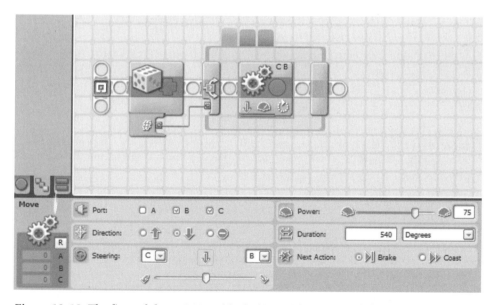

Figure 12-18. The first tab has a MOVE block that executes if SPOT picks 1.

I'll do the same thing for the second and third tabs. When the RANDOM block generates a number from 1 to 3, that number is passed to the SWITCH block. The SWITCH block takes this Number value and compares it to the values in its Condition section. If the RANDOM block sends a 3, the SWITCH blocks takes that value, notices that it equals the 3 in the third condition, and then executes any blocks found on the third tab. Easy!

One final warning, though—what happens if the RANDOM block goes crazy and sends a value of 4 or 5 to the SWITCH block? There is no condition that has a matching value of 4 or 5, so what will happen? Well, remember when you selected a condition and clicked the * button and a checkmark appeared next to the condition? That checkmark also specifies the *default condition*. Look back at Figure 12-17. The checkmark is next to the third condition. This means that if a value of 4 or 5 is provided by the RANDOM block, the default path will be chosen. So the blocks in the third tab will execute for a value of 4, 5, 100, or any other number except for 1 and 2.

The SWITCH block is a very useful block for giving your robots some powerful decision-making skills. The SWITCH block can use Logic values (True or False), Numbers, Text, and sensors to determine which paths are chosen by your robot to execute. Keep this in mind when you need to give your robots the ability to make different decisions based on different types of input.

As your programming skills progress, you'll find the SWITCH block one of your favorite tools to use.

Now, before leaving this chapter and moving on to some of the more advanced NXT-G blocks, I'd like for you to try creating an NXT-G program that satisfies the requirements found in Exercise 12-1. I've provided the answer at the end of the chapter if you get stuck.

Exercise 12-1 Left or Right?

Program SPOT to examine his surroundings and make some decisions based on sensor input. SPOT should move around the room as defined by these rules:

- Move forward until the Color sensor detects a red or yellow piece of tape on the floor.

- If a red piece of tape is detected, turn left 90 degrees and move forward 10 rotations.

- If a yellow piece of tape is detected, turn right 90 degrees and move forward 10 rotations.

What's Next?

In the next few chapters, you'll be looking into some specialty blocks. You'll learn about a block to stop your robot's program execution. Believe it or not, stopping and doing nothing is sometimes exactly the right thing to do. After stopping, you'll learn about randomizing. There's much more to follow too, so don't stop reading.

Exercise Solution

The solution to Exercise 12-1 can be seen in Figures 12-19 through 12-24. Notice that the WAIT block is first used to detect a colored piece of tape (red or yellow), specified by dragging the condition bars on the COLOR SENSOR WAIT block's configuration panel. Once a red or yellow piece of tape is discovered, the SWITCH block will examine the tape and determine if it is red in color. If it is, the condition specified in Figure 12-21 is true and the MOVE block in the top portion of the SWITCH block will execute (see Figure 12-22). If the tape isn't red, then it must be yellow (because the COLOR SENSOR WAIT block stops only for red or yellow) and this will force the lower portion of the SWITCH block to execute its MOVE block seen in Figure 12-23 (rotating the robot to the right). After a turn is made, the final MOVE block (see Figure 12-24) will have the robot roll forward 10 rotations.

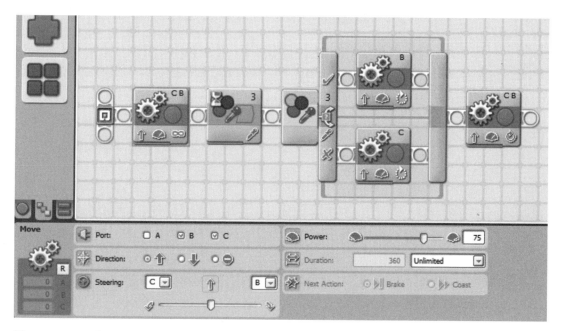

Figure 12-19. The complete program and the first MOVE block's configuration panel

Figure 12-20. The COLOR SENSOR WAIT block's configuration panel

Figure 12-21. The SWITCH block's configuration panel

Figure 12-22. The true path MOVE block's configuration panel

Figure 12-23. The false path MOVE block's configuration panel

Figure 12-24. The final MOVE block's configuration panel

■ ■ ■

CHAPTER 13

Stop It!

This will be another short chapter. How much can one really say about a block that simply stops your program from running?

The STOP Block

The most important thing you need to know about the STOP block is this: if your robot encounters a STOP block at any point in the program, the robot will simply stop at that point with no further action (there is one exception and that is when you are using data wires—more on that later).

Why would you need a STOP block? Your robot will always stop when it reaches the end of your program unless you have a LOOP block somewhere in the program that keeps the program running (or a LOOP block surrounding all other programming blocks, which means the program will run forever until you press the Cancel button or a STOP block is encountered somewhere in the inner workings of your program).

So why a STOP block? It's because once you begin looping, you need a way to stop looping.

A Looping Example

The STOP block is shown in Figure 13-1. Notice in its data hub that it only has one input data plug and one output data plug, which can use a Logic data type.

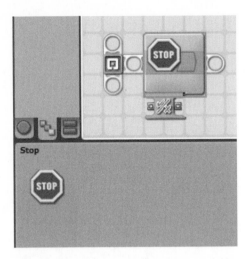

Figure 13-1. The STOP block and its configuration panel

As I mentioned earlier, the STOP block will immediately stop the program when the STOP block is reached *unless* a data wire is providing a False input (signal) to the STOP block's input data plug. Let's look at the example in Figure 13-2.

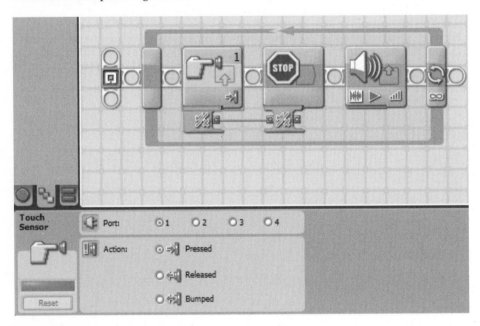

Figure 13-2. A simple program using the STOP block

In Figure 13-2, I've got a small program for SPOT. It's a LOOP block that contains a TOUCH SENSOR block, a STOP block, and a SOUND block. When the program is run, every time the LOOP block loops, SPOT will beep (using the SOUND block). This will continue until the Touch sensor is pressed. When the Touch sensor is pressed, a True response is sent (using the data wire) to the STOP block's input data plug. And the program will stop. As long as the Touch sensor is not pressed, the STOP block will continue to receive a False response from the Touch sensor and will not stop the program. Simple!

An Unconditional STOP

Now, what do you think would happen if I didn't connect a data wire between the Touch sensor and the STOP block, as shown in Figure 13-3?

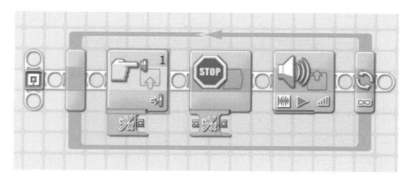

Figure 13-3. Modifying the sample program's data wire completely changes the way it works.

You can load the program and try it, but if you walk through the simple program visually I think you'll figure it out.

When the program runs, the LOOP block starts. The Touch sensor block runs, followed by the STOP block. Will the program execute the SOUND block? The answer is, "No." Remember my initial rule: the program will stop running when it executes a STOP block and will perform no further actions. This program will stop immediately and never execute the SOUND block (run the program to prove it to yourself).

A SWITCH to a STOP

You might be wondering when you would ever want to put a STOP block in the middle of a program. Well, one answer involves the SWITCH block. Recall that using the SWITCH block allows your robots to choose different action paths to take. One path might send your robot into some more complex programming behavior while the other path might be a simple STOP block. Take a look at Figure 13-4, which shows an example of this process.

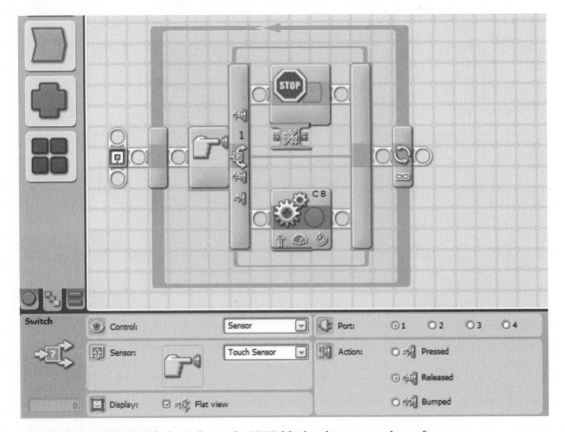

Figure 13-4. A SWITCH block might need a STOP block to keep your robot safe.

In this example, I've placed SPOT on a tall table. SPOT's Touch sensor is mounted facing downward on the table, so the button is pressed. If SPOT reaches the edge of the table, the Touch sensor button will no longer be pressed, right? (There's no table surface to continue to press against the button.)

Figure 13-4 shows a simple LOOP block that contains a SWITCH block. I've configured the SWITCH block to test whether the Touch sensor button is Released. If it is, the True path will be selected. If the button is still pressed, the False path will be selected. I want SPOT to stop immediately when the Touch sensor button is released, so I place a STOP block in the True path and a MOVE block in the False path. As long as the button is pressed, SPOT will keep moving forward. But for SPOT's safety, once the button is released (and he's reached the edge of the table), I want the program to immediately end. The trick to this program is placing the Touch sensor far out in front of SPOT, so he's still safely back from the edge when the button is released. Try it!

STOP for Testing

The STOP block is extremely easy to use. As a testing tool, you can always place a STOP block in your program if you're testing a robot but don't want it to continue past a certain point in the program. For example, let's say you have a robot that performs three separate tasks, one after the other. Placing a STOP block after the programming blocks for the first task will allow you to run your program and test to make certain the program works for that task. This is seen in Figure 13-5. If all is well, remove the STOP block and place another STOP block after the programming blocks for the second task. Now when you run the program, your robot will perform the steps for the first and second tasks, but not for the third.

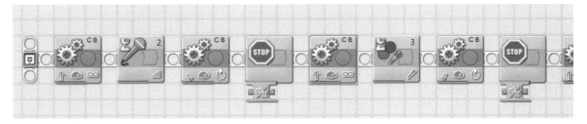

Figure 13-5. Use a series of STOP blocks when testing a long program.

In the program in Figure 13-5, SPOT will begin rolling forward for an Unlimited duration. Only when the SOUND SENSOR WAIT block is triggered will SPOT rotate a specific number of degrees. I want to test different values for the number of degrees to rotate, so I've placed a STOP block in the program so that SPOT doesn't begin to roll forward again (controlled by the third MOVE block in the program). Once I've got the proper number of degrees configured in the second MOVE block, I'll remove the first STOP block, upload the new program to SPOT, and proceed with the next portion of the program (which performs the same action but will be triggered by the COLOR SENSOR WAIT block).

The STOP block is there when you need it—for testing or for building in a method for automatically stopping your robots when a specific condition is reached (or not reached). It's one of the simplest NXT-G blocks around, but it's also one of the most helpful.

What's Next?

Now it's time to STOP this chapter and MOVE on to the "NXT" one; it's not a RANDOM chapter, but it does cover the RANDOM block. Sorry, I couldn't resist.

CHAPTER 14

■ ■ ■

Pick a Card, Any Card

Have you ever had someone perform a card trick and ask you to pick a card from the deck? There are 52 cards in a standard deck (the two jokers don't count), and if it's been properly shuffled, you should be able to pick a random card from the deck.

It's the same with rolling a pair of dice. Each die has the potential to roll a number from one to six. When you roll a normal pair of dice, the numbers that appear are random. The odds of rolling a two on one die are the same as rolling a six; they all have the same likelihood of appearing. What allows this to occur is simple randomness.

Your robots also have the ability to generate random numbers. You might want to build a robot that can roll a virtual set of dice or maybe pick a number between 1 and 1,000. Read on to learn how to have your robots generate random numbers *and* display them on the LCD screen.

The RANDOM Block

Your robots can use the RANDOM block to generate numbers in a range (a minimum value and maximum value) that you define. Data wires can also be used to provide the minimum and maximum values that will be generated. The RANDOM block is found on the Complete Palette in the Data fly-out menu. Take a look at the block and its configuration panel in Figure 14-1.

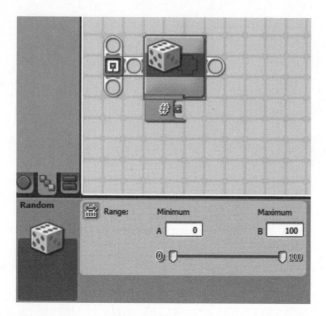

Figure 14-1. The RANDOM block and its configuration panel

The RANDOM block is another one of those blocks that is very simple to use. There are not a lot of options to configure, but what is there is important.

The first thing I want you to notice in the configuration panel is the Minimum and Maximum number fields in the Range section. In these boxes, you can type in the upper and lower values for the numbers you want the RANDOM block to generate. For NXT-G version 1.0, the minimum value can never be less than zero, and the maximum value can never be greater than 32,767. For NXT-G version 2.0, the minimum value can be negative.

There is one other method you can use for defining the minimum and maximum values. There are two small tabs on the slider bar below the minimum and maximum values. You can drag the leftmost small tab to set the minimum value. The rightmost small tab can be dragged to set the maximum value.

■ **Note** One thing you should be aware of is that the slider bar can be used only for defining a range between 0 and 100. If you wish to use a maximum value greater than 100, you need to type the number into the maximum number field. If you are using version 2.0, you must also type in a negative value for the minimum number field; the slider bar is not capable of setting values less than zero.

Now, let's do an example with SPOT using pseudo-code:

Me: SPOT, show a random number on your LCD screen between 20 and 80 until I press the left button.

To do this, I'll first drop a RANDOM block on the beam (see Figure 14-1). I've told SPOT that I want the minimum value to be no less than 20, so I'll use the slider bar to set the minimum value (see Figure 14-2).

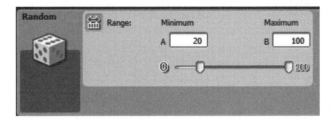

Figure 14-2. The RANDOM block with the minimum value set to 20

Now, what if I had wanted the value to be between 20 and 80 but not include 20? Remember, the minimum and maximum values you define will be included in the possible numbers generated by the RANDOM block. So if I didn't want 20 to be a possible number, I would simply drag the slider bar again to set the minimum value to 21. By doing this, 21 would be a possibility, but 20 would be no longer allowed.

My final step is to set the maximum value; I drag the slider bar to set the maximum value to 80 (see Figure 14-3).

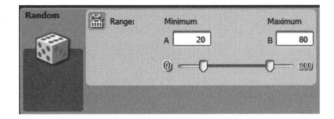

Figure 14-3. The RANDOM block with the maximum value set to 80

Now all that's left to do is to have SPOT display the value on the LCD screen. To do this, I need to introduce you to another NXT-G programming block: NUMBER TO TEXT.

The NUMBER TO TEXT Block

The NUMBER TO TEXT block is also found on the Complete Palette in the Data fly-out menu. I'll drag and drop it after the RANDOM block, so you can see its configuration panel (shown in Figure 14-4).

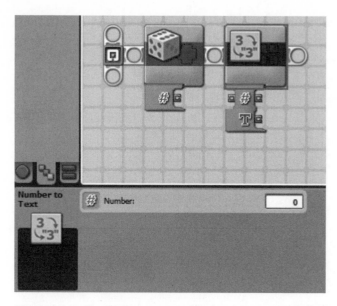

Figure 14-4. The NUMBER TO TEXT *block is for displaying numbers on the LCD screen.*

Why do I need to use the NUMBER TO TEXT block? Remember, the DISPLAY block is capable only of displaying an image, text, or a drawing, Since it cannot display a number value, we have to convert a number into text. The text "1" is not the same as the number value "1"—the text "1" is treated just like any other character in the alphabet.

The NUMBER TO TEXT block requires the number it will send to the LCD screen to come into its single-input data plug or be typed into the Number field on the configuration panel. The number is then converted to text that can be displayed using the DISPLAY block. So, let me go ahead and drag a wire from the output Number data plug on the RANDOM block into the input Number data plug on the NUMBER TO TEXT block. You can see this in Figure 14-5.

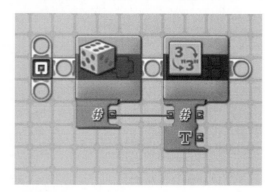

Figure 14-5. Drag a wire from the RANDOM block to the NUMBER TO TEXT block.

As you can tell from Figure 14-5, the text you want to display will come from the output data plug on the NUMBER TO TEXT block. I'll drop in a DISPLAY block and drag another wire from the output Text data plug on the NUMBER TO TEXT block into the input Text data plug on the DISPLAY block (see Figure 14-6). Remember to set the DISPLAY block to display text, not images or drawings, in its configuration panel.

One mistake often made is to drag a wire out of the RANDOM block's plug and drag it into the DISPLAY block's last data plug, the one that has the # symbol and looks like it should take a number. That data plug controls the radius of a circle (if a circle is drawn on the LCD screen), so all you'd be doing is using the RANDOM block to control the radius of a circle instead of displaying the value on the screen. The only way to display the number generated by the RANDOM block is to use the NUMBER TO TEXT block.

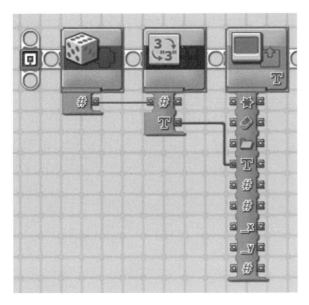

Figure 14-6. Drag a wire from the NUMBER TO TEXT block to the DISPLAY block.

Instead of using a TIME WAIT block to keep the text on screen as I've done with past examples, I'm going to use an NXT BUTTON WAIT block this time. The RANDOM number generated will stay on the LCD screen until I press the Left button.

To do this, I drop in an NXT BUTTON WAIT block and configure it as shown in Figure 14-7.

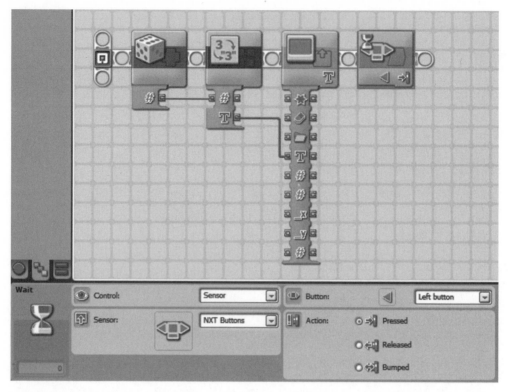

Figure 14-7. The generated number will stay on the LCD screen until the left button is pressed.

I've used a WAIT block with the Control section set to Sensor. In the Sensor section, I selected NXT Buttons from the drop-down menu. For the Button section, select Left button from the drop-down menu, and finally, in the Action section, I selected Pressed. By configuring the WAIT block this way, the random number will stay on the LCD screen until I press the left button on the NXT Brick. Then the program ends.

Not too difficult, huh?

One final thing I want to point out on the NUMBER TO TEXT block is the output Number data plug. This block will still allow you to keep and use the random number you generated in a Number format. You might need that random number later in the program. If so, you can drag a data wire out of the output Number data plug—it will still be a number and not changed to text.

So now you know how the RANDOM block is configured and used. If you want your robot to move randomly around the room, for example, you could configure a RANDOM block to generate a number between one and four. Program your bot to go left if the number is one, right if the number is two, forward if the number is three, and in reverse if the number is four. By using a random number to control the bot's direction, you can give the bot some unpredictable behavior. Refer to Chapter 12's discussion of the SWITCH block for using conditions such as a random number to control movement.

Now let's see if you've got a grasp of how the RANDOM block works. Read over Exercise 14-1 and create a new program for SPOT. If you get stuck, I've provided one possible solution at the end of the chapter.

Exercise 14-1

Create a program that will have your robot move forward (from its START position) a random number of degrees (and stopping at its END position). You are then going to have the robot reverse direction and move backwards a random value so that it ends up somewhere between the START position and the END position. Have your robot display the number of degrees it has moved forward (to the END position) and also display the number of rotations it rolls backwards. Keep both these values displayed on the screen. When the movement has completed, use a WAIT block to allow you time to view the values on the LCD screen before the program ends.

What's Next?

Next, in Chapter 15, we'll look at the COMPARE block. The COMPARE block uses two types of data—number and logic. It compares two number values and then provides a logical data type—True or False—depending on how you've configured the two number values to be compared. Confusing? It'll all be cleared up in the next chapter.

Exercise Solution

Figures 14-8 through 14-16 provide you with the complete program and the configuration panels for Exercise 14-1.

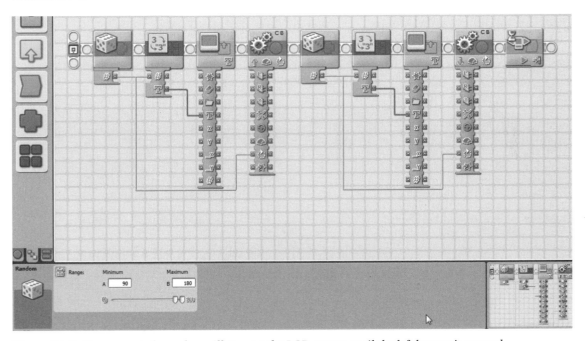

Figure 14-8. The generated number will stay on the LCD screen until the left button is pressed.

In Figure 14-8, I've configured the RANDOM block to select a value between 90 and 180. So the maximum distance the robot's wheels will travel is 180 degrees and the minimum is 90 degrees.

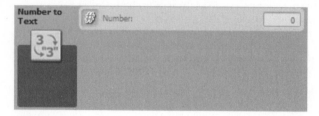

Figure 14-9. The generated number will stay on the LCD screen until the left button is pressed.

Figure 14-9 is grayed out because I'm using a data wire to carry a number value into the block.

Figure 14-10. The generated number will stay on the LCD screen until the left button is pressed.

Figure 14-10 shows that I've selected Text as the Action for the DISPLAY block. For this first DISPLAY block, I've also left the Display setting checked (to clear the LCD screen).

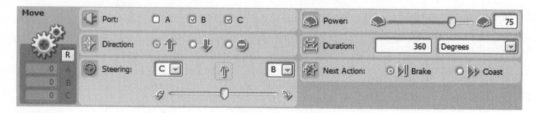

Figure 14-11. The generated number will stay on the LCD screen until the left button is pressed.

Figure 14-11 shows that the robot has been configured to roll forwards using Degrees.

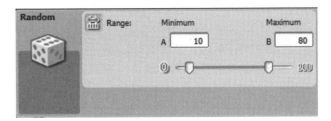

Figure 14-12. The generated number will stay on the LCD screen until the left button is pressed.

Figure 14-12 shows the second RANDOM block. This time, I've configured it to select a value between 10 and 80. This will ensure that when the robot rolls backwards it ends up somewhere between its START and END positions.

Figure 14-13. The generated number will stay on the LCD screen until the left button is pressed.

Another NUMBER TO TEXT block is shown in Figure 14-3. This will pass the second random number generated to the next DISPLAY block.

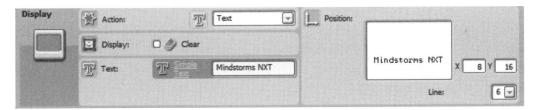

Figure 14-14. The generated number will stay on the LCD screen until the left button is pressed.

Notice in Figure 14-14 that I've unchecked the Display setting and changed the Line to display the second value to Line 6. This will ensure that the original random number and the new random number are both displayed on the LCD screen.

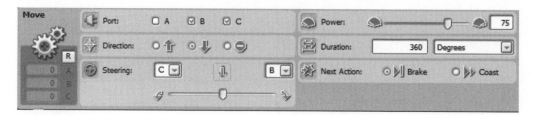

Figure 14-15. The generated number will stay on the LCD screen until the left button is pressed.

Another MOVE block is used to roll the robot backwards a random number of degrees, shown in Figure 14-15.

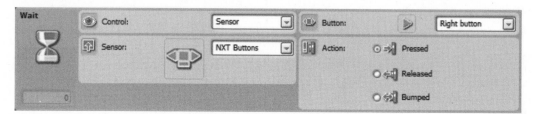

Figure 14-16. The generated number will stay on the LCD screen until the left button is pressed.

Finally, when the robot has completed its movement, both random numbers will be displayed on the screen until the user (you) presses the right button, as configured in Figure 14-16.

CHAPTER 15

Apples and Oranges

There's an old saying, "That's like comparing apples to oranges." What it means is that it's sometimes unfair to compare dissimilar objects. I said "sometimes," because at other times it's completely fair. Suppose I hand you one apple and one orange. Which one is heavier? Which one has a larger diameter? These aren't unfair questions, are they?

So sometimes you *can* compare apples to oranges! And when it comes to your robots, there's a way for your robots to compare things, too—not apples and oranges, but numbers.

Logic

Remember that we discussed the concept of Logic back in Chapter 8? True or False? (If you said False, you need to go back and read Chapter 8 again!)

Well, NXT-G comes with a programming block called the COMPARE block that relies on your understanding of Logic.

Suppose I ask you, "Is five greater than three?" Your answer would be, "Yes." When you program, the same question is given to a computer or robot in the form of a statement, "Five is greater than three." This statement, to your robot, is either True or False.

Similarly, if I ask you, "Is the Earth square-shaped?" you would answer, "No." A robot would not be asked this question, but instead told, "The Earth is square-shaped." And it would respond with False.

So, here's an important item to remember: robots respond to statements with True or False. And to do this, robots will rely on the COMPARE block.

A Random Example

Before I show you the COMPARE block, let's create a test program for SPOT using pseudo-code:

Me: SPOT, I want you to create two random numbers between one and nine (number A and number B), show them on the LCD screen, and tell me if A is greater than B.

To do this, we'll start by dropping two RANDOM blocks (see Chapter 14) on to the beam, as shown in Figure 15-1. I've configured both RANDOM blocks with identical settings, as shown in the configuration panel.

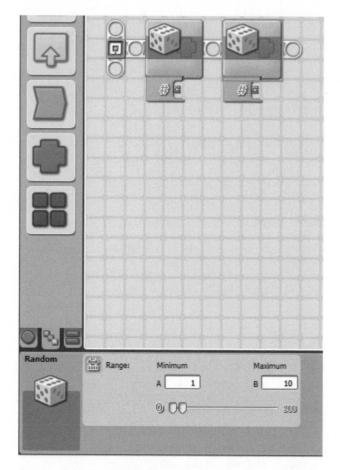

Figure 15-1. *Two* RANDOM *blocks will generate numbers for comparison.*

Next, I'll convert them to text using two NUMBER TO TEXT blocks (see Figure 15-2). Review Chapter 14 for information on the NUMBER TO TEXT block.

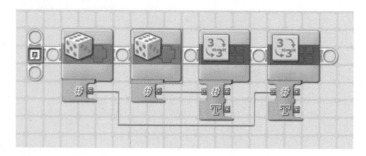

Figure 15-2. *Convert the random numbers to text.*

And before we get to the COMPARE block, I'll use a TEXT block to create a statement in the form of "A greater than B," as shown in Figure 15-3. The TEXT block will allow you to enter up to three bits of text in the A, B, and C text fields shown in Figure 15-3. You can also submit text to one of those three text fields using data wires as I've done with the NUMBER TO TEXT blocks (also shown in Figure 15-3).

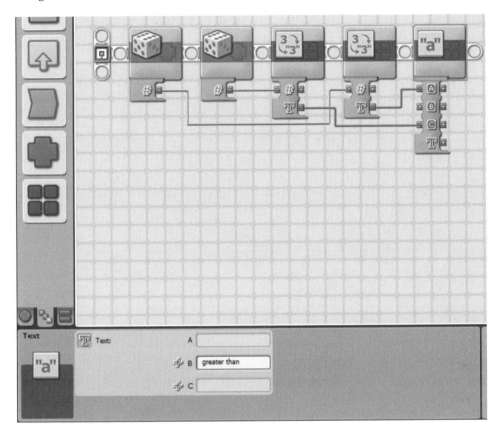

Figure 15-3. Create a text statement to be displayed on the LCD screen.

As you can see from Figure 15-3, the first RANDOM block number is used as input in the second NUMBER TO TEXT block (the fourth block from the left). The second RANDOM block number is used as input in the first NUMBER TO TEXT block (the third block from the left).

For the TEXT block, I have taken the first number (now converted to text) and used it as input to the A data plug. Also, I have taken the second number (now converted to text) and used it as input to the C data plug. I enter the words "greater than" in the B text box. This will create a single sentence (also called a *statement*): A greater than C (where A and C will be numbers between one and nine).

I now send the combined text to a DISPLAY block configured to display text on Line 3 with position X=2 and Y=40 (see Figure 15-4).

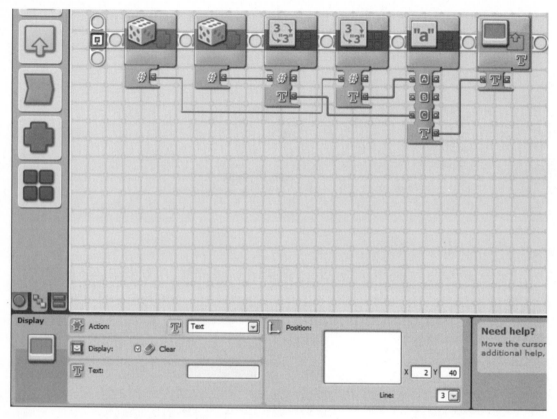

Figure 15-4. The DISPLAY *block will display a statement on the LCD screen.*

The COMPARE Block

Now we're ready to see how the COMPARE block works. (Sorry it took so long to get here, but the COMPARE block by itself can't do anything—we need a good example with things to compare to see it in action.)

I'm going to break off a new beam to run in parallel. To do this, I hold down the Shift key and drag an extra beam, shown in Figure 15-5.

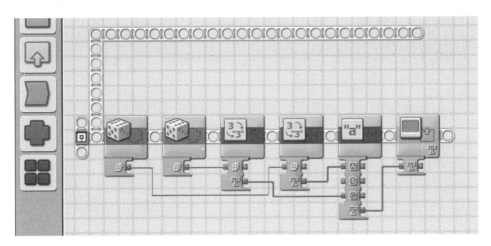

Figure 15-5. An extra beam will be used to compare values.

This parallel beam will let me compare value A to value B at the same time that the numbers are being converted to text. Remember, I want to check the statement "A greater than B" and determine if it is True or False, so not only do I want to put the statement on the screen, but I also need to determine whether A really is greater than B.

The first thing I need to do is drop the COMPARE block onto the new beam, as shown in Figure 15-6.

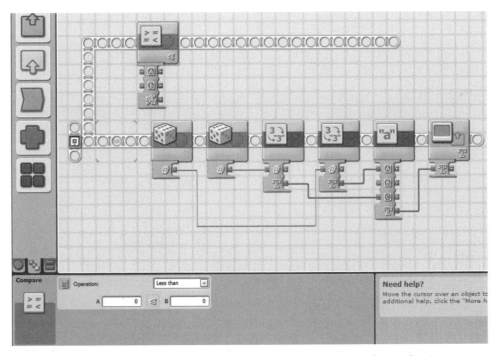

Figure 15-6. The COMPARE block will check to see if value A is greater than value B.

Notice in Figure 15-6 that the COMPARE block has two input data plugs. I'll take the original random numbers from the NUMBER TO TEXT blocks' output Number data plugs and drag data wires into the two COMPARE block input data plugs.

■ **Note** Back in Chapter 14, I told you that the NUMBER TO TEXT block had an output Number data plug that could be used to keep the number in Number format and not Text format. You'll use this ability now to send these original random numbers into the COMPARE block.

Carefully drag a data wire out of the second NUMBER TO TEXT block (the fourth one from the left) and into value A's input data plug. Do the same for the first NUMBER TO TEXT block (the third from the left) but drag this wire into value B's input data plug. This configuration is shown in Figure 15-7.

■ **Note** Sometimes NXT-G will try to fix your wiring to keep it from becoming a tangled mess. In Figure 15-7 you might notice that the wires coming out of the RANDOM blocks have been split. This happened automatically for me, even after I dragged the wire out of the NUMBER TO TEXT block. After I released my mouse button to complete the wire, NXT-G changed it so the RANDOM block wire split.

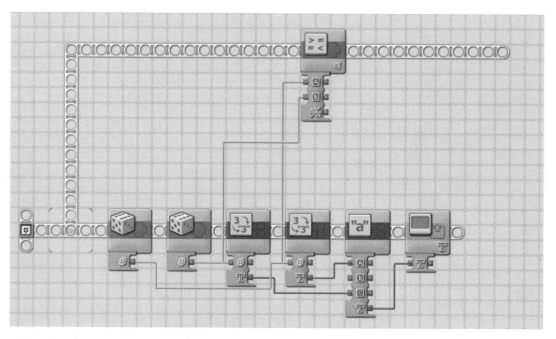

Figure 15-7. Use the original number values as input for the COMPARE block.

Now, click the COMPARE block to view its configuration panel (shown in Figure 15-8).

Figure 15-8. The COMPARE block's configuration panel

The COMPARE block's configuration panel has a drop-down menu in the Operation section. Click this drop-down, and you'll see three options: Less than, Greater than, and Equals.

If you choose the "Less than" option, the COMPARE block will evaluate the statement "A Less than B" and determine if it is True or False. If you choose the "Greater than" option, the COMPARE block will evaluate the statement "A Greater than B" and determine if it is True or False. And if you choose the "Equals" option, the statement "A Equals B" will be evaluated.

For my example, I chose the "Greater than" option, as shown in Figure 15-8. Now, my program will take the values for A and B and check to see if A is greater in value than B. The COMPARE block does this, and the answer will come from the output Result data plug. A logic data type (True or False) can then be accessed using the COMPARE block's Result data plug, which will supply a logical True or False data signal.

The Display of Logic Values

If we go back to the pseudo-code, we'll see that I wanted True or False to be displayed on the LCD screen along with the original statement "A greater than B." To do this, I'm going to use the SWITCH block I covered in Chapter 12.

There are a bunch of items I need to configure for this to work. I drop a SWITCH block after the COMPARE block, and in the Display section, leave the Flat view box checked (see Figure 15-9). In the Control section, I choose Value, and in the Type section, I choose Logic. I also drag a data wire out of the output Result data plug on the COMPARE block and connect it to the input data plug on the SWITCH block.

169

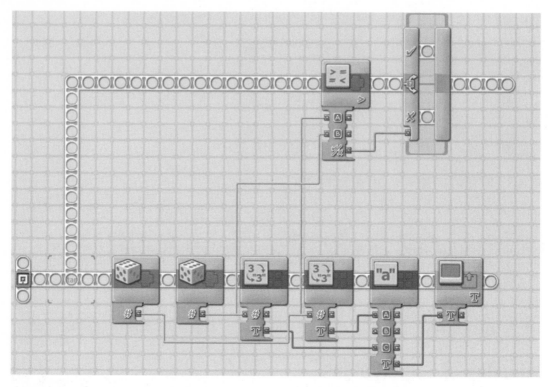

Figure 15-9. *The* SWITCH *block will help me display True or False on the screen.*

Next, I need to decide what will happen when the SWITCH block receives a True or a False signal from the COMPARE block. Let's start with the True path in the top portion of the SWITCH block, shown in Figure 15-9.

I want to send the word "True" to the LCD display if the statement is True, so I'll drop in a DISPLAY block that will contain the word "True." This is shown in Figure 15-10.

I also unchecked the Clear box so the statement "A greater than B" doesn't get cleared off the LCD screen. I also set the text to display at X=2 and Y=8 so the word "True" appears below the original statement "A greater than B."

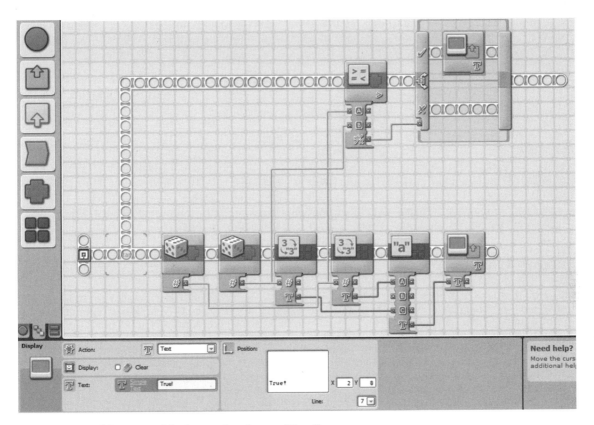

Figure 15-10. This DISPLAY block contains the text "True!"

Now I need to configure another DISPLAY block in the False portion of the SWITCH block. Figure 15-11 shows the new DISPLAY block.

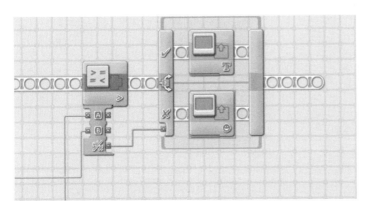

Figure 15-11. This DISPLAY block contains the text "False!"

Figure 15-12 shows how I've configured the "False!" DISPLAY block—notice that I've configured it to display the text in the same location, with X=2 and Y=8, and that I've unchecked the Clear box.

Figure 15-12. The configuration panel for the False! DISPLAY block

Finally, I drop in a NXT BUTTON WAIT block configured to wait for the left button to be pressed. This will give me time to view the results on the LCD screen (see Figure 15-13).

A Test Run

Let's walk through the program and see how it works. First, two RANDOM blocks generate two numbers, A and B. These numbers are converted to text (with the NUMBER TO TEXT blocks) and these "text numbers" are combined to create a text statement, "A greater than B," which is fed into a DISPLAY block.

After the random numbers are generated, these numbers are also fed into the COMPARE block, which takes the two numbers and looks to see if A is greater than B. If it is, the SWITCH statement executes the DISPLAY block on the True path and displays the word "True!" on the LCD screen. If A is not greater than B, the SWITCH statement executes the DISPLAY block on the False path and displays the word "False!" on the screen.

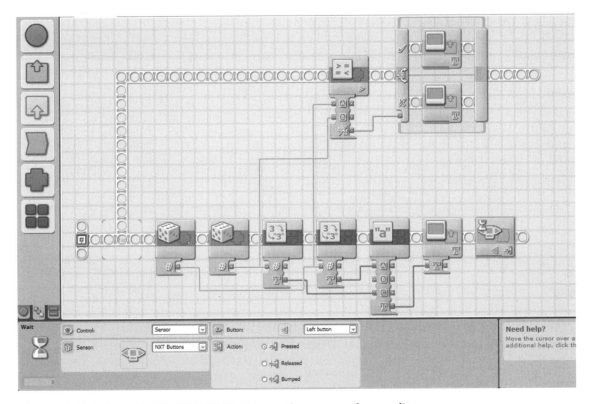

Figure 15-13. A final NXT BUTTON WAIT *block keeps the program from ending.*

I encourage you to create this program and test it yourself. You'll gain a better understanding of using wires, and you can tinker with it. Play around with changing the condition to "Less than" or "Equals" and see how the results change.

Think you've got the COMPARE block figured out? Try out Exercise 15-1 before moving on to the next chapter. If you need help, I've placed one possible solution at the end of the chapter.

Exercise 15-1 Happy or Sad

Write a program that generates a random number between 50 and 150. Display this number on the screen with the text "Less than 100?" After the user presses the left button, display a smiley face if the statement is true and a frowning face if the statement is false. Keep displaying the face until the user presses the right button. Then end the program.

What's Next?

When you are finished, continue on to the next chapter, where I'll introduce you to the RANGE block.

Exercise Solution

Figures 15-14 through 15-23 provide the full program and configuration panels for the solution to Exercise 15-1. Notice that I entered the value of 100 manually in the COMPARE block for the B value.

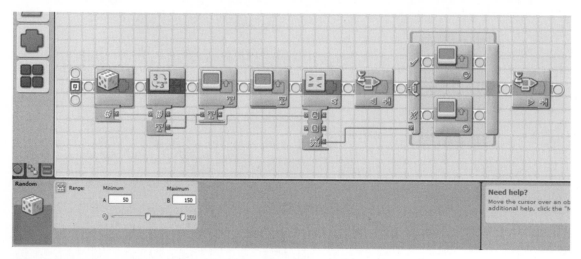

Figure 15-14. *The complete program and the* RANDOM *block's configuration panel.*

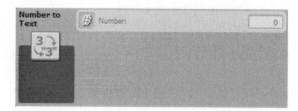

Figure 15-15. *The* NUMBER TO TEXT *configuration panel.*

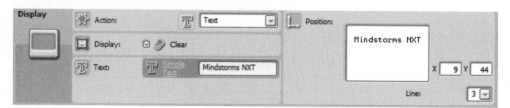

Figure 15-16. *The first* DISPLAY *configuration panel.*

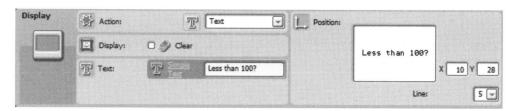

Figure 15-17. The second DISPLAY configuration panel.

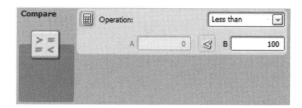

Figure 15-18. The COMPARE configuration panel.

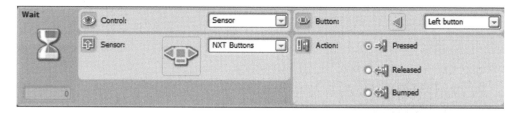

Figure 15-19. The first NXT BUTTONS WAIT block's configuration panel.

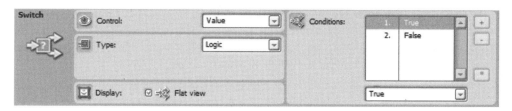

Figure 15-20. The SWITCH block's configuration panel.

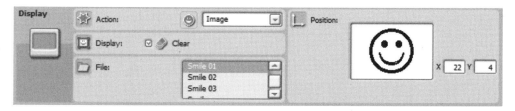

Figure 15-21. The third (True path) DISPLAY block's configuration panel.

Figure 15-22. The fourth (False Path) DISPLAY *block's configuration panel.*

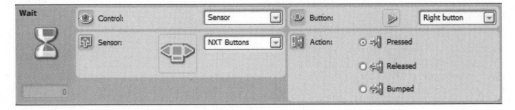

Figure 15-23. A final NXT BUTTON WAIT *block keeps the program from ending.*

CHAPTER 16

Inside or Out?

In the last chapter, you learned how to use the COMPARE block to test whether a value was less than, greater than, or equal to another value. The block compares the two numbers and determines whether the statement (A Less than B, A Greater than B, or A Equals B) is True or False.

Sometimes, however, you want to check to see if a value falls inside or outside a range of numbers: Is 28 inside the range 2 through 30? True. Is 50 outside the range 1 through 60? False.

NXT-G provides a block that allows you test the condition of a number (A) to determine whether it falls inside or outside the range of two other numbers (B and C). Here's how it works.

The RANGE Block

Just like the COMPARE block, the RANGE block uses the following rule: robots respond to statements with True or False.

The statements that a RANGE block will evaluate look like these:

- A is inside the range of numbers beginning with B and ending with C.
- A is outside the range of numbers beginning with B and ending with C.

That's it. The RANGE block evaluates the statement and returns a True or False response. Let's build a small program for SPOT that can use the RANGE block. As usual, we'll start with the pseudo-code.

Me: SPOT, I want you to create a random number between 1 and 100, show it on the LCD screen, and tell me if it is inside the range of 40 to 60.

To do this, we place one RANDOM block onto the beam and configure it as shown in Figure 16-1.

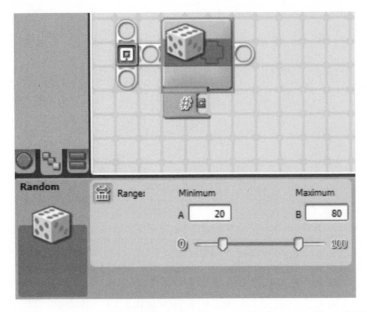

Figure 16-1. A RANDOM block generates a number between 20 and 80.

Next, I convert the number to text using a NUMBER TO TEXT block (see Figure 16-2). I have to do this because I want to display the random number on the LCD screen.

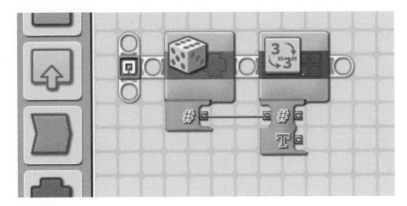

Figure 16-2. Convert the random numbers to text.

Next, I'll add a TEXT block to create a statement in the form of "A inside range 40 and 60," as shown in Figure 16-3.

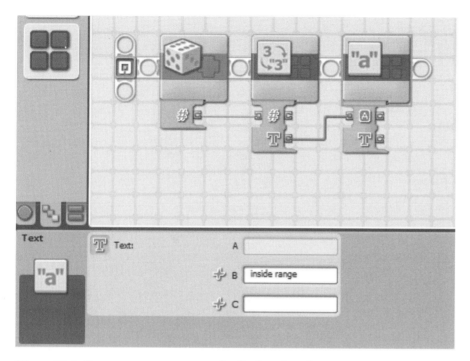

Figure 16-3. *Create a text statement to be displayed on the LCD screen.*

In Figure 16-3, the RANDOM block number is used as input to the NUMBER TO TEXT block. The TEXT block then takes this bit of text (A) and combines it with the statement "inside range."

In Figure 16-4, I use a data wire to send the text from the TEXT block to a DISPLAY block configured to display text on Line 3 with position X=2 and Y=40 (see Figure 16-4).

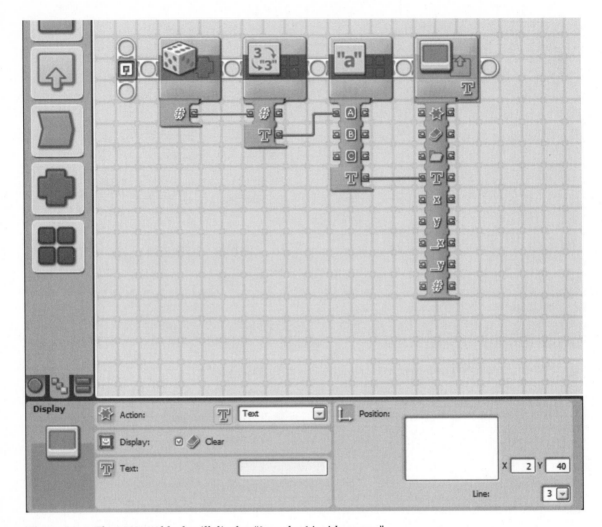

Figure 16-4. The DISPLAY block will display "[number] inside range."

I need to add one more DISPLAY block, so I can add the text "40 and 60" on Line 4 with position X=2 and Y=32 (see Figure 16-5). Remember to remove the check from the Clear box, so the text in the first DISPLAY box doesn't disappear!

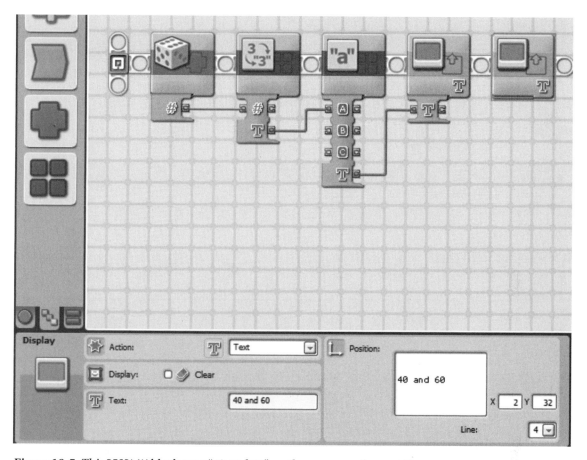

Figure 16-5. This DISPLAY block puts "40 and 60" on the screen on the next line.

And now it's time to use the RANGE block to evaluate the statement. I drop the RANGE block onto the beam, as shown in Figure 16-6.

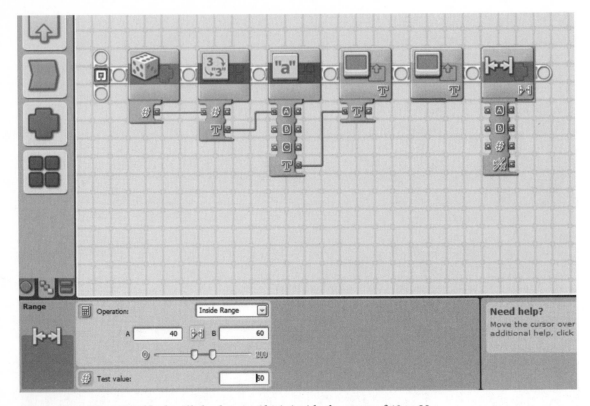

Figure 16-6. The RANGE block will check to see if A is inside the range of 40 to 60.

In Figure 16-6, you can see that I've selected Inside Range in the drop-down menu for the Operation section. I've also entered a value of 40 in the A field and 60 in the B field. I could have used the Slider bar to select the Lower Limit and Upper Limit for the range, but keep in mind that the Slider bar will only allow you to define a range between 0 and 100. If you need a larger range, you'll have to enter the values manually.

Also, I won't need to enter a value into the Test value field because I'm using a data wire to submit the random number to the RANGE block.

■ **Note** The other option in the Operation drop-down menu is Outside Range. If I select this option, the statement will be True if the random number is outside the range of 40 to 60 and False if it is inside the range. Also notice that a Test Value can be entered in the Test value field. You can use this if you do not have a number from an outside block (a RANDOM block, for example) to use as input. And finally, the Upper Limit and Lower Limit can also be provided to the RANGE block dynamically by using data wires to provide input (in Number format) to the Upper Limit data plug and the Lower Limit data plug.

My next step is to run a data wire into the RANGE block that contains the original random number. There are two ways to do this. The first is to drag a data wire out of the NUMBER TO TEXT block (remember that this block has an output data plug for the original Number). I used that method in Chapter 15 for the COMPARE block. Now I want to show you the other method.

If you click the output Number data plug on the RANDOM block, you can drag a data wire to the input Test Value data plug on the RANGE block. I've done this in Figure 16-7. Notice that the original data wire going into the NUMBER TO TEXT block now splits into two wires—one still goes in the NUMBER TO TEXT block, and the other goes into the RANGE block.

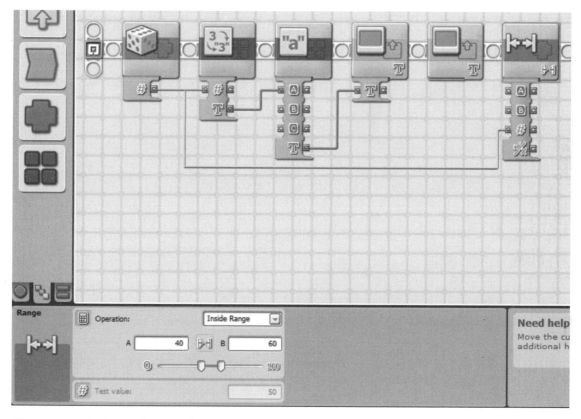

Figure 16-7. The Test Value is evaluated to see if it is inside the range of 40 to 60.

The pseudo-code tells SPOT to display on the LCD screen whether the statement "[number] inside range 40 and 60" is True or False. To do this, I've dropped a SWITCH block after the RANGE block. In the Display section, I uncheck the Flat view box; in the Control section, I choose Value; and in the Type section, I choose Logic. I also drag a data wire out of the output Result data plug on the RANGE block and connect it to the input data plug on the SWITCH block (see Figure 16-8).

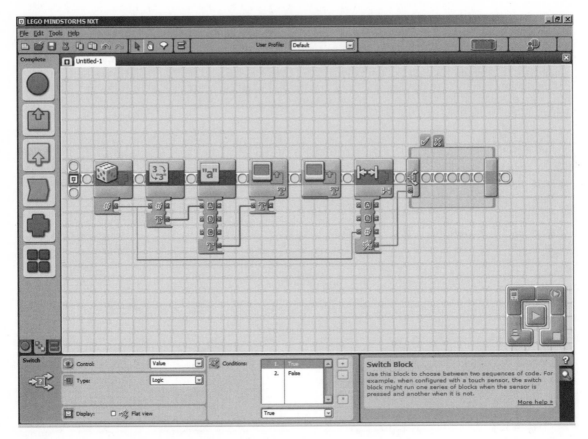

Figure 16-8. The SWITCH block will help me display True or False on the screen.

Now all that is left is for the LCD screen to display "True" or "False." This is simple enough: I'll drop one DISPLAY block in the True tab (see Figure 16-9) that puts the word "True" on the LCD screen on Line 7. I'll drop another DISPLAY block in the False tab (see Figure 16-10) that puts the word "False" on the LCD screen on Line 7 (remember to remove the check from the Clear box so text on the LCD screen doesn't get erased). I'll position the True and False text so they are displayed on the LCD screen where X=12 and Y=8.

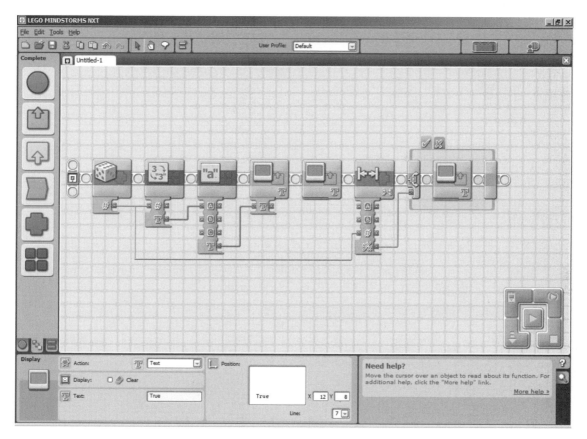

Figure 16-9. This DISPLAY block puts the word "True" on the screen.

Now, if the statement is evaluated as True, the SWITCH block will execute the DISPLAY block found in the True tab. And if the statement is evaluated as False, the SWITCH block will execute the other DISPLAY block found in the False tab.

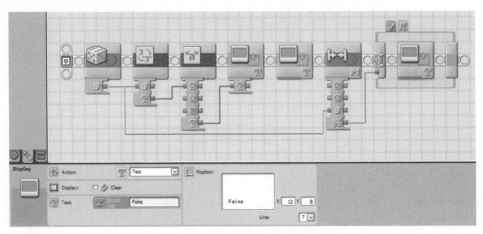

Figure 16-10. *This* DISPLAY *block puts the word "False" on the screen.*

Next, I'll drop in a NXT BUTTON WAIT block and configure it to wait for the left button to be pressed (see Figure 16-11). This will allow me time to view the results.

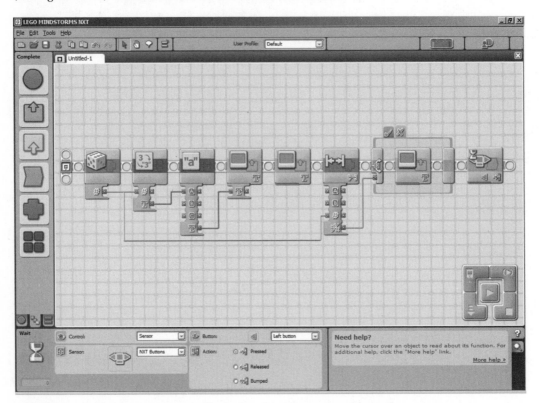

Figure 16-11. *The* NXT BUTTON WAIT *block gives me time to view the results.*

And now I've got an exercise for you. It shouldn't be too difficult if you understand the program we've just created. One possible solution to the exercise is at the end of the chapter.

Exercise 16-1 Outside a Range

Modify the program to use two RANDOM blocks to create the Upper and Lower values used by the RANGE block. The Lower value should be between 30 and 40. The Upper value should be between 50 and 60. Use a third RANDOM block to generate the Test value between 5 and 95 and test whether this value falls outside the range. Use DISPLAY blocks to display the Upper and Lower values as well as the Test value and display True or False depending on whether the Test value falls outside the range.

What's Next?

When you're finished, continue on to Chapter 17, where I'll cover the LOGIC block. You should have a good understanding of Logic and how True and False statements are evaluated; the LOGIC block will add some more power to your robots by allowing you to control how items are evaluated before obtaining a True or False answer.

Exercise Solution

Figures 16-12 through 16-23 provide the full program and configuration panels for Exercise 16-1. Remember to uncheck the Clear boxes in the DISPLAY blocks so the text is not erased.

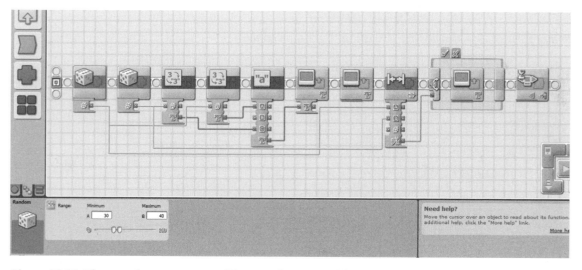

Figure 16-12. The complete program and Lower value RANDOM block's configuration panel

Figure 16-13. The Upper value RANDOM block's configuration panel

Figure 16-14. The first NUMBER TO TEXT configuration panel.

Figure 16-15. The second NUMBER TO TEXT configuration panel

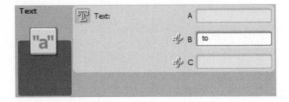

Figure 16-16. The TEXT block's configuration panel

Figure 16-17. The first DISPLAY block's configuration panel

Figure 16-18. *The second DISPLAY block's configuration panel*

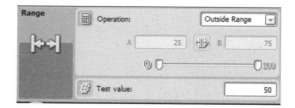

Figure 16-19. *The RANGE block's configuration panel*

Figure 16-20. *The SWITCH block's configuration panel*

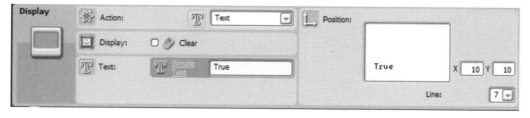

Figure 16-21. *The True path's DISPLAY block configuration panel*

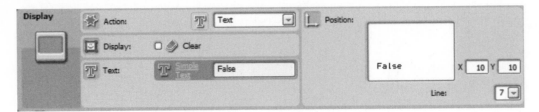

Figure 16-22. *The False path's* DISPLAY *block configuration panel*

Figure 16-23. *The* NXT BUTTON WAIT *block's configuration panel*

■ ■ ■

CHAPTER 17

Yes? No? Maybe?

In Chapter 15, I introduced you to the COMPARE block, which takes two numbers, A and B, and examines them to determine if A is greater than, less than, or equal to B (depending on the option you select). The result of this comparison is then converted to a Logic data type (either True or False) that can be used as output using a data wire. In Chapter 16, I showed you how the RANGE block examines a value and determines whether it falls between an upper and lower value—a True or False response is then generated.

In this chapter, I'm going to show you a block that is similar to the COMPARE and RANGE blocks, but not quite the same. Instead of comparing two numbers, this block will compare two Logic data type inputs and also output a True/False Logic data type response.

The LOGIC Block

The Logic block is an interesting one (shown in Figure 17-1).

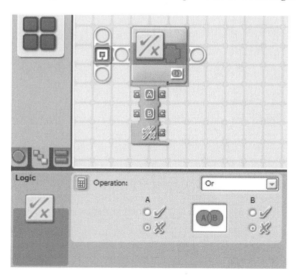

Figure 17-1. The LOGIC block and its configuration panel

Let me set up a scenario for SPOT that I think will help you understand how this block works. I've attached a Light sensor and a Sound sensor to SPOT. Here's my first bit of pseudo-code for SPOT to try out.

Me: SPOT, I want you to move forward three rotations if two conditions are True.

Me: The first condition is that the Light sensor detects a light level below 30.

Me: The second condition is that the Sound sensor detects a sound level below 20.

What will happen here? Well, SPOT will check to see if his Light sensor detects a low light level in the room (<30). He'll also check to see if his Sound sensor is detecting a quiet room (<20). Recall from the discussion of sensors that a sensor can return a True or False reply based on the conditions you have configured the sensor to detect.

Let's start your program by dropping a Light sensor block on the beam and configuring it, as shown in the configuration panel in Figure 17-2.

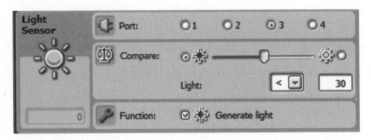

Figure 17-2. Configure the Light sensor as shown in the configuration panel

Next, you'll add a Sound sensor block and configure it as shown in Figure 17-3.

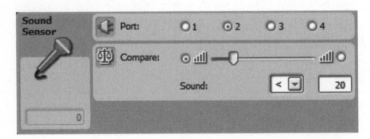

Figure 17-3. Configure the Sound sensor as shown in the configuration panel

Now you have two sensors that will check the conditions of the light and sound in the room.

If you look back at your pseudo-code, SPOT will move forward *only* if both of the sensors are triggered. This means the Light sensor must receive a value less than 30 for the room's lighting level, and the Sound sensor must receive a value less than 20 for the room's sound level—both conditions *must* exist or SPOT will not move forward.

What will happen if the room is bright and quiet? SPOT will not move.

What will happen if the room is dark and loud? SPOT will still not move.

What happens if the room is bright and loud? SPOT will get a headache. Just kidding—he still won't move.

As you can tell, he's only going to move if the room is both quiet *and* dark.

So, how can SPOT quickly examine the lighting and sound conditions of the room and decide if he can move forward or not? Simple—he'll use the COMPARE block.

Go ahead and drop the LOGIC block on the beam, as shown in Figure 17-4.

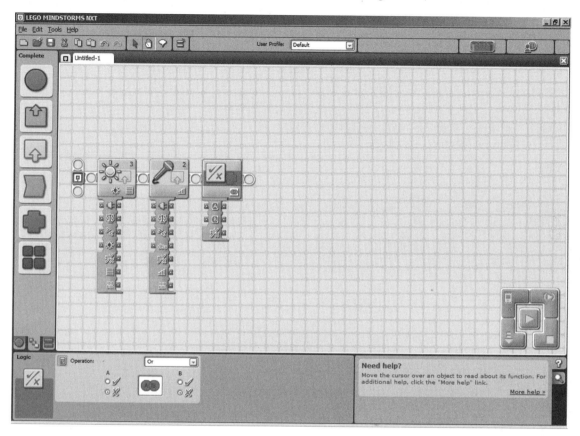

Figure 17-4. The LOGIC block helps SPOT to examine the light and sound conditions.

Take a look at the drop-down menu in the Operation section. The drop-down menu has four options: And, Or, Xor, and Not. For now, select the And option (I'll explain the other three options shortly).

Next, I want you to drag a wire out of the Yes/No data plug on the Light sensor block and connect it to the A input data plug on the LOGIC block, as shown in Figure 17-5.

Drag another wire out of the Yes/No data plug on the Sound sensor block and connect it to the B input data plug on the LOGIC lock, as shown in Figure 17-6.

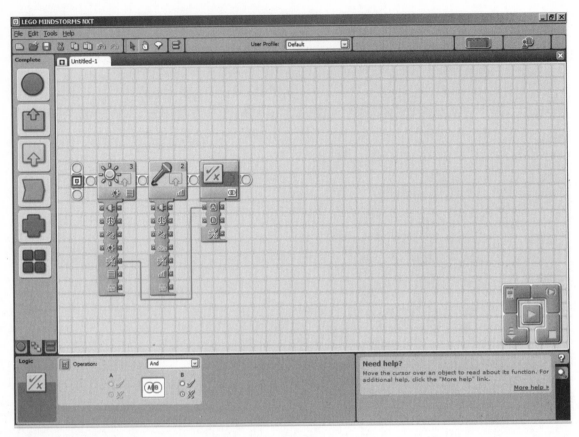

Figure 17-5. Connect the Light sensor block to the LOGIC block

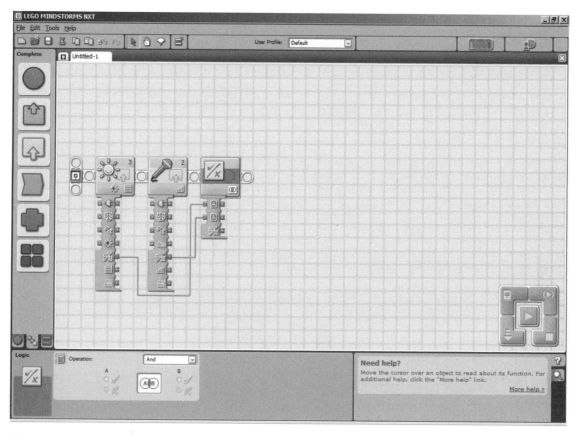

***Figure 17-6.** Connect the Sound sensor block to the LOGIC block*

Now, let me explain what is happening so far. The LOGIC block is taking a Yes/No response from the Light sensor. It is also taking a Yes/No response from the Sound sensor. By selecting the And option on the LOGIC block, you are forcing the LOGIC block to take the result in plug A (Yes or No) and the result in plug B (Yes or No) and *add* them together to create a single Yes/No response. I can already hear you asking, "How do you add Yes/No responses?"

Well, the answer is fairly simple and relies on the option you selected in that drop-down menu (the And, Or, Xor, and Not options):

And option: If you select the And option, *both* responses must be Yes for a final Yes result to be generated. If plug A is Yes and plug B is No, then the final result will be No. Likewise, if plug A is No and plug B is Yes, the final result will still be No. And if plug A is No and Plug B is No, the final result is No. *Only* when both inputs are Yes will a Yes result be generated.

Or option: If you select the Or option, only *one* response must be Yes for a final Yes result to be generated. If plug A is Yes and plug B is No, then the final result will be Yes. Likewise, if plug A is No and plug B is Yes, the final result will still be Yes. If both plug A and plug B are both Yes, then the final result will be Yes. Only if plug A is No and Plug B is No, the final result is No.

Xor option: This is a weird one. If you select the Xor option, only *one* plug value *can* be Yes for a final Yes result to be generated. If plug A is Yes and plug B is No, then the final result will be Yes. Likewise, if plug A is No and plug B is Yes, the final result will still be Yes. However, if plug A and plug B are both Yes, the final result will be No. And if plug A and plug B are both No, the final result is No. Remember, for a Yes output response, only one of the logic input values can be Yes…*only one.*

Not option: This is another strange one. This option doesn't really return a final value— it simply changes the Logic value input for plug A to its opposite. For example, if plug A is Yes, then the output for plug A will be No. This option reverses the Logic value for you and nothing else. Be aware that plug B is disabled for the Not option.

Now, let's finish up your sample program. If you look back at Figure 17-6, you now have the LOGIC block ready to provide a Yes/No response (using a data wire).

If you recall, you are testing to see if the Sound sensor detects a value below 30 and the Light sensor detects a value below 20. If these conditions are both true, then SPOT will be allowed to move forward three rotations. If either of these two conditions is not true, SPOT will not be allowed to move.

So, your next step is to drop in a SWITCH block to test the condition of the LOGIC block. First, select Value from the Control section drop-down menu. Next, choose Logic from the Type section drop-down menu. You can leave the Flat View box checked, because you only have two possible options (True or False). This configuration is shown in Figure 17-7.

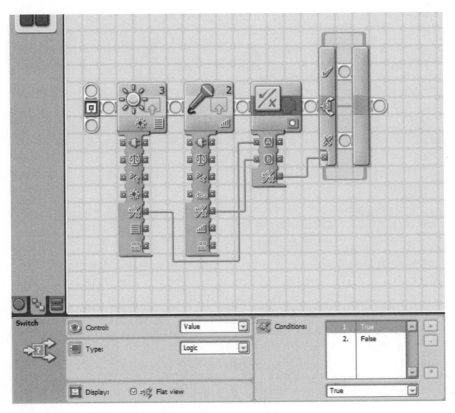

Figure 17-7. A SWITCH block will use the LOGIC block output to control SPOT's actions.

Now, here's where it can get a little tricky. If the Light sensor detects a light value below 30, then it sends a True value to the LOGIC block. If the Sound sensor detects a sound value below 20, then it sends a True value to the LOGIC block. You have configured the LOGIC block using the And option, because you want to test if both conditions are True. If they are, the LOGIC block will send a True (or Yes) value to the SWITCH block. If either of the conditions is False, the LOGIC block will send a False value to the SWITCH block.

All that's left is to drop in a MOVE block for the True condition in the SWITCH block, as shown in Figure 17-8.

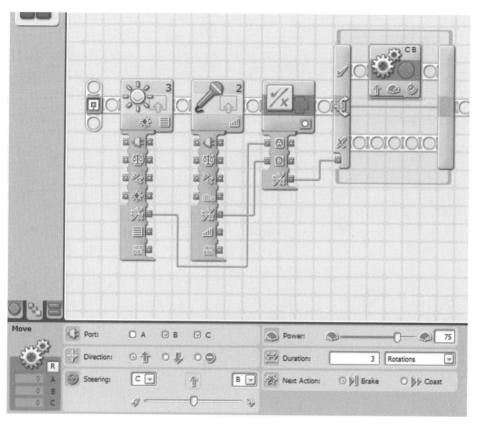

Figure 17-8. *A MOVE block is configured for three forward rotations.*

If the SWITCH block detects a True response from the LOGIC block, the MOVE block executes (three forward rotations), and the program ends. If the SWITCH block detects a False response from the LOGIC block, there are no additional blocks to run, and the program ends without SPOT moving. All that's needed is to add a NXT BUTTON WAIT block at the end of the program that will allow the MOVE block to finish and wait for the user to push a button to end the program.

Think you've got the hang of the LOGIC block? Then take a look at Excerise 17-1. If you get stumped, I've placed one possible solution to the exercise at the end of the chapter.

Exercise 17-1: SPOT Finds a Spot

Place a series of blue and red circles on the floor in a long straight line. Have SPOT roll forward and follow the line of circles. When SPOT is over a red circle, yell out "STOP!" Create a program that will only stop SPOT's movement when both the color red is detected and the Sound sensor detects a noise over a level of 75.

What's Next?

The LOGIC block is a useful tool for you to take two Logic data type responses (Yes/No or True/False) and "add" them together to produce one Logic data type. Are you wondering what you would do if, for example, you had four Logic data type inputs and needed to combine them? You would need to use two LOGIC blocks: each block would take two of the Logic data type input values and provide a final Logic response. You can see this in Figure 17-9. These two Logic responses would then be combined using a third LOGIC block to obtain the true "final" Logic response. Confusing? A little. But when you start using the LOGIC block, you'll begin to see how it can be used with LOOP and SWITCH blocks to give your robots even better decision-making abilities.

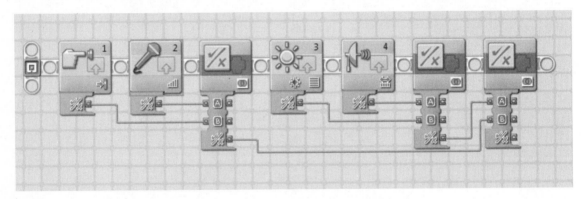

Figure 17-9. Multiple LOGIC blocks feeding into a single LOGIC block.

Exercise Solution

Figures 17-10 through 17-14 show the complete program and configuration panels for Exercise 17-1. The MOVE block will continue to spin the motors indefinitely until the Loop is broken and the program ends.

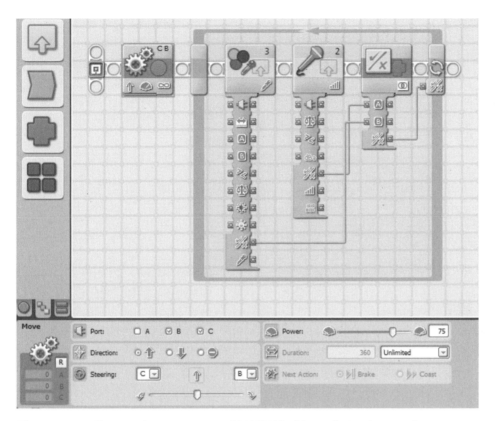

Figure 17-10. The complete program and MOVE block's configuration panel

Figure 17-11. The LOOP block's configuration panel

Figure 17-12. The Color sensor's configuration panel

Figure 17-13. *The Sound sensor's configuration panel*

Figure 17-14. *The LOGIC block's configuration panel*

CHAPTER 18

Title = Anything You Like

That's a strange title, isn't it? You can pick anything you like and make it the title. But that doesn't mean the material covered in this chapter will change. Nope, this chapter covers two special types of block called the VARIABLE block and the CONSTANT block. You'll find these blocks useful when you need to store a piece of information for later use. This is a lengthy chapter, so there won't be any exercises. But the information here is very valuable for giving your robots the ability to save information and use it later, so take it slow and really try to understand how and when to use both new block types. So let's take a look.

The VARIABLE Block

Let's imagine for just a moment that you want to give SPOT some information to remember. This information consists of some words, a few numbers, and a couple of logical True/False values. SPOT has the ability to place each piece of information in a virtual folder that exists in his memory. That information, however, will disappear when the program ends or the brick is turned off. Here's the pseudo-code:

Me: SPOT, will you please store the words "pizza" and "cheesecake" in your memory?

Me: SPOT, I also need you to store the numbers "50" and "200" in your memory.

Me: SPOT, will you also please store one logical "True" and one logical "False" in your memory?

Now, before we convert this pseudo-code to an NXT-G program, I need to tell you a little bit about how an NXT-G program stores information, changes it, and retrieves it. All of this can be done using the VARIABLE block or the CONSTANT block. I'm going to cover the VARIABLE block first because once you understand how it works, you'll also know how to use the CONSTANT block because it works in an almost identical manner (but with one big exception that I'll reveal later).

A VARIABLE block can be used to do one of two things:

- Information can be *written* to a virtual folder that is stored in memory.

- Information can be *read from* a virtual folder that is stored in memory.

These virtual folders are also known as variables. An NXT-G variable can be configured to hold only one of three types of data: Text, Number, or Logic (True or False).

Text is easy enough; my pseudo-code tells SPOT to store "pizza" and "cheesecake," but it could just as easily have told SPOT to store the letter "A" or the sentence "My name is SPOT."

Numbers are even easier: when an NXT-G 2.0 VARIABLE block is configured to hold a number, it can be *only* a positive or negative number. Examples include 5, -3.0, and 101.25. For NXT-G 1.0 software users, however, the VARIABLE block is limited to only positive and negative integer values, so numbers such as 4.5 or -10.2 will be rounded to the nearest integer (5 and -10 for my examples).

Logic values have only two choices: True or False. An NXT-G VARIABLE block configured to hold a logical value can hold *only* True or False and nothing else.

Exploring the VARIABLE Block

OK, now it's time to take a look at the VARIABLE block. This block is found on the Complete Palette on the Data fly-out menu. Select the VARIABLE block, and drop it on the beam (see Figure 18-1).

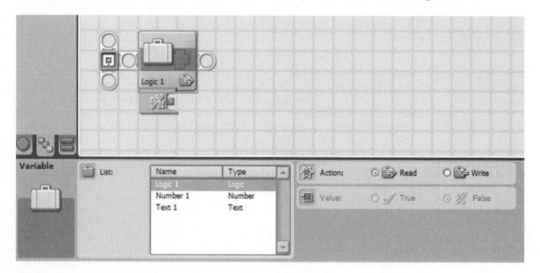

Figure 18-1. *The VARIABLE block and its configuration panel*

I mentioned to you that information can be *read from* or *written to* a VARIABLE block. In Figure 18-1, you'll notice that, by default, the first time you drop a block on the beam it is configured to Read (in the Action section) a Logic Type value. The variable also has a Name assigned to it: Logic 1.

This means that if True or False is stored in the variable, this value can be *read from* the variable. Notice that the Value section is grayed out; it isn't available for you to edit. Also notice that the default value selected in the Value section is False.

Before I show you how to change this, select the variable named Number 1 in the VARIABLE block's configuration panel (see Figure 18-2).

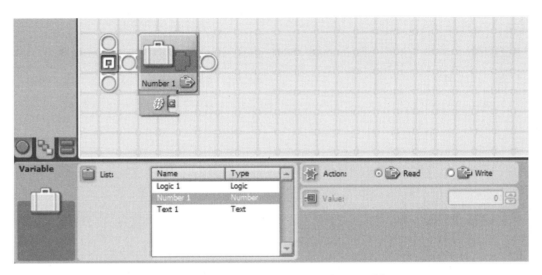

Figure 18-2. The VARIABLE block with Number 1 selected as the variable name

If you choose Number 1 as the variable name, you'll see that the default value stored is zero (0). This number is the value that will be *read from* the variable named Number 1.

Next, choose Text 1 in the VARIABLE block's configuration panel (see Figure 18-3).

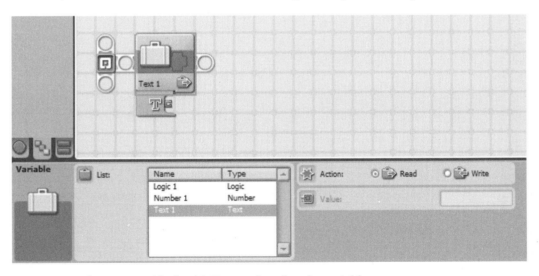

Figure 18-3. The VARIABLE block with Text 1 selected as the variable name

If you choose Text 1 as the variable name, the default value stored is blank; there is no text stored in the Text 1 variable.

Reading from a VARIABLE

In Figures 18-1, 18-2, and 18-3, notice also that the each of the blocks has only one output data plug. This matches what we know about a VARIABLE block with the Action section configured to Read. The variables can *only* be *read from*; other blocks (a DISPLAY block, for example) would use a data wire from this output data plug as input. This is "reading from" the variable.

I want to make sure you understand this concept, so take a look at Figure 18-4, and I'll explain it further.

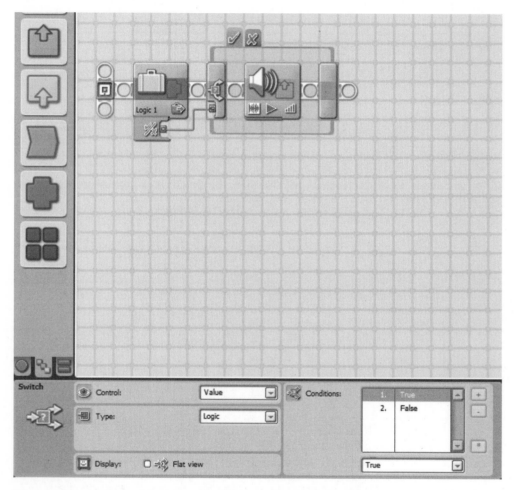

Figure 18-4. A VARIABLE block providing its variable value to another block

In Figure 18-4, I've connected a VARIABLE block called Logic 1 to a SWITCH block. The SWITCH block's configuration panel is visible in Figure 18-4, and you can see that I've configured it to check for a Logic value in the Type section. When the program is executed, the SWITCH block will *read* the value from the VARIABLE block. If the value is True, the SWITCH block will execute the SOUND block I've dropped in the True tab. If the value is False, the SWITCH block will execute a MOVE block that I dropped in the False tab.

Writing to a VARIABLE

Now, that example involved reading the data directly from the VARIABLE block. What if I want to put some data in? Then I'd have to *write* some data into the block. Here is how you do it.

Take a look at Figure 18-5. In this figure, I've selected Write in the Action section.

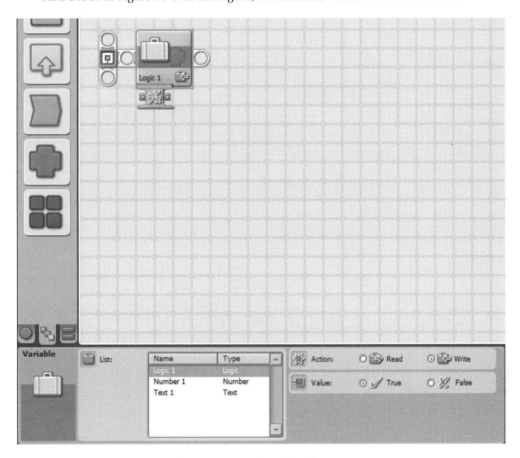

Figure 18-5. *The VARIABLE block with Write selected in the Action section*

In Figure 18-5, I can change the logic value. Remember that the default is False, so I've changed it to True. Did you also notice the input data plug that was added on the data hub? This means that I could actually have the True or False value determined by a data wire from another block. (In this example, the data wire *must* carry a logic value of True or False; anything else would give me a broken wire that wouldn't work. Likewise, if the List section has Number or Text selected, the input data wire *must* be providing a data type of the selected item.)

Figure 18-6 shows the configuration panels for the Number 1 and Text 1 blocks. I'm including them, because I want you to see how you can modify the data when the Action option is set to Write. For the Number 1 variable, you can type either a positive or a negative value in the Value field. For the Text 1 variable, you can type words, sentences, or even entire paragraphs in the Value field.

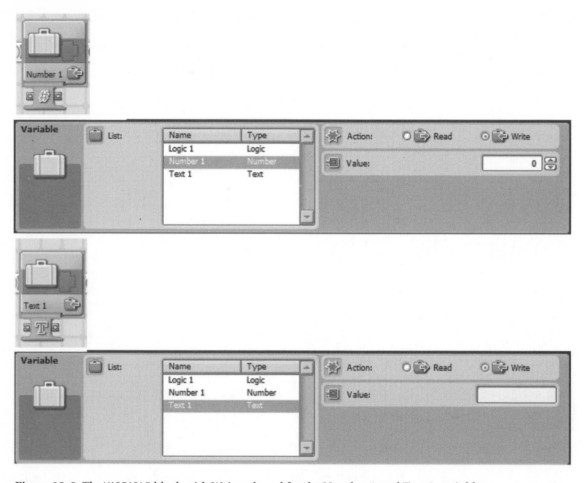

Figure 18-6. The VARIABLE block with Write selected for the Number 1 and Text 1 variables

After you've modified the data in a variable block, you can either close the variable by selecting Read in the Action menu (this prevents the data from being changed) or leave the block alone. If you choose to leave the Action section option as Write, you can drag a data wire from another block to the input data plug on the variable block (just remember that the type of data wire going into the input data plug must match the type of data the variable is configured to hold—Text, Number, or Logic).

Storing Many Values

Now, let's go back to the original pseudo-code I gave SPOT:

Me: SPOT, will you please store the words "pizza" and "cheesecake" in your memory?

Me: SPOT, I also need you to store the numbers "50" and "200" in your memory.

Me: SPOT, will you also please store one logical "True" and one logical "False" in your memory?

Do you see a problem? I've got two pieces of text to store and two number values. I already know that a variable block can hold only *one* piece of data. If I store the number 50, for example, in the Number 1 variable, where will I store the number 200? And I can store "pizza" in the Text 1 variable, but what about "cheesecake?"

The answer is simple. NXT-G allows you to create as many variables as you need. You can even rename a variable from something like Text 1 to something easier to remember like "Food," or Number 1 to something like "Test Scores." Here's how it's done.

If you need to create another variable, start by clicking the Edit menu at the top of the NXT-G software. Click the menu option labeled Define Variables.

A small window, like the one shown in Figure 18-7, opens.

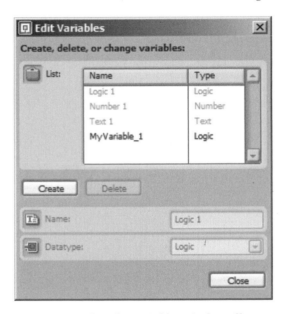

Figure 18-7. The Edit Variables window allows you to create new variables.

Click the Create button, and a new variable will appear in the List section with a default name like MyVariable_1 (see Figure 18-8).

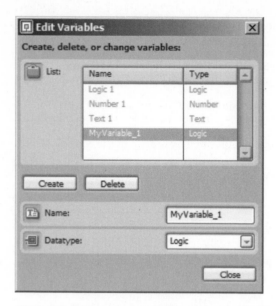

Figure 18-8. Your new variable appears in the List section.

You can change the name of the variable by typing a new name in the Name field. Select the type of data the variable will contain in the drop-down menu in the Datatype section. I've named my new variable Test Scores and configured it to hold a Number (see Figure 18-9). You can click the Create button again to make another variable. Click the Close button when you are finished.

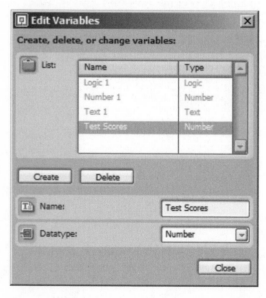

Figure 18-9. Give the new variable a Name and a Datatype to hold.

Now, when you drop a VARIABLE block on the beam, you'll notice that your new variable appears as a selection in the List section (see Figure 18-10). Using this method, you can create as many Text, Number, and Logic variables as you need.

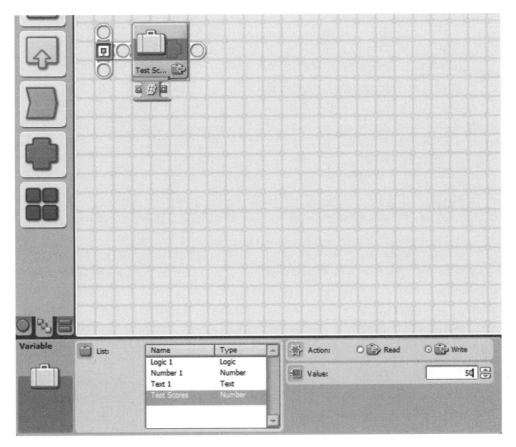

Figure 18-10. Your new variable now appears in the List section of the configuration panel.

Solving the Example Problem

OK, now you know how to put data into a variable (Write) and how to get data from a variable (Read). You also know how to create additional variables. Now you need to learn how to use variables throughout your programs.

Here's a bit of pseudo-code for SPOT:

Me: SPOT, count from one to three and then check whether your Left button is pressed. If it is pressed, send a True logic value to a VARIABLE block titled Pressed. If it is not pressed, send a False logic value to the VARIABLE block.

Me: Next, count down from three to one. When finished counting down, display on the LCD screen "Pressed" or "Not Pressed" depending on the True/False logic value read from the VARIABLE block.

Me: End the program after your right button is pressed.

I'll first start off by dropping three SOUND blocks configured to count up from one to three. All three SOUND blocks are shown in Figure 18-11 along with the last block's configuration panel.

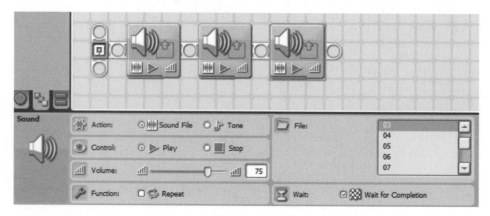

Figure 18-11. The first three SOUND blocks will count from one to three.

I'll next drop in an NXT BUTTONS SENSOR block and configure it to detect the press of the Left button (see Figure 18-12).

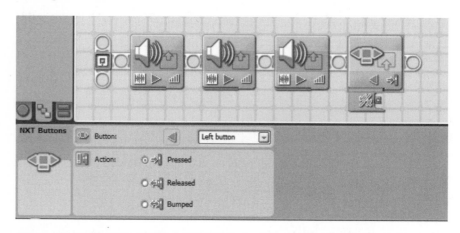

Figure 18-12. The NXT BUTTONS SENSOR block will monitor the Left button.

I created a new VARIABLE block called "Pressed" that holds a Logic value. I next drop a VARIABLE block after the NXT BUTTONS SENSOR block. I choose my new variable, Pressed, and in the Action section, I choose Write. I also drag a data wire out of the NXT BUTTONS SENSOR block's output data plug into the input data plug on the VARIABLE block (see Figure 18-13).

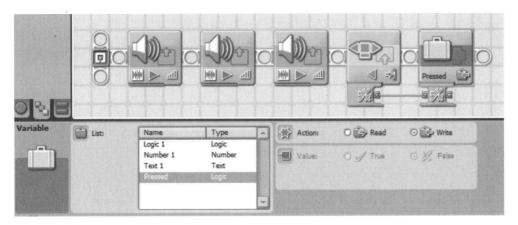

Figure 18-13. *The variable Pressed will hold True or False.*

If the Left button is pressed immediately after the count-up from one to three, the NXT BUTTONS SENSOR block will detect the press and change the logic value to True. When the program starts, the initial value will be False, but it will change to True if the Left button is bumped at the end of the count-up.

Next, I want SPOT to count down from three to one. I'll drop another three SOUND blocks into the program. Figure 18-14 shows these three SOUND blocks and the configuration panel for the last SOUND block.

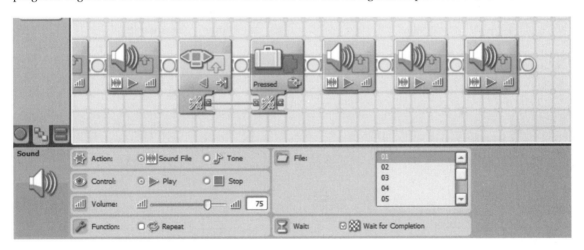

Figure 18-14. *SPOT will count down from three to one.*

After the countdown ends, we need to display "Pressed" or "Not Pressed" on the LCD screen. To do this, we'll drop in another VARIABLE block. This time I'm going to choose my Pressed variable again, but I'm changing its Action section option to Read (see Figure 18-15).

211

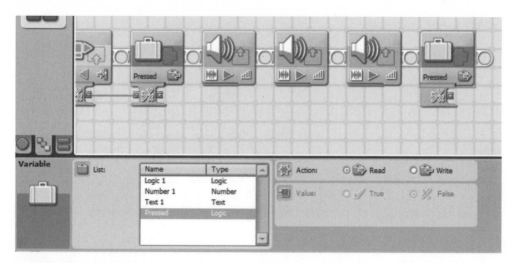

Figure 18-15. *A SWITCH block will read the Pressed variable's value.*

Now, I drop in a SWITCH block and configure it to read a Logic value (see Figure 18-16), and I've turned off Flat view so the SWITCH block is visible in its tabbed format. I've also dragged a data wire from the VARIABLE block to the SWITCH block that contains the value True or False. I've also dropped a DISPLAY block in the True tab (of the SWITCH block) and configured it to display "Pressed" (this isn't shown in the configuration panel in Figure 18-16, but it is easy enough to figure out).

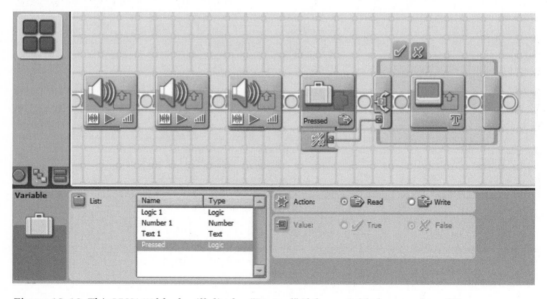

Figure 18-16. *This DISPLAY block will display "Pressed" if the variable has a value of True.*

On the False tab, I place another DISPLAY block that clears the LCD screen and puts the words "Not Pressed" on the screen (see Figure 18-17).

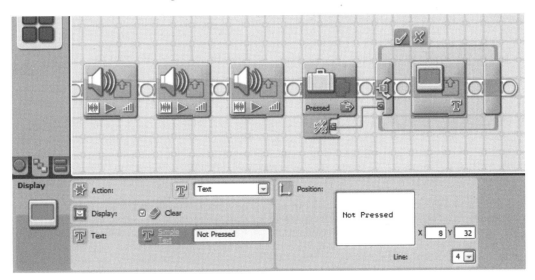

Figure 18-17. The words "Not Pressed" will display if the variable has a value of False.

Finally, I drop in an NXT BUTTON WAIT block to wait until the Right button is pressed; this will give me time to view the results on the screen (see Figure 18-18).

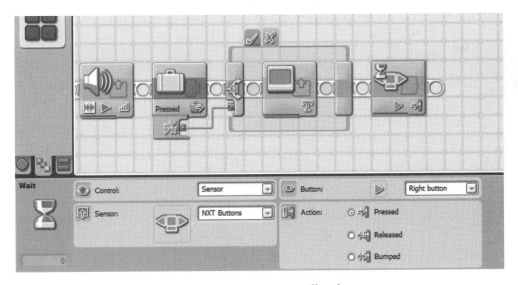

Figure 18-18. If I press the Right button, the program will end.

Now run the program. Try it a few times—press the Left button immediately after the count-up ends, or don't press it. Your decision to press or not press the button will be converted to a True or False value that is written to the Pressed variable. After the countdown, the Pressed variable is read by the SWITCH block, and the proper text is written on the LCD screen.

Variables are a powerful way for your robot to store away information—and to use that data later. Once the variable has been created and data written to it, that data will be available anytime you need it—well, at least until the program ends. If you want to store data for use after the program ends and/or after the power has been turned off, you'll need a different type of block. And that's where the CONSTANT block becomes useful.

The CONSTANT Block

When you use the VARIABLE block in a program, any variable value (Number, Text, or Logic) will be saved only while the program is running. Once the program ends, your variable data is gone. Normally this isn't a big deal; you typically program your robots to use variables that are useful only at the time the program is running.

But what if there's a value that often changes but is used by multiple programs uploaded to your robot? For example, let's imagine a program (Program 1) that stops the robot 12 inches from a FINISH LINE and has the robot do a little dance before finishing. Let's say that the initial distance between the STARTING LINE and the FINISH LINE is 24 rotations. Program 1 could instruct the robot with a MOVE block to roll 20 rotations (four rotations short of the FINISH LINE) to stop just before it crosses the FINISH LINE and do a little dance before finishing.

Let's also imagine another program (Program 2) that should have the robot roll half the distance between the STARTING LINE and FINISH LINE before doing its dance; you'd program it with a MOVE block configured to roll the robot forwards 12 rotations. When the robot reaches this point, it stops, does a dance, and then continues to the finish line.

Finally, let's have a third program (Program 3) that rolls the robot forward 1/4 of the total distance or six rotations, has the robot do a little dance, and then continues rolling it to the FINISH LINE. Once again, you could just configure the MOVE block to roll forward six rotations before beginning the dance routine.

You should be able to program these three programs easily. But what happens if I change the distance between the STARTING LINE and FINISH LINE to 48 rotations? Now you have to go into all three programs (Program 1, Program 2, and Program 3) and change a bunch of MOVE blocks' configuration panels.

There should be an easier way to save important values between programs… and there is! It's called the CONSTANT block.

Like the VARIABLE block, the CONSTANT block can store a single value—a number, a logic value, or a string of text. This value is then stored on the NXT brick and is referred to as a "global constant." As long as you don't delete the program, this value will stay on the brick even when the power is turned off! Because it stays on the brick, you can use the CONSTANT block in other programs to read the value stored as a constant on the brick. That's the "global" part—it's available everywhere (well, at least by any program that's stored on your brick).

To show you how it works, I'm going to create new program (with the name Distance) that creates a constant called "StartToFinish" that holds a value equal to the distance (in inches) between the STARTING LINE and the FINISH LINE. Figure 18-19 shows the single block contained in this program.

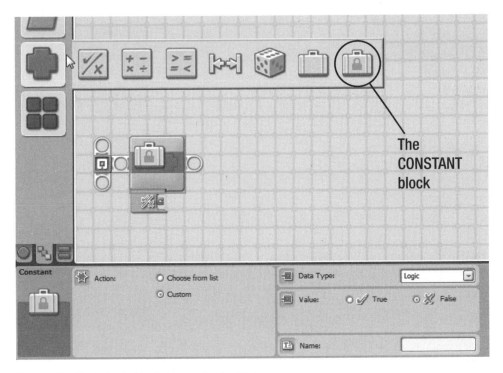

Figure 18-19. A single block is used in the Distance program.

Before I use this CONSTANT block I need to create a constant that will hold the distance (in inches) between the STARTING LINE and FINISH LINE. To do this I click on the Edit menu and select the Define Constants option. A window appears, as shown in Figure 18-20.

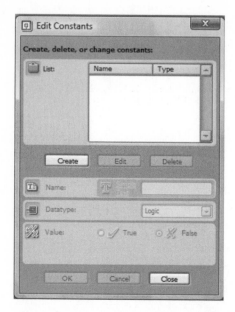

Figure 18-20. *Create a constant to hold a value available to other programs.*

Now I need to provide a name and data type for the constant. I click the Create button (see Figure 18-20) and enter "StartToFinish" for the Name, and I select Number from the Data Type drop-down menu and enter a value (24 for this example) in the Value section, as shown in Figure 18-21.

Figure 18-21. *Provide a name, data type, and a value for the constant.*

Click the OK button and then click the Close button to close the Edit Constants window.

Now, click on the single CONSTANT block in your program (see Figure 18-19) and select the "Choose From List" option in its configuration panel. The new constant, StartToFinish, is listed in the right column of the configuration panel. Click on it to select it. Save the program (name it "Distance") and upload it to the brick.

Now it's time to create Program 1 that will use the value stored in the constant StartToFinish. I'll create a new program called Program1 and drop in a CONSTANT block, as shown in Figure 18-22.

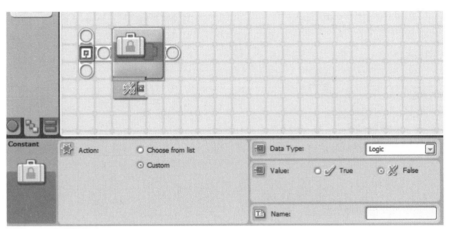

Figure 18-22. A new program's CONSTANT block configuration panel

Notice in Figure 18-22 that I can define a new constant by simply entering the name of the constant in the Name section and selecting the Data Type from the drop-down menu (rather than selecting Define Constants from the Edit menu). But because I've already configured a constant named "StartToFinish" and uploaded it to my brick I want to select the "Choose from list" option shown in Figure 18-22. When I select that option, a list of available constants is displayed on the right side of the configuration panel, as shown in Figure 18-23.

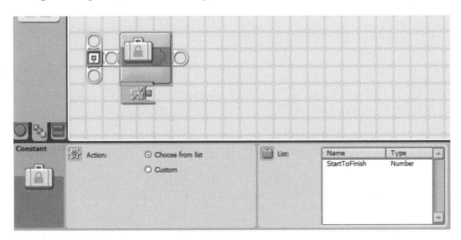

Figure 18-23. Select a constant from the list.

217

If you'll remember, the function of Program 1 was to have your robot roll forward the total distance minus four rotations before doing a dance. Before we knew about the CONSTANT block, we would simply have dropped in a MOVE block and configured it to roll the robot forward for 20 rotations.

But now, we can use the CONSTANT block (that's holding a value of 24) with a MATH block to do a little calculation. I'll cover the MATH block in more detail in Chapter 20, but for now just know that the MATH block can be used to add, subtract, multiply, and more. Figure 18-24 shows that I'll be using it to take the CONSTANT block's value (24) and subtract four from it. I first drag a data wire out of the CONSTANT block and into the input plug A for the MATH block. I've also used the MATH block's configuration panel to set the value of B to four and configured the Operation to perform a Subtraction operation. B will be subtracted from A and that value will be supplied to a MOVE block.

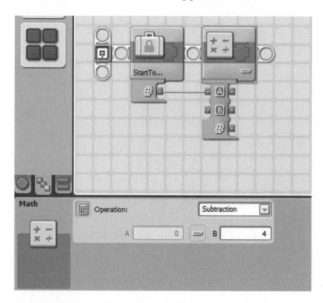

Figure 18-24. The CONSTANT block provides its value to the MATH block.

Next, I drop in a MOVE block configured for Rotations and drag a data wire out of the MATH block and into the MOVE block's Duration data plug. This is shown in Figure 18-25.

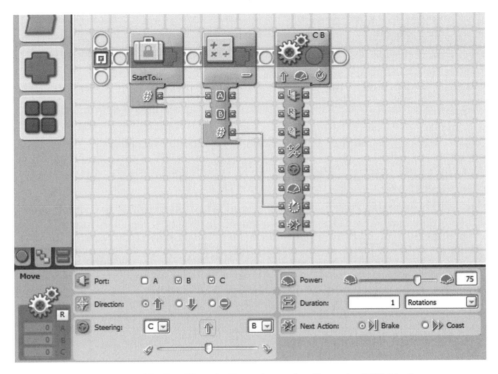

Figure 18-25. *The* MOVE *block will get its Duration value from the* MATH *block.*

Now all that's left is to drop in a few MOVE blocks to get the robot to dance and then roll forward four rotations to the FINISH LINE. (I'll leave that up to you to program—make it as simple or as complex a dance as you like.)

With Program 2, you'll create a similar program but you can use the MATH block to divide the value provided by the CONSTANT block by two (divide it in half) and send that value to the MOVE block. Program 3 will use a MATH block to divide the CONSTANT block value by four and send that value to the MOVE block (1/4 the total distance).

So, why not simply use a bunch of MOVE blocks instead of the CONSTANT and MATH blocks? Think about this—what happens now when I change the total distance between the STARTING LINE and FINISH LINE to 48? Or 100? With MOVE blocks, you'll need to open up all three programs (Program 1, 2, and 3) and change the values in the specific MOVE blocks.

But not with CONSTANT blocks. Now, all I need to do is open up the original program titled "Distance" and change the value (24) to the new distance. I save the program, upload it to my brick, and run the program. Now the constant value has been changed, and Programs 1, 2, and 3 do not have to be opened and modified. They will each take the current value stored in the constant StartToFinish and use it to calculate the proper distance to move. Cool, huh?

VARIABLE vs. CONSTANT

Deciding when to use a VARIABLE block vs. when to use a CONSTANT block shouldn't be confusing. Here are a few suggestions to help you determine when to use one over the other:

- Use a VARIABLE block to hold a value needed only in a single program.

- Use a CONSTANT block to provide a fixed value to multiple programs stored on your brick.

- Use a VARIABLE block if you need a value to be changed while running a single program.

- Use a CONSTANT block to provide a value that will *not* change while running multiple programs.

Keep in mind that the CONSTANT block can provide text as well as logic data values. You could easily program a CONSTANT block to hold your name (text) and provide that on the LCD screen for every program you run. When someone runs a program, it could display "Program by YOUR NAME" where YOUR NAME is provided by a CONSTANT block stored on the brick.

Likewise, a CONSTANT block could hold a True logic value that you'll always use with a COMPARE block (refer back to Chapter 15). When performing an AND operation with this CONSTANT value, only a second True logic type will produce a True output from the COMPARE block.

Variables and constants are important concepts to understand when it comes to programming your robots. If you wish to build and program more complex robots, you'll need to understand the VARIABLE and CONSTANT blocks and how best to use them to give your robots better decision-making abilities.

What's Next?

In the next chapter, I'll show you how to use the TEXT block. It's a handy way to provide information on the LCD screen, including instructions as well as results from tests your robot performs. The TEXT block allows for a bit of formatting and combining of text to give you some control over how text is displayed.

CHAPTER 19

■ ■ ■

Basic Text

For a chapter dealing with words, this one won't be too wordy. See, it even has a short introduction. You're going to learn to use the TEXT block to give your robot the ability to combine text into sentences and letters into words.

The TEXT Block

Mindstorms NXT robots can make a lot of noise using the SOUND block. However, if you want to give your robots control over the written word, you'll need to understand the TEXT block and how to use it properly (see Figure 19-1).

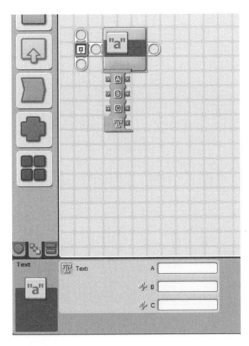

Figure 19-1. *The TEXT block and its configuration panel*

Here's another programming word for you to add to your list: *string* (and I don't mean the kind you use to fly a kite).

"String" is a term that's been around in programming circles forever and is fairly simple to define. A string is a collection of letters, numbers, spaces, special characters, or a combination of any of them. The following are five examples:

- THISISASTRINGOFTEXT

- So is this.

- 123456789

- !@#$%^&*( )

- These are all strings, including this one.

The reason I've introduced you to the concept of a string is that the TEXT block has the ability to take up to three different strings and merge them into one larger string value.

Look again at Figure 19-1. The TEXT block can hold three string values: A, B, and C. Notice that all three strings can be entered manually (by you, the programmer) using the configuration panel or they can be submitted to the TEXT block using the input data plugs. Also, keep in mind that the value A will always be on the far left, B in the middle, and C on the right. You cannot change the order in which the three strings will be combined.

As an example, take a look at Figure 19-2.

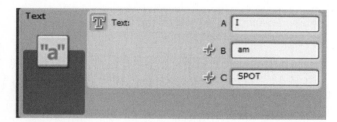

Figure 19-2. Three string values for the TEXT block

For value A, the text I entered is "I", with no spaces. Value B contains " am" (with a leading space), and value C is " SPOT" (with a leading space). The leading spaces will keep the combined text from looking like "IamSPOT"; instead, the combined text will look like "I am SPOT" when displayed on the screen. Once the text items are combined, how do you display the new string on the screen? You'll first add in a DISPLAY block to show the text on the screen (see Figure 19-3). Then, drag a wire from the output Text data plug (of the TEXT block) into the input Text data plug (on the DISPLAY block). The output Text data plug provides the combined text from A, B, and C.

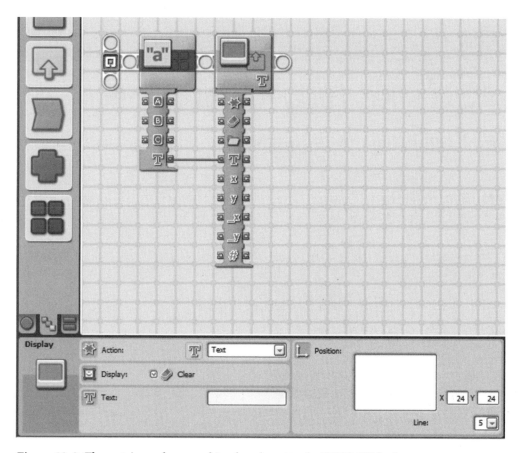

Figure 19-3. Three string values combined and sent to the DISPLAY block

Next, add a TIME WAIT block, so you can view the text before the program ends and the text disappears. You'll configure the WAIT block for 10 seconds (see Figure 19-4).

223

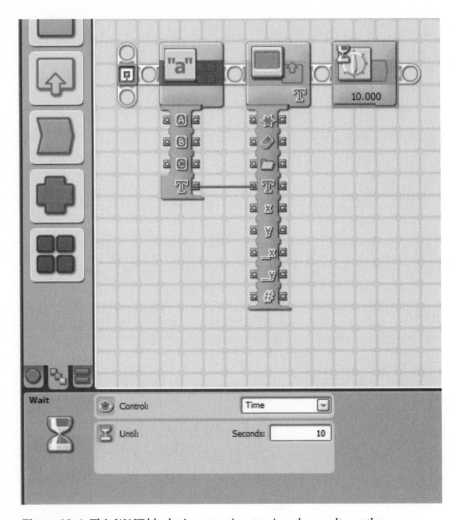

Figure 19-4. *This WAIT block gives you time to view the results on the screen.*

When you run the program, it now displays "I am SPOT" on the LCD screen. In Chapter 18, I showed you how to use the VARIABLE block. You could use this block to send text to the TEXT block using the input data plugs (A, B, and/or C). To do this, you would configure three VARIABLE blocks to each hold a bit of text. Drag a wire out of each VARIABLE block into ports A, B, and C and let the TEXT block do the rest!

Exercise 19-1: Counting Characters

Now for a short and easy exercise. Create a program that uses the TEXT block to combine three separate strings, each with a length of 10 characters. Use a combination of characters that when displayed on the LCD screen will make it easy for you to count the maximum number of characters that can be displayed on a single line.

The information from this exercise will be useful when it comes time to determine how much text can be squeezed on to a single line. I've included one possible solution at the end of the chapter.

What's Next?

Continue on to the next chapter where I'll show you how to program your robot with some basic math skills. Believe it or not, the more complicated your robot becomes, the more likely it is that it will need to perform some addition, subtraction, or possibly even multiplication and division. Your robot isn't smart enough to do the math itself, so it's going to require a special block that assists it with performing calculations.

Exercise Solution

Figures 19-5 to 19-13 show the complete program and configuration panels for Exercise 19-1. Notice that I've configured the DISPLAY block to start displaying any text it receives at a position where X=1. This will place the first character in any string all the way to the left side of the LCD screen. I've also created three variables (String1, String2, and String 3). See Chapter 14 for instructions on creating a variable, one for each of the VARIABLE blocks.

The first three VARIABLE blocks have their Action setting set to Write so I can enter a string of text. The next three VARIABLE blocks (wired to the TEXT block) have their Action setting set to Read so the data stored inside can be read by the TEXT block. (Try wiring the TEXT block using the first three VARIABLE blocks—you'll see that a VARIABLE block set to Write cannot be used to provide that data via its output data plug.)

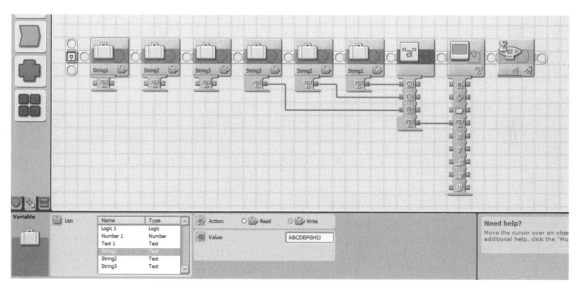

Figure 19-5. The complete program and the first VARIABLE block's configuration panel

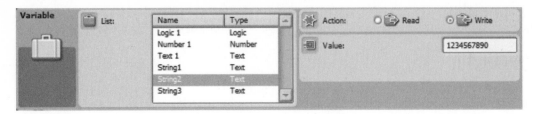

Figure 19-6. The second VARIABLE block's configuration panel

Figure 19-7. The third VARIABLE block's configuration panel

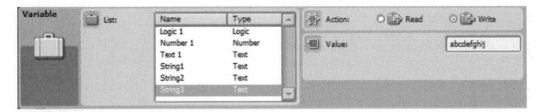

Figure 19-8. The fourth VARIABLE block's configuration panel

Figure 19-9. The fifth VARIABLE block's configuration panel

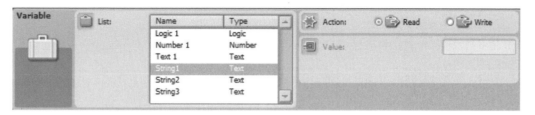

Figure 19-10. The sixth VARIABLE block's configuration panel

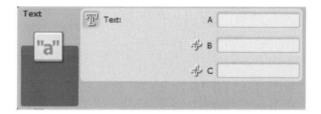

Figure 19-11. The TEXT block's configuration panel

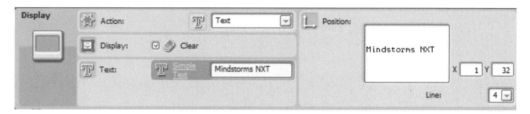

Figure 19-12. The DISPLAY block's configuration panel

Figure 19-13. The NXT BUTTON WAIT block's configuration panel

CHAPTER 20

■ ■ ■

Basic Math

Don't you just love short chapters? Well, I promise this is going to be another extremely short chapter. So get ready to add another programming block to your collection of tools—you're going to turn your robot into a calculator.

The MATH Block

Your robots can do some very simple math: addition, subtraction, multiplication, and division. Take a look at Figure 20-1, which shows the MATH block and its configuration panel.

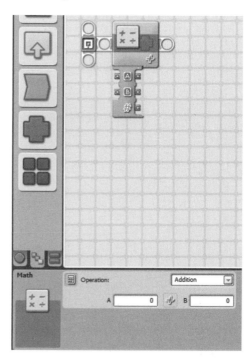

Figure 20-1. The MATH block and its configuration panel

The MATH block uses two values: A and B. For NXT-G 1.0 users, these values can be positive or negative integers. An *integer* is a whole number with no decimal values. If you attempt to enter in a number such as –4.3 or 10.8 the MATH block will round the values up or down to the nearest integer (–4 and 11 for my examples). But for NXT-G 2.0 users, you are not limited to integer math. Decimal values are allowed.

In the Operation section, there is a drop-down menu for you to select the type of operation to be performed. If you click the drop-down menu, you should see the following options:

- *Addition:* This option will add values A and B.

- *Subtraction:* This option will subtract value B from value A.

- *Multiplication:* This option will multiply value A by value B.

- *Division:* This option will divide value A by value B.

- *Absolute value:* This option will calculate the absolute value of A.

- *Square root:* This option will calculate the square root of value A.

■ **Note** NXT-G 1.0 does not offer the ability to calculate Absolute Value or Square Root.

Notice in Figure 20-1 that I've opened the data hub on the MATH block. There are two input data wire plugs (one for value A and one for value B) and three output data wire plugs. The MATH block requires one or two integer values, depending on the option you selected in the Operation section: if A or B is left blank, its value defaults to 0, except for Absolute Value or Square Root where only Value A is used.

Numbers can be entered manually by typing a value for A and a value for B in the configuration panel, or they can be provided to the MATH block by running one data wire into plug A and another data wire into plug B (see Figure 20-2).

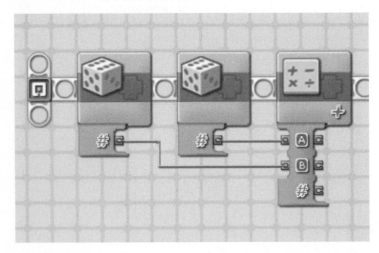

Figure 20-2. The MATH block can receive data wires for values of A and B.

Figure 20-2 shows a sample program that creates two random numbers (generated by two RANDOM blocks). Each RANDOM block uses its output data plug to run a wire into the A and B input data plugs on the MATH block.

You should understand that you really can't do anything with the MATH block without having its data hub open. The reason for this is simple: no matter what operation (addition, subtraction, multiplication, or division) you choose to perform on values A and B, the answer can only be obtained from the Result data plug (using a data wire).

Once values A and B have been added together, you want to see the answer on the LCD screen. To do this, you have to first convert the number to text. Drop in a NUMBER TO TEXT block (see Figure 20-3) and drag a data wire from the Result data plug on the MATH block into the Number data plug on the NUMBER TO TEXT block.

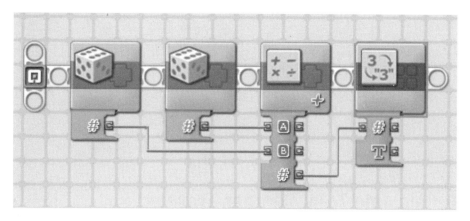

Figure 20-3. *The NUMBER TO TEXT block will convert the numeric answer to text.*

In order for you to see the answer on the Brick's LCD screen, you drag a data wire out of the Text data plug on the NUMBER TO TEXT block and into the Text data plug on the DISPLAY block; see Figure 20-4 (remember to change the DISPLAY block to show Text). Also, add in a small WAIT block, so you can see the results before they disappear off the screen.

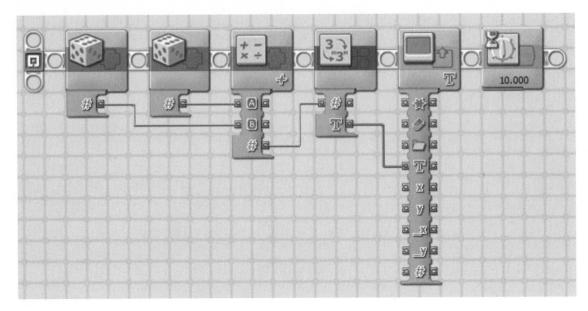

Figure 20-4. The DISPLAY block will show the result on the LCD screen.

Exercise 20-1: Calculate Total Degrees Traveled

Program your robot to roll a random number of degrees. The random number should be between –360 and –1 (negative values). After the movement is complete, generate another random number using the same range and have the robot roll that number of degrees. Display on the screen the total number of degrees turned as a positive integer. Check your solution against mine that I've provided at the end of this chapter.

What's Next?

That's it for the MATH block! Remember, value A and value B must be positive or negative integers and will default to *zero* (0) if you don't configure a value for them. If you plan on displaying the results of your MATH block, you'll need to convert the number to text before sending it to a DISPLAY block. Have fun! Up next, I'll show you how to prevent your robots from falling asleep.

Exercise Solution

Figures 20-5 through 20-14 show the complete program and all configuration blocks for Exercise 20-1. Notice that the values generated by the RANDOM blocks are negative values. These will be sent to a MATH block and an absolute value calculated for both values before sending to the MOVE blocks.

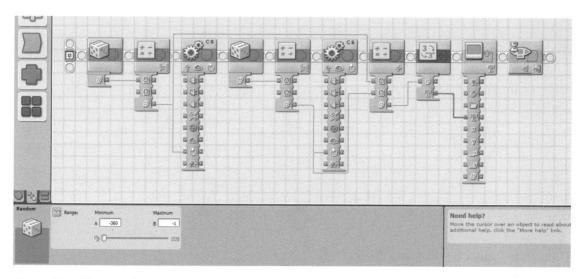

Figure 20-5. The complete program and the first RANDOM block's configuration panel

Figure 20-6. The first MATH block's configuration panel

Figure 20-7. The first MOVE block's configuration panel

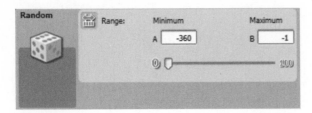

Figure 20-8. The second RANDOM block's configuration panel

Figure 20-9. The second MATH block's configuration panel

Figure 20-10. The second MOVE block's configuration panel

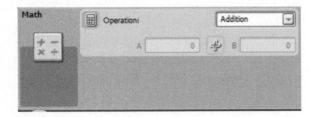

Figure 20-11. The third MATH block's configuration panel

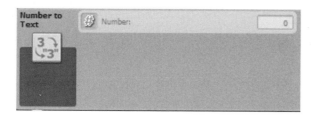

Figure 20-12. The NUMBER TO TEXT block's configuration panel

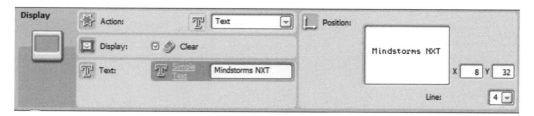

Figure 20-13. The DISPLAY block's configuration panel

Figure 20-14. The NXT BUTTONS WAIT block's configuration panel

■■■

CHAPTER 21

Staying Alive

Another short chapter? Of course! You can learn something and then get back to playing around with your NXT robots. But you won't get to play much if your robots keep falling asleep. This chapter will show you how to keep your robots working, even if the Sleep option on the Brick has been set to a short period of time like 2 minutes or 5 minutes.

The KEEP ALIVE Block

Your NXT Brick has a built-in feature that automatically turns off your robot after a certain amount of time has passed. This Sleep timer is configured on the Brick, and you can choose for the Brick to shut down after 2, 5, 10, 30, or 60 minutes of inactivity, or you can choose Never.

The Sleep timer is a useful feature, and you should definitely set it to a reasonable time. It can help save battery power if you accidentally leave the Brick turned on. If a program finishes executing, for example, and the robot stops moving while you're away for a little bit, the Sleep timer can make sure your robot turns itself off. But what if you want to build a robot that, for example, monitors the movement of a door using the Ultrasonic sensor? Think of a room alarm system that protects against intrusions from nosy brothers and sisters. If you program the robot to sit and monitor the door, you could easily set the Sleep setting to Never so it won't turn off on its own. However, an easier way is to use the KEEP ALIVE block.

The KEEP ALIVE block and its configuration panel are shown in Figure 21-1.

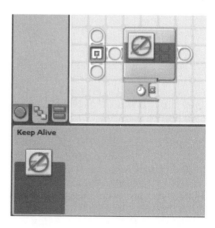

Figure 21-1. *The KEEP ALIVE block and its configuration panel*

Notice that the configuration panel is blank! There are no settings to configure with the KEEP ALIVE block.

Here's how it works: During the execution of your program, if at any time a KEEP ALIVE block is executed, the Sleep timer resets to its initial starting time. So, if you configured your Brick for a 5-minute Sleep timer and 1 minute into the program a KEEP ALIVE block is encountered, the Sleep timer will reset to 5 minutes.

Now, to make this useful, you'll probably need to place the KEEP ALIVE block in a location where it will frequently be executed. The best location is a LOOP block that will occasionally (or continually) run the blocks inside it, including the KEEP ALIVE block. This is one method for continually resetting the Sleep timer. (Remember, the Sleep timer starts counting when you turn on the brick, but resets when you run a program. If you don't run a program and the Sleep timer is set to 2 minutes, then after 120 seconds have elapsed, the Brick will turn itself off.)

An example is shown in Figure 21-2.

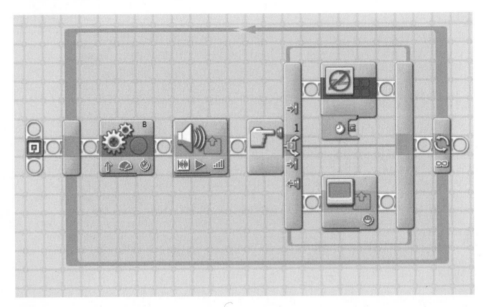

Figure 21-2. Put a KEEP ALIVE inside a LOOP and you can repeatedly reset the Sleep timer.

In this simple program, the robot will spin around a few times, say "Hello", and then do it again and again and again . . . if the Touch sensor button is ever pressed, the SWITCH block will execute the KEEP ALIVE block, which resets the Sleep timer. If the button is never pressed, the robot will eventually turn off when the default Sleep timer value has been reached (assuming the Sleep timer is not set to Never).

This is important: always check the Sleep timer setting on your Brick before running a program. Once the time has expired, the program will stop. This happens frequently when the Sleep timer is set to 2 minutes or 5 minutes, so double-check this before running a program, and be certain to set the Sleep timer to a setting that is longer than you expect the program to run.

To close out this chapter, the last item I want to mention about the KEEP ALIVE block is that it does have an output data plug in its data hub. This data plug will *only* supply a Number data type, and that number will always be the Sleep timer default value in milliseconds (1,000 milliseconds = 1 second). You might not find this data plug very useful, but it could be used as input to a COMPARE block that looks to see which is greater—a value from one of the Brick's three internal timers or the default Sleep timer value. Depending on the condition of the COMPARE block, your robot might perform some final action before letting the robot shut down using a STOP block or, as mentioned earlier, it might execute a KEEP ALIVE block to reset the Sleep timer value.

For some reason, a lot of people don't believe me that the brick will simply shut down when the Sleep timer value is reached. Exercise 21-1 is a small sample program to test the validity of this statement. I've included a short sample program at the end of the chapter if you need help.

Exercise 21-1: Loop Forever or Sleep?

Create a program to test whether the brick will automatically shut down after two minutes even while running a program that loops forever. Be sure to set your brick to use a value of 2 for the Sleep timer.

What's Next?

Well, that's it for the KEEP ALIVE block. Up next in Chapter 22 is the FILE ACCESS block. You'll learn how to program your robot to store data in files that can be accessed at any time, now or later.

Exercise Solution

Before you run the program, make certain the brick's Sleep setting is set to two minutes. To do this, turn on the brick, use the left or right buttons to navigate to the Settings selection and then press the Enter button (orange button). Use the left or right buttons again to navigate to the Sleep selection and press the Enter button. Use the left or right button to count up or down and change the value on the screen to 2. (Options include 2, 5, 10, 30, 60, and Never.)

Figures 21-3 through 21-7 show the complete test program and configuration panels for testing Exercise 21-1. Notice that the LOOP block is configured to loop for a duration of Forever. When the program runs, the brick will play a sound first, wait 3 seconds, rotate motors B and C a single rotation, wait 3 seconds, and then will repeat the entire process. Use a stopwatch or timer to verify that after the program starts that the brick shuts down after 120 seconds have elapsed.

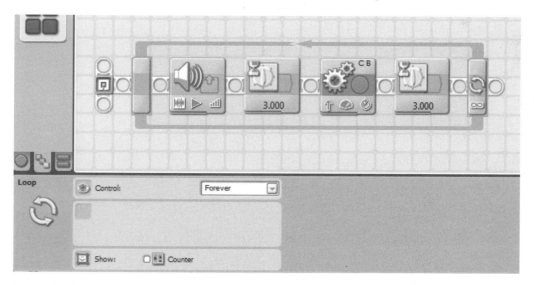

Figure 21-3. The complete program and the LOOP block's configuration panel

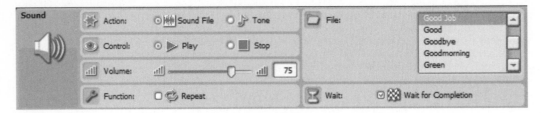

Figure 21-4. The SOUND block's configuration panel

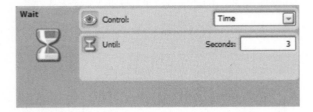

Figure 21-5. The first WAIT block's configuration panel

Figure 21-6. The MOVE block's configuration panel

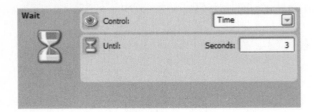

Figure 21-7. The second WAIT block's configuration panel

CHAPTER 22

■■■

Your Own Filing Cabinet

In Chapter 18, I showed you how to use VARIABLE and CONSTANT blocks to hold data such as Numbers and Text. But the problem with the VARIABLE block is that when the program ends, the data disappears! Even worse, if the batteries die or the power is turned off on your robot while it's running, the VARIABLE blocks all lose whatever values they were holding. The CONSTANT block solves this problem by allowing you to create a global variable that can be reused by multiple programs, but you must create the constant and its value ahead of time, either using the Define Constants menu option (see Chapter 18) or the CONSTANT block's configuration panel. Another limitation to the CONSTANT block is the amount of data this block can hold.

Fortunately, your NXT robots have access to a block that can hold a larger amount of data in memory and this data doesn't have to be pre-defined. That block is the FILE ACCESS block. It allows you to store data in a text file that doesn't disappear—even if you turn off the robot's power or the program ends. Your data is stored in a file that is kept in the NXT Brick's memory, and it stays there until you delete it, just like a program.

Introducing the FILE ACCESS Block

The FILE ACCESS block is shown in Figure 22-1 along with its configuration panel.

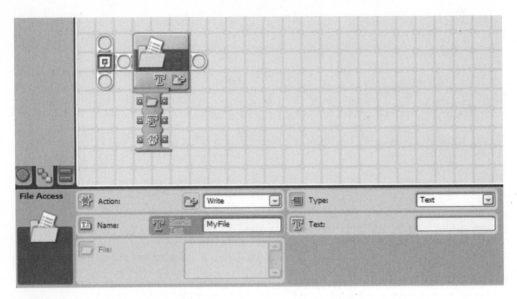

Figure 22-1. The FILE ACCESS block and its configuration panel

Now, before I get into showing you how to use this block, let me first explain some simple rules that you must obey when using the FILE ACCESS block:

Rule 1: The block can only hold Number or Text data, not Logic.

Rule 2: The block can perform four actions: Read, Write, Close, and Delete.

Rule 3: Each FILE ACCESS block can only perform one of the actions; this means that you need to use one FILE ACCESS block per action type.

Rule 4: When you write data to a file, the data is added to the end of any existing data already in the file.

Suppose that your Text data file has the following data stored in it: 15429823. Now, what will happen if you add 34 to it? Well, according to rule 4, the file will now be holding 1542982334. The 34 is *appended* to the end.

There are just a few more rules for you to remember:

Rule 5: To read the data written to a file, you must first close the file.

Rule 6: To overwrite the file (but keep the same filename), you must delete the file and create a new one with the same name.

The FILE ACCESS block does require some experimentation to learn how to properly use it. I highly encourage you to perform the following examples and then experiment by making changes. Try to read a mixture of values (of Number and Text types). Next, close the file and try opening it again and reading back your values. By playing with the block, you'll quickly figure out how best to use it with your own robots.

But for now, let me go over the basics of how to use the block.

Let's start with the Action section in the configuration panel. The Action section has a drop-down menu with four options: Read, Write, Close, and Delete. Easy enough—choose the Read option to read the contents of a file; choose the Write option to write data to a file; choose the Close option to close the file; and choose Delete to delete the file.

The Name section is where you specify the name of the file you will be working with (you might be writing, reading, closing, or deleting it). If you are creating a new file, keep the name short and unique but descriptive enough so you'll remember what kind of data it holds. Good examples are "RightTurns" (it could hold the total number of right turns a robot makes) and "TeamName" (this could hold a team's name for use in different programs).

The File section will list any files that currently exist on the NXT Brick when the Brick is connected and communicating with the software. You can choose a file from this list rather than specifying a new filename.

The Type section has a drop-down with two options: Number and Text. Choosing Number creates a Number section where you can type in a numeric value or use the small buttons to increase or decrease the number (if you are writing to the file). Choosing Text will create a Text section where you can type in a bit of text (also if you are writing to a file).

If you are reading from a file, you must specify if you are reading a Number or Text value from the file. If the file contains 1234, for example, and you select to read a text value, the data will be treated as text and not as a number. Keep that in mind, and remember to always select the proper type of data to read or write to a file.

If you are closing a file, this simply protects the file from being written or deleted. It's a good practice to always close a file when you are finished using it and before opening a different file.

Let me give you a small example of a program that uses the FILE ACCESS block.

First, I'll create a new file called LuckyNumber, as shown in Figure 22-2. Choose to write 15 as a Number value into the file.

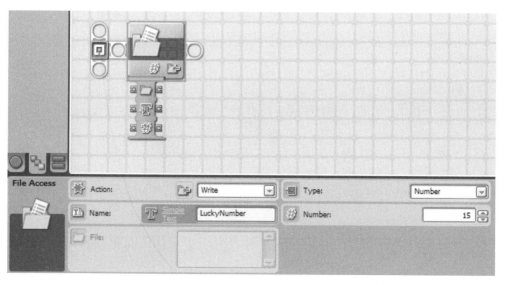

Figure 22-2. Creating a new file

You'll need to close the file after the number has been written to the file. This will allow you to later read the data. So add another FILE ACCESS block that closes the file (see Figure 22-3).

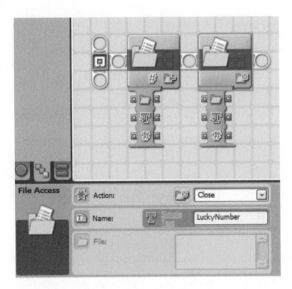

Figure 22-3. Closing the file will allow you to read from it later.

Now, here's some pseudo-code for SPOT:

Me: SPOT, I've stored a file in your memory called LuckyNumber. I want you to move forward three rotations and then display my lucky number on your LCD screen.

Here's how the program will look. First, drop in a MOVE block that will move SPOT forward three rotations (see Figure 22-4).

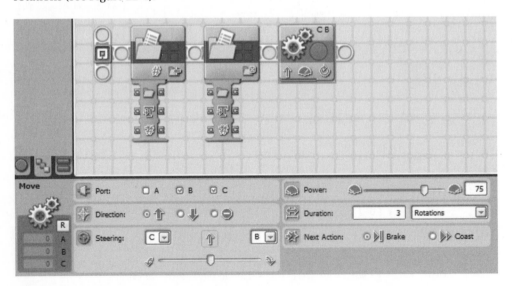

Figure 22-4. Move forward three rotations.

Now, you'll need to read the number stored in the LuckyNumber file and have SPOT display that value on his LCD screen. Fortunately, you can use a NUMBER TO TEXT block that will take a Number value and send that to a DISPLAY block. So, your first step is to read that value from the file. This is done by dropping in another FILE ACCESS block and reading the data (see Figure 22-5).

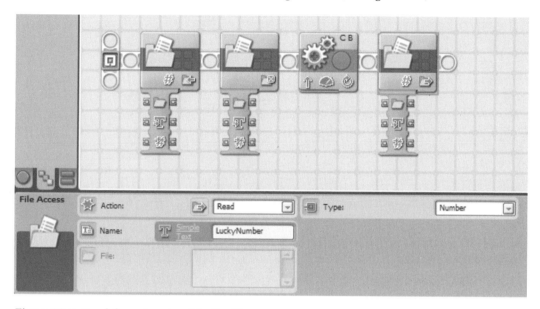

Figure 22-5. Read the value stored in the file.

Now, you need to drop in a NUMBER TO TEXT block and configure it to read the value stored in the file. You'll then pass this Text value on to a DISPLAY block. This is shown in Figure 22-6 along with the final WAIT block and its configuration panel.

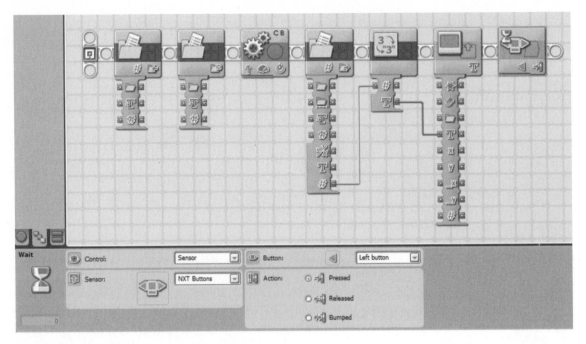

Figure 22-6. Read the value stored in the file.

Be sure to notice that there are two output data plugs that have the pound (number) symbol: #. One is used to provide the current number being written to the FILE ACCESS block (the block is set to the Write action), and the other is used to read data from the file. This sounds confusing but remember that you can be writing a number or text to a file that contains many numbers or many strings of text. When a FILE ACCESS block is set to the Read action, it will read the first bit of data it encounters in the file. Dropping another FILE ACCESS block and setting it to the Read action will read the next bit of data stored in the file. (You can also place a FILE ACCESS block set to Read in a LOOP block and every loop will cause it to read the next number or bit of text in the file.)

Figure 22-6 shows a data wire running from the output data plug. Be careful to select the correct one when using a FILE ACCESS block, or you'll receive a broken wire. Once this is completed, the FILE ACCESS block will provide the number stored as data that can be read by the NUMBER TO TEXT block. You'll just have to test this to prove it to yourself. The NUMBER TO TEXT block provides this to the DISPLAY block; the program waits for you to press the Left button (using the final WAIT block), and the program then ends.

The FILE ACCESS block is a great way for you to store data that your robot obtains during its explorations. You could use files to store things like number of motor rotations and left and right turns it makes. Your robot could later read from these files and find its way back home. There are many ways to use files stored on your Brick, and now you know how to create them, add to them, and delete them.

Before I close out this chapter, I want to mention a couple of useful tips. The first is to always get in a habit of closing your file. By doing this, you reset the file, and any values stored inside will be read in order (first to last). If you are using a FILE ACCESS block in other programs, I also suggest that you place a FILE ACCESS block at the beginning of the program and configure it to close the file. Again, do this to ensure that the file's data will be read in proper order.

Remember, because the data stored in a file is in sequential order, to read another value simply requires adding another FILE ACCESS block set to Read, *or* you can place a FILE ACCESS block inside a LOOP block so that every time the program loops, the FILE ACCESS block will read the next value in the file.

Finally, do remember that the file has an end. When the end of the file is reached, the FILE ACCESS block will not read any more values. To determine if this is happening, the FILE ACCESS block has a very useful Error data plug that returns a True or False Logic value (this uses a data plug and not a stored value of True or False inside the actual file). You can drag a data wire out of the Error data plug and use it as a condition to monitor. For example, a LOOP block could be configured to break when a True value is received from the Error data plug—the loop breaks and the program continues.

This chapter has only touched lightly on the power of the FILE ACCESS block. Believe me; there are many more uses for this block, and you'll find that giving your robots the ability to record data (and later retrieve it) will be a powerful tool. You can use it to keep track of light values, left and right turns, and more. Play around and experiment with the FILE ACCESS block to learn the little tricks that will allow you to give your robot a long-term memory!

Exercise 22-1: Left, Right, Left

Create a program for SPOT that generates a series of five random turns, left or right, and pauses for a few seconds between each turn. Count the number of left turns. Write the number of left turns to a file that will be stored on the brick for later use. Also, display the value stored in the file on the LCD screen before the program terminates.

This exercise will test what you've learned about a variety of NXT-G blocks, including the VARIABLE, LOOP, SWITCH, and MATH blocks. If you have trouble, I've included one possible solution at the end of this chapter.

What's Next?

Up next, make sure your Light and Sound sensors are working properly using the CALIBRATION block. I find this block isn't used as often as it should be, and that many errors related to these sensors are often related to the fact that trigger values are often set in one condition (a bright room, for example) while the robot and its program is executed in a different condition (a dimly lit room, for example). The CALIBRATION block can help eliminate these types of inconsistent conditions.

Exercise Solution

Because Exercise 22-1 is rather lengthy, I'll provide a little extra discussion on why I've used certain blocks. Figures 22-7 through 22-22 provide the complete program and configuration panels for Exercise 22-1.

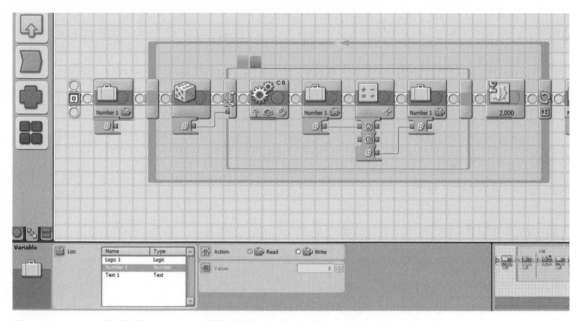

Figure 22-7. First half of program and the VARIABLE block's configuration panel

The VARIABLE block is initially configured to hold a value of 0. This variable will hold the number of left turns made during the program's execution.

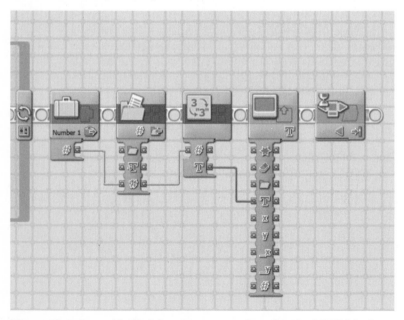

Figure 22-8. Second half of the program starting after the LOOP block

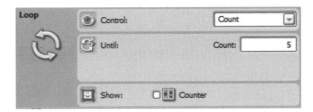

Figure 22-9. The LOOP block's configuration panel

Figure 22-10. The RANDOM block's configuration panel.

Because I want to make random left or right turns, I'll configure a RANDOM block to generate two values—1 or 2. I'll then use this value with the SWITCH block next.

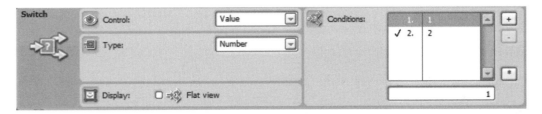

Figure 22-11. The SWITCH block's configuration panel

Remember to set it to a Number type and change the default values for the two possible conditions to 1 and 2. (See Chapter 12 for information on configuring a SWITCH block.)

Figure 22-12. The MOVE block's configuration panel for condition 2

The SWITCH block will take the value from the RANDOM block (1 or 2) and use this to select a path. Condition 2 will have the robot make a right turn. Condition 1 will have the robot make a left turn. Note that the MOVE block for Condition 2 is not seen in Figure 22-7; this figure shows the SWITCH block's tab for Condition 1.

Figure 22-13. The MOVE block's configuration panel for Condition 1

This is the MOVE block that will have the robot make a left turn. In addition to this MOVE block, a few other blocks are required in order to track the number of left turns made.

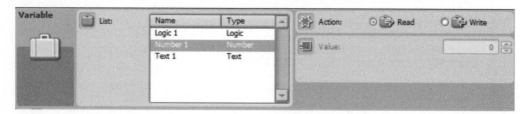

Figure 22-14. The second VARIABLE block's configuration panel

Here is where the current value stored in the VARIABLE block is read into the MATH block.

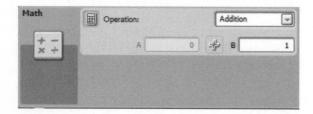

Figure 22-15. The MATH block's configuration panel

The MATH block increments the value stored in the VARIABLE block by 1. Every time Condition 1 is executed, the value stored will increase by a value of 1.

Figure 22-16. The third VARIABLE block's configuration panel

After the value increases by 1, it must then be rewritten to the VARIABLE block. Notice in Figure 22-16 that the block is set to the Write option.

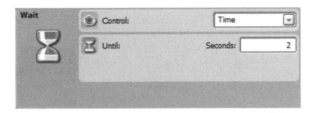

Figure 22-17. The WAIT block's configuration panel

Figure 22-18. The fourth VARIABLE block's configuration panel

After the looping is completed, the value stored in the VARIABLE block must be written the FILE ACCESS block, so make certain the action is set to Read.

Figure 22-19. The FILE ACCESS block's configuration panel

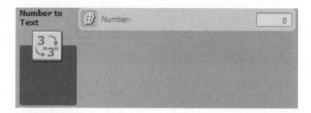

Figure 22-20. The NUMBER TO TEXT block's configuration panel

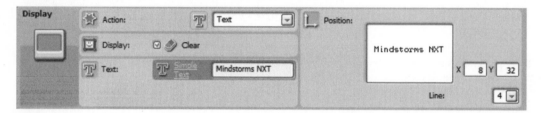

Figure 22-21. The DISPLAY block's configuration panel

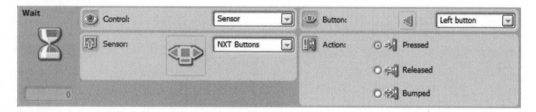

Figure 22-22. THE WAIT block's configuration panel

CHAPTER 23

■ ■ ■

Calibration

When it comes to the Sound and Light sensors, you will find that the minimum and maximum values of these two sensors can change from environment to environment. If your robot, for example, is located in a well-lit room, the minimum value (darkest spot in the room) will be substantially different from the minimum value the sensor obtains in a poorly lit room.

■ **Note** The NXT 2.0 robotics kit does not come with the Light or Sound sensors, but you may still find yourself using them one day, so it's worth knowing not only how to use these sensors with your 2.0 brick but also how to calibrate them.

This chapter will show you how to use the CALIBRATE block (and the Calibrate Sensor tool built into the 2.0 software), so you can trust the values your Sound and Light sensors are receiving. There's no exercise in this chapter, but I do encourage you to plug in a Sound and Light sensor to your brick and test the Calibrate Sensors Tool if you are an NXT-G 2.0 user.

The CALIBRATE Block

The CALIBRATE block is available only for the Light sensor (both NXT and RIS versions) and the Sound sensor. Figure 23-1 shows the basic CALIBRATE block and its configuration panel.

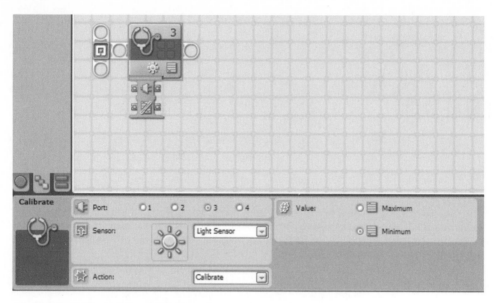

Figure 23-1. The CALIBRATE *block and its configuration panel*

Using the drop-down menu in the Sensor section, you can choose Light sensor or Sound sensor. The Port section is simple enough; just select the port number where the sensor you wish to calibrate is plugged in.

The Action section has a drop-down menu with two options: Calibrate and Delete. Calibrate is the typical option you will select, but if you wish to reset the minimum or maximum values for a sensor, choose the Delete option to delete the current settings, and then use additional CALIBRATE blocks to obtain new values.

The Value section is where you will choose to calibrate or delete the minimum or maximum value. This is important to remember: one CALIBRATE block is required to calibrate (or delete) the minimum value and an additional CALIBRATE block is needed to calibrate (or delete) the maximum value. However, if you choose to use only one CALIBRATE block, the good news is that calibrating one value (the minimum value, for example) will automatically calibrate the other value. To be safe, though, it's probably best to always use one CALIBRATE block for the minimum value and another for the maximum value.

There is one additional feature of the CALIBRATE block you need to know about, and it relates to multiple Sound or Light sensors. If you are using two or more of the same type of sensor, the minimum and maximum values obtained from two CALIBRATE blocks will apply to all sensors of that type. There is no need, for example, to have six CALIBRATE blocks for three Sound sensors—one block can be used to set the minimum values for all three Sound sensors and another block to set the maximum values.

Put the CALIBRATE Block to Work

And how do you actually calibrate your robot's sensors to the environment where it will be performing actions? The answer is simple, and I'll give you examples for both the Sound sensor and the Light sensor.

Let's look at the Light sensor first. If you've built a robot with a Light sensor (or multiple Light sensors) and you want to calibrate them to the current surroundings, the first thing you need to do is place two CALIBRATE blocks inside your program, preferably at the beginning of the program. The help documentation included with your NXT kit has a great suggestion, and I'm going to use it here with a sample of the NXT-G program code.

Take a look at Figure 23-2.

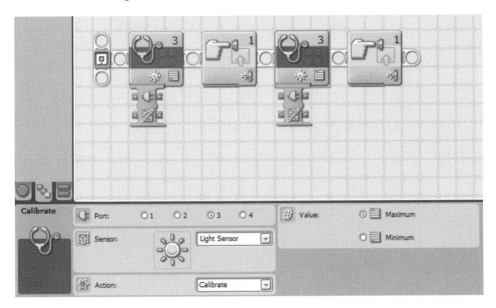

Figure 23-2. Calibrating a Light sensor

In this example, I've placed two CALIBRATE blocks. The first one is set to calibrate the minimum value for the Light sensor. The second block is set to calibrate the maximum value for the Light sensor. After the first CALIBRATE block, I've placed a TOUCH SENSOR WAIT block that simply waits for the sensor's button to be pressed. I've done the same thing for the second CALIBRATE block. This bit of NXT-G code can be placed at the beginning of your NXT-G program for your robot.

Now, the first thing I do is place the robot in the darkest (or least lighted) area of the room. When I've done this, I press the Touch sensor button. This allows the first CALIBRATE block to obtain the minimum value for the room.

Next, I take the robot and place it in the brightest area of the room. I press the Touch sensor button, and the second CALIBRATE block obtains the maximum value for the room.

And that's it! Now, if I've programmed my robot to use the Light sensor at any point in its program, the Light sensor should react properly based on any conditions I've programmed (such as "Turn Left if the Light sensor obtains a value over 30").

For the Sound sensor, I perform the exact same steps. Figure 23-3 shows the same NXT-G code but with the Sound sensor configured for calibration.

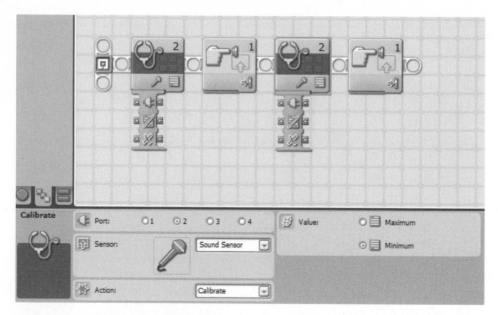

Figure 23-3. Calibrating a Sound sensor

In this example, I would try to place the robot in the quietest point in the room. This could be difficult, as I cannot predict factors such as observers or other potential sources of sound, but I'll do my best. I press the Touch sensor button, and the first CALIBRATE block will obtain the minimum value for the Sound sensor. Next, I'll place the robot in what I think will be the noisiest part of the room and press the Touch sensor button. The maximum value for the Sound sensor is now set.

One thing to note with the Sound sensor is the proximity of the sensor to the NXT motors. Keep in mind that when your robot is using any or all of its motors, the sound from the motors can influence the Sound sensor if you have programmed it to use the sound level for decision-making. You'll have to experiment and test your robots to determine the proper settings to configure for your Sound sensor triggers. You might program SPOT to turn left if the sound level is less than 20, but the sound coming from the NXT motors might cause the Sound sensor to evaluate the sound level as 22 or 23 when all other conditions are correct for a left turn. That's why it always pays to test, test, test.

The Calibrate Sensors Tool

The CALIBRATE block allows you to calibrate the sensors wherever the robot is located. This means that during a competition or a test where you don't have access to your computer or laptop, you will still have the ability to set the minimum and maximum values for these sensors and have them calibrated to the specific lighting and sound conditions your robot is experiencing. There is also a tool that you can use that exists outside your program.

A few CALIBRATE blocks won't substantially increase the size of your program, but if you do have access to your computer or laptop, you can save a little bit of storage space on your brick by removing the CALIBRATE blocks and instead using the Calibrate Sensors Tool, shown in Figure 23-4.

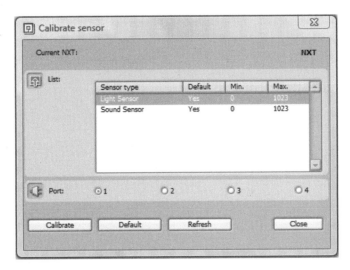

Figure 23-4. The Calibrate Sensors Tool user screen

To open the Calibrate Sensors Tool, connect your brick to your computer or laptop with a USB cable and turn the brick on. You'll also need to connect at least one of the sensors, or the List area shown in Figure 23-4 will be grayed out and unavailable.

After connecting your brick and turning it on, open the NXT-G software, click on the Tools menu, and select Calibrate Sensors from the drop-down menu. This will open the screen shown in Figure 23-4.

Using the Calibrate Sensors Tool works best with a laptop, when you can carry your brick (or robot) and the laptop to various locations where your robot will execute a program. If you've got the Light Sensor plugged in, for example, carry the laptop and robot to the darkest location where your robot will operate. Examples include under a table or maybe inside a tunnel.

On the tool's screen, make sure you select the sensor you'll be using (Light sensor for this example) as well as the port number you've got it plugged into (Port 1 for this example). Place the robot in the darkest location and press the Calibrate button. On the brick's screen, you'll hear a beep after the calibrate program is executed. The LCD screen will indicate it is taking a minimum reading and that you should press the Enter button (orange button) to capture the reading. Press the Enter button once.

Next, carry your robot and laptop to the brightest location where your robot is likely to operate. Examples include directly under a light or as close to a window as possible. Look at the LCD screen and you'll see a message asking you to press the Enter button to capture the maximum value. Press the Enter button once.

Finally, click the Refresh button on the Calibrate Sensors Tool and you'll see that the minimum and maximum values change to reflect the robot's current lighting conditions. This is shown in Figure 23-5.

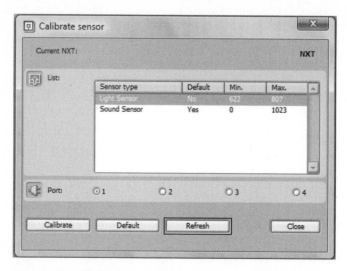

Figure 23-5. *The Calibrate Sensors Tool will update the minimum and maximum values for a sensor.*

The process works the same for the Sound sensor. In this case, you'll want to carry your robot and laptop to the quietest spot where the robot will operate. Press the Calibrate button and follow the on-screen instructions to capture the minimum value. Next you'll carry the robot and laptop to the loudest area the robot might encounter and perform the same steps to capture the maximum value.

Disconnect your robot from the laptop when done and your robot's Sound and Light sensors will be properly calibrated. To reset the sensors to the default conditions, simply reconnect your brick, launch the Calibrate Sensors Tool, and click the Default button, which will reconfigure the minimum and maximum values to their original settings.

What's Next?

Well, that does it for the CALIBRATE block. In Chapter 24, I'm going to show you how to program your bot to reset its motors, which is useful if you are monitoring motor rotation, for example. Keep reading to find out how it works.

■■■

Motoring

Throughout this book, I've used the MOVE block for control of the motors. I use it in just about every robot I've ever designed, but if you've been paying attention to the NXT-G software as you've worked through the book's exercises, you may have noticed a block that I've yet to cover—the MOTOR block. You'll also look at the RESET MOTOR block, which you might find handy for diagnosing and correcting movement problems.

The MOTOR Block

Figure 24-1 shows the MOTOR block. It works almost exactly like the MOVE block, with but a few exceptions. First, the MOTOR block can only be used to control a single motor; you cannot use it to control two or more motors, so you'll have to drop in two (or more) MOTOR blocks if you wish to have precise control over two or more motors.

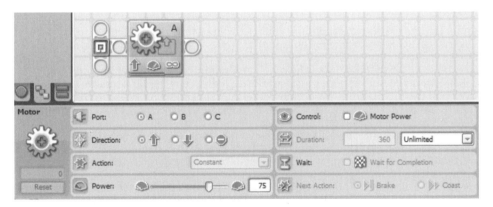

Figure 24-1. The MOTOR block and its configuration panel

You can use the MOTOR block just like a MOVE block to control the Direction, Power, Duration, and Next Action sections, but the Action, Control, and Wait sections work a little differently. If you leave the Duration set to Unlimited, the Action and Wait sections will be grayed out and unavailable. Only when you configure the MOTOR block to allow for precise control of the Duration (rotations, degrees, or time) will you have access to the Action and Wait sections. Figure 24-2 shows that I've elected to control Port B (Motor B) and wish to configure that motor using degrees for the Duration.

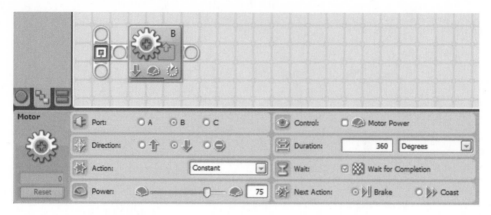

Figure 24-2. The MOTOR block will use degrees for control of Motor B.

In the Action section, you now have three options from the pull-down menu, as seen in Figure 24-3. These include Ramp Up, Ramp Down, and Constant.

Figure 24-3. Three options are available for the Action section of the MOTOR block.

If you choose Ramp Up and execute the program, you'll find that Motor B will increase its rotation speed at a constant rate until it reaches its maximum value for Power (75 in this example). Ramp Down will instruct the motor to reduce its current Power value to zero at a constant rate. In effect, you'll see the robot speed up or slow down at a fixed rate. This is helpful if you're finding your robot jumping and possibly changing its direction due to the sudden acceleration experienced when the motors kick in.

The Constant option in the Action drop-down menu does the exact opposite as Ramp Up or Ramp Down. If you configure a motor's Action section to Constant, the motor will attempt to reach the set Power immediately when the block is executed. This is great if you wish to give your robot an immediate boost of speed, but as I mentioned earlier you may find that your robot may lose some accuracy when it comes to moving in a specific direction. The sudden jump of the motors to maximum speed can often cause the robot to move off course due to slippage of the wheel(s) on a slick surface or a resistance to spin on a difficult surface such as sand or grass, for example.

How might you reduce the chance of this happening? Simple! Place a check in the Control section box labeled Motor Power. This will force the motor to attempt to compensate for slippage or resistance and force all motors to spin at the speed and keep the same velocity.

Finally, if you leave the box labeled Wait for Completion checked, no NXT-G blocks placed after the MOTOR block will execute until the MOTOR block has completed its programmed movement. If, for example, you program motor B to rotate 720 degrees and leave this box checked, only after the motor has completed two rotations will the block placed after it execute. This works similar to the SOUND block; if you wish to allow your program to continue running while the motors are rotating, uncheck this box.

The RESET MOTOR Block

The RESET MOTOR block is shown in Figure 24-4 along with its configuration panel. It does just one thing—reset a motor's internal record-keeping (for how many rotations a motor has made), and that one thing is something you may rarely (or never) use. I have actually never found a strong use for it, but who knows? This may very well be the one block that you've been looking for to make your new robot function properly.

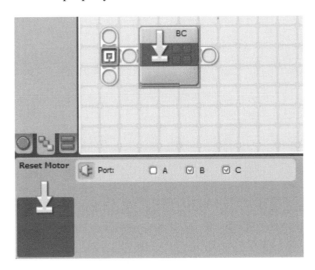

Figure 24-4. The RESET MOTOR block and its configuration panel

One of the first things you might notice about this block is that its configuration panel is extremely simple. You simply check the ports for the motors (A, B, and/or C) on which you wish to use the RESET MOTOR block. Why would you want to do this? I'll explain.

One of the great things about the NXT servo motors is the ability to pair them, so your robots can move in a more accurate straight line. The Brick sends the proper signal to motors B and C (I'm assuming you're using B and C for your movement control) and ensures that they spin at the same rate. By doing this, your robot is able to travel in fairly accurate straight lines. Imagine if one motor was spinning a little faster or farther than the other—your robot would end up moving in a not-so-straight line. Also, by pairing the motors, you can ensure that both motors are spinning with the same duration, such as 300 degrees or 2.5 rotations. This behavior is one of the advantages of the NXT motors.

Take a look at the following pseudo-code:

Me: SPOT, move forward 360 degrees and wait 3 seconds.

Me: Now, move forward 270 degrees and wait 3 seconds.

Me: Now, move forward 90 degrees and stop.

The NXT-G program for this pseudo-code looks like the one shown in Figure 24-5.

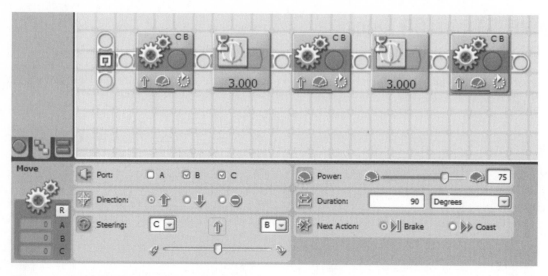

Figure 24- 5. An NXT-G program to move SPOT

In the program, I've added three MOVE blocks and a couple of WAIT blocks. The first MOVE block moves SPOT forward 360 degrees, and then SPOT waits for 3 seconds. The second MOVE block moves him forward 270 degrees, and then he waits for 3 more seconds. Finally, the third MOVE block moves him forward 90 degrees, and he stops. In all, SPOT has moved forward 720 degrees, or 2 rotations, for motors B and C. Now, I also configured the first two MOVE blocks to Coast in the Next Action section and the third MOVE block to Brake. I did this because I want to demonstrate a little trick that your NXT Brick and its motors perform.

Let's say that after SPOT's first MOVE block executes, SPOT actually rolls forward 380 degrees with the slight coast. On SPOT's second movement, he rolls forward 278 degrees with the coast. Now, if SPOT's final movement forward is 97 degrees, he will have moved a total of 755 degrees, not the expected 720 degrees. But if you upload this program to SPOT and run it, you'll find that SPOT will actually move forward 720 degrees, or 2 rotations. How?

The Brick and motors keep track of the distance SPOT coasts (by continuing to monitor the number of rotations the wheels make during the coasting) and reduce the final movement of the third MOVE block (configured to Brake) to a value of 62 degrees, not 90 degrees. By reducing the final MOVE block to 62 degrees, SPOT is still able to move forward a total of 720 degrees with accuracy (if the final MOVE block was set to Coast instead of Brake, this accuracy could not be guaranteed). It is this "error correction" that the Brick and motors provide that allows your robot to make very precise movements.

What if you don't care about the preciseness of the moves and want to shut off the "error correction" activity of the Brick and motors? Well, that's where the RESET MOTOR block comes into the picture.

Take a look at Figure 24-6, and you'll see SPOT's original program slightly modified.

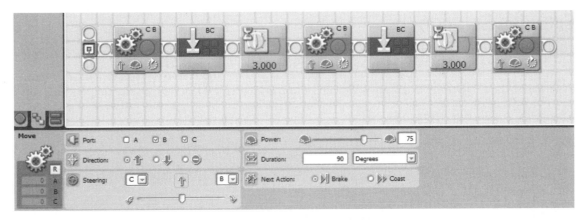

Figure 24-6. Another NXT-G program to move SPOT

In this program, SPOT will perform the same actions, but after the first MOVE block has been executed, the RESET MOTOR block will perform its action. Recall that your Brick and motors are communicating and keeping track of the number of degrees that you've programmed SPOT to move. If the first MOVE block causes SPOT to move forward 380 degrees, the RESET MOTOR block simply clears that value (resets to 0), and it's as if SPOT never moved at all. The second MOVE block may move SPOT forward another 277 degrees, but the second RESET MOTOR block resets that value to 0, too. Finally, the third MOVE block moves SPOT forward 90 degrees and then brakes. All in all, SPOT has moved forward a total of 747 degrees, not 720. SPOT moved an additional 27 degrees, because the "error correction" built into the motors has been disabled by the RESET MOTOR blocks.

Exercise 24-1: True Readings

That's it for the MOTOR and RESET MOTOR blocks. If you decide that you're not concerned with your robot keeping track of its movement durations and prefer to use the Coast feature with your MOVE blocks (maybe to save battery power), then the RESET MOTOR block may be useful to you. For now though, here's an exercise:

Create a program that will spin a single motor a set number of degrees (using the MOTOR block) and then coast to a stop. Send to the LCD display the actual value that the wheel spins due to coasting.

Running this exercise will show how using the Coast feature effects the actual distance a robot will travel versus the programmed value. It gives you a chance to observe the coasting effect and see for yourself how the actual number of wheel rotations might not match up to the programmed value. If you need help, I've included a sample solution at the end of the chapter.

What's Next?

Up next, I'll go over the use of Bluetooth and the SEND MESSAGE and RECEIVE MESSAGE blocks, and you'll learn how to program your NXT robot to communicate with other NXT robots.

Exercise Solution

Figures 24-7 through 24-12 show the complete program and configuration panels for Exercise 24-1. Note that the MOTOR block has its Wait for Completion box checked and the Next Action section is set to Coast. After Motor B has completed its rotation, I've added a NXT BUTTON WAIT block that will wait for you to press the Left button. Don't press the Left button until motor B has completely stopped. This will allow the ROTATION SENSOR block to get an accurate reading of the total number of degrees that motor B spun. This value will be sent to the NUMBER TO TEXT block and then to the DISPLAY block so you can see that the actual number of degrees rotated will be greater than the programmed value (of 360). The final WAIT block will wait for you to press the Right button to end the program.

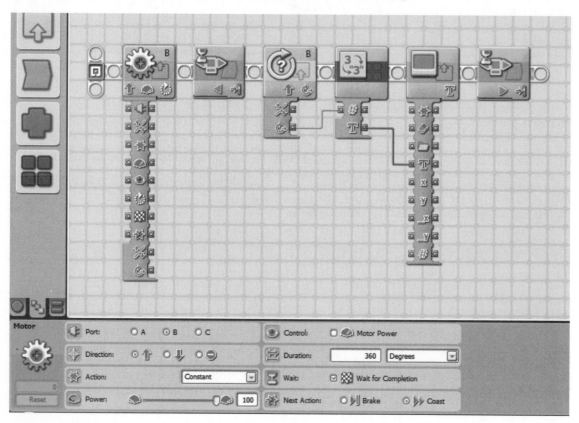

Figure 24-7. The complete program and the MOTOR block's configuration panel

Figure 24-8. *The first WAIT block's configuration panel*

Figure 24-9. *The ROTATION SENSOR block's configuration panel*

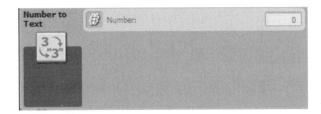

Figure 24-10. *The NUMBER TO TEXT block's configuration panel*

Figure 24-11. *The DISPLAY block's configuration panel*

Figure 24-12. The second WAIT block's configuration panel

■ ■ ■

CHAPTER 25

Messages

There may come a time when you'd like your NXT robot to be able to communicate and share information with other NXT robots. Or, if you have a second NXT kit, you could build a remote control for your robot and give it commands using the second NXT brick.

To make all this happen requires a handful of blocks that will be covered in this chapter. Many people find these blocks difficult or confusing, but they're really very simple if you understand the basic concept behind sending and receiving messages.

Of course, sending and receiving messages requires that the NXT bricks be connected via a Bluetooth connection. Connecting two or more NXT bricks via Bluetooth is fairly straightforward and I'll cover the basics here, but if you need more help with this task, check the built-in Help file with your NXT software. You can find instructions for connecting two or more NXT devices using the BLUETOOTH CONNECTION block in addition to the SEND MESSAGE or RECEIVE MESSAGE block's documentation.

The BLUETOOTH CONNECTION Block

If you have more than one NXT brick, you can use a variety of NXT-G blocks to allow communication between them. NXT robots can use Bluetooth communication to share information such as distances or recorded sensor values (the brightness of a room, for example). Using Bluetooth is fun, but it does have a small disadvantage in that it can drain the batteries when it's being used.

■ **Note** Without getting too technical, Bluetooth is a way for devices to communicate wirelessly over short distances. Bluetooth requires that both devices identify themselves to one another and that a password (also called a passcode) be swapped to give the devices permission to communicate. For more information (and a slightly more technical discussion), visit http://en.wikipedia.org/wiki/Bluetooth.

Some Preliminaries

You can turn Bluetooth on using the brick's buttons and menu system; you'll use this same menu system to find other NXT bricks and perform what's called Discovery and Handshake. Discovery and Handshake is simply allowing each NXT brick to identify itself to other bricks and then exchanging passwords that will allow bricks to securely communicate. The Discovery part is where the two bricks send out signals for the other device to listen for and receive. Once the devices "see" one another, they must exchange a password (also called a passcode) in order to obtain permission to start communicating and sharing information.

■ **Note** If you wish to have your NXT brick communicate with one or more NXT bricks, you will need to make certain that you have gone through the Discovery and Handshake process. Ideally, you'll want to do this while your brick is connected to your computer or laptop so that a list of other NXT devices can be gathered and listed in the NXT-G software. Consult the Help documentation for more information on how to perform this task.

Once the Discovery and Handshake process is completed by both bricks, you can use NXT-G programs to send and receive data between bricks. Sending and receiving information is covered a bit later in this chapter, but with NXT-G 2.0, you can now turn on and off the Bluetooth communication ability. This is a useful feature that will help save battery power.

Configuring a Connection

Figure 25-1 shows the BLUETOOTH CONNECTION block and its single setting, which you can configure.

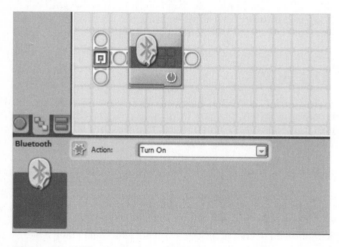

Figure 25-1. The BLUETOOTH CONNECTION block and configuration panel

The Action section's drop-down menu offers four options: Turn On, Turn Off, Initiate Connection, and Close Connection.

The Turn On and Turn Off options do exactly as you'd imagine. Turn On will turn on the Bluetooth function on your brick, allowing it to communicate with any other bricks that have been identified and exchanged passwords with. Turn Off will disable the Bluetooth function on your brick. If you intend to use an NXT-G program to communicate and send and receive data with another brick, I highly encourage you to use the Turn On and Turn Off ability. You simply drop a BLUETOOTH CONNECTION block at the beginning of the program and configure its Action setting to Turn On, and drop another BLUETOOTH

CONNECTION block at the end of the program and configure its Action setting to Turn Off. By doing so, you won't have to remember to turn off the Bluetooth feature on the brick.

During the Discovery and Handshake task, you will need to make note of the ID of the other NXT bricks. The ID is the same thing as the brick's Name. The Name is stored on your NXT brick and appears at the top of the LCD screen when your brick is turned on. You can also view the Name in the NXT Data window shown in Figure 25-2. Click the button indicated in Figure 25-2 to open up the NXT Data window.

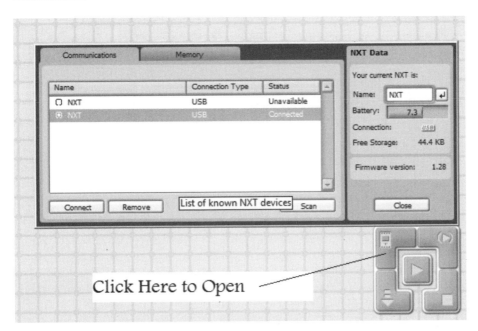

Figure 25-2. The NXT data window will show you the name of your connected brick.

You may notice that there are two devices in the list, both with the name NXT. Ideally, all bricks should have unique names. You can change the name of the currently connected brick by typing a new one in the Name field in the upper-right corner of the window, shown in Figure 25-3. I'm changing this brick's name to Jim. Now I can give that name to other NXT brick owners and they will be able to use it to send and receive data—but only after one more task is performed.

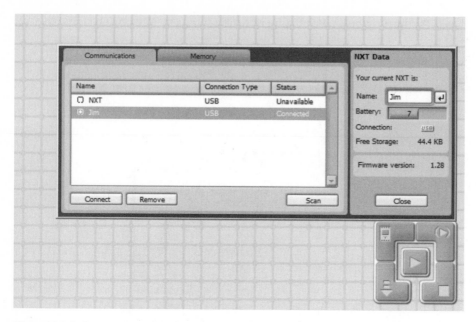

Figure 25-3. Rename your brick to something unique and easy to remember.

Initiating a Connection

Once all the bricks have identified themselves to one another and exchanged passwords entered by their owners, you will still need to tell your program the name of the brick with which you wish to communicate. This is especially important if you have multiple NXT bricks.

Fortunately, it's extremely simple. Drop in another BLUETOOTH CONNECTION block early in your program and select the "Initiate Connection" setting in the Action section, as shown in Figure 25-4.

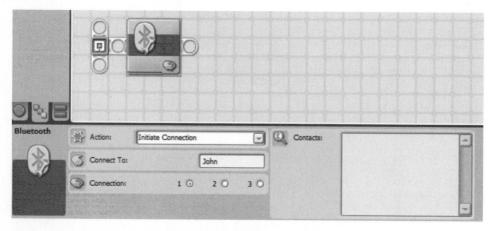

Figure 25-4. Initiating connection with another brick to share data

Type in the name of another brick (in this case, John) in the Connect To section and select a Connection port—1, 2, or 3. As you can see, this will allow your NXT brick to communicate with up to three additional bricks, each having its own communication port. You'll see in a moment how this is useful when sending and receiving data between bricks.

Closing a Connection

Finally, if you are done sending and receiving information from another NXT brick, it's useful to close a connection with another brick using the "Close Connection" option in the Action section. This can be useful to the other NXT brick's owner as it will free up a communication port that might be needed for that owner to communicate with another brick (not yours). Figure 25-5 shows that I've closed the connection with the brick named John. The Connections section on the configuration panel will also show you any other NXT bricks that have been identified and are in communication with your brick.

Figure 25-5. Closing a connection will free up a communication port on another brick.

You may have noticed the Contacts section in Figure 25-4. This list will show all the names of any NXT bricks that have been connected to your laptop or computer. It can be useful to you to ask the other NXT brick owners to connect their bricks to your laptop or computer so the name of their bricks will be stored in this list. Otherwise, you'll have to type in the name manually when initiating a connection.

So, now that you know how to turn Bluetooth on and off and how to select the particular brick you wish to communicate with, it's time to learn how to actually send and receive data between bricks. This is done with two easy-to-remember blocks, the SEND MESSAGE and RECEIVE MESSAGE blocks.

The SEND MESSAGE Block

The SEND MESSAGE block is shown in Figure 25-6 along with its configuration panel.

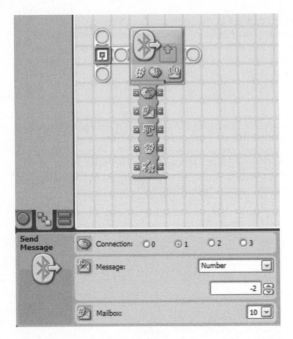

Figure 25-6. *The SEND MESSAGE block and its configuration panel*

There are a couple of items you really need to understand in the configuration panel. The first one is found in the Message section. The drop-down menu has three options: Text, Number, or Logic. By selecting one of these, you supply the correct type of message in the text box immediately below the drop-down menu. If you choose Text in the drop-down, the text box must contain some form of text content. Likewise, if you choose Number in the drop-down menu, the text box must contain a positive or negative integer value. And last, selecting Logic from the drop-down menu requires that you must select the True or False value.

■ **Note** As with most of the advanced NXT blocks, the SEND MESSAGE block can be configured to receive Text, Number, or Logic values using data wires, as shown in Figure 25-6. Note that the Connection data plug is a value between 0 and 3 and is used to identify the master or slave NXT device. The master device is always configured to use the value 0, and up to three additional NXT bricks can be linked via Bluetooth, with each being identified by 1, 2, or 3. Earlier in the chapter you saw how the BLUETOOTH CONNECTION block is used to select a communication port—1, 2, or 3—to assign to a brick. When sending and receiving data between bricks, you'll want to pay attention to the port configured in the SEND MESSAGE and RECEIVE MESSAGE blocks so you get the proper data from the proper brick.

Now, this is a great way for one NXT brick to send a single item to another brick. One NXT brick could, for example, monitor the number of times the Touch sensor is triggered and send this value to another robot. But what if you want to send even more information? What about sending the Light sensor's value as well as the number of rotations motor B has made to the second robot? Is this possible?

Well, if you think of each potential message as a variable (covered in Chapter 18), then the answer is "Yes." The SEND MESSAGE and RECEIVE MESSAGE blocks allow for up to ten unique messages to be sent back and forth between bricks using a concept called *mailboxes*.

Each NXT brick has ten mailboxes, and each mailbox is numbered. The first mailbox is called Mailbox 1; the second mailbox is called Mailbox 2, and so on. If you look at the configuration panel for the SEND MESSAGE block, you'll see that the last section is called Mailbox, and it contains a drop-down menu. Select this drop-down menu, and you'll see that you can select from numbers 1 to 10. It's simple! When you place a Text, Number, or Logic value in Mailbox 3, for example, that value is held in that mailbox (remember, a Text value can be a single character or multiple characters but is still considered a single value to a mailbox). Up to five values can be held per mailbox, *but* the values held *must* be of the same type (Text, Number, or Logic). If, for example, a SEND MESSAGE block attempts to put a sixth value in Mailbox 5, the first value inserted into Mailbox 5 drops out and is lost. So be careful about putting too many values into a Mailbox before they are retrieved!

Now, can you guess how the other robots will retrieve a value held in a mailbox? If you said by using a RECEIVE MESSAGE block, you're right. Take a look at Figure 25-7, and you'll see the RECEIVE MESSAGE block and its configuration panel.

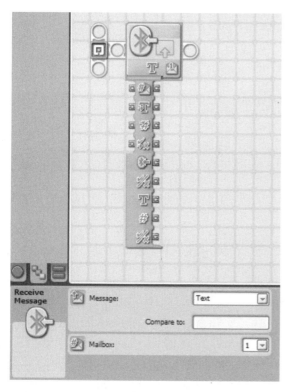

Figure 25-7. The RECEIVE MESSAGE block and its configuration panel

The RECEIVE MESSAGE block works similarly to the SEND MESSAGE block. Select the mailbox number from the drop-down menu in the Mailbox section. Again, the mailboxes are numbered 1 to 10. You must also select the type of data you are expecting to receive from the SEND MESSAGE block (Text, Number, or Logic) in the drop-down menu in the Message section.

You'll notice that in the Message section there is a "Compare to" text box. If you enter a value in this box, a True or False logic value will be determined, and using an output data wire, you can obtain this logic value to give it to another block. For example, if Mailbox 3 is holding a Number data type value of 250, your RECEIVE MESSAGE block is configured to read a Number value from Mailbox 3, and you've entered 250 in the "Compare to" text box, a True value will result from the comparison.

Now, for a quick example of a simple program, let's take the following pseudo-code and convert it to an NXT-G program:

Me: SPOT, move forward until your Ultrasonic sensor detects an object at least 10 inches in front of you.

Me: Read the value on your Light sensor.

Me: Send the Light sensor Intensity value to SPOT2 using Mailbox 3.

As you can see from Figure 25-8, I've created a simple program that causes SPOT to start moving forward (unlimited duration) while monitoring his Ultrasonic sensor. When the Ultrasonic sensor is triggered, the second MOVE block stops motors B and C. The Light sensor takes a reading, and this value is sent to the SEND MESSAGE block using a data wire configured to hold a Number value.

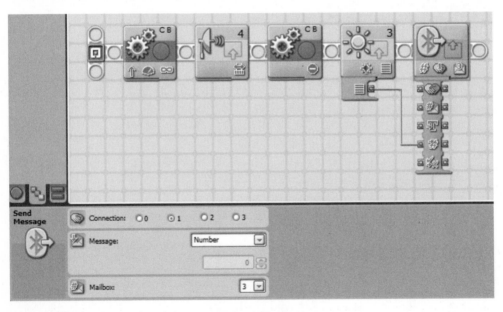

Figure 25-8. A program using the SEND MESSAGE block

Now, if I have a second robot (called SPOT2), I can convert the following pseudo-code into another NXT-G program that will obtain the Light sensor value:

Me: SPOT2, check Mailbox 3 for a Number value.

Me: Compare that value to your Light sensor reading.

Me: If your Light sensor reading matches the value in Mailbox 3, move forward eight rotations.

Now, take a look at Figure 25-9 to see how I've converted the pseudo-code to an NXT-G program.

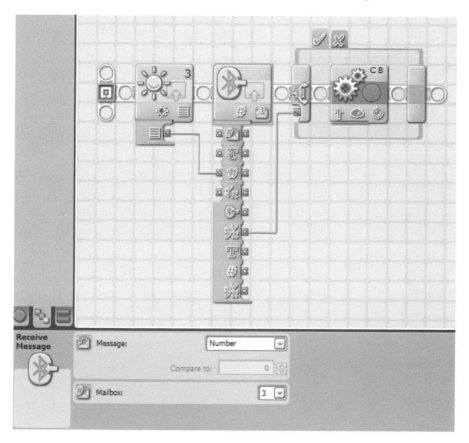

Figure 25-9. A program using the RECEIVE MESSAGE block

In this program, SPOT2's Light sensor takes a reading, and this value is passed to the RECEIVE MESSAGE block using a data wire. Now, when SPOT2 checks Mailbox 3 and reads the value, a comparison is made between the stored value and the value obtained by SPOT2's Light sensor. This comparison is done automatically, because a number value has been provided to the RECEIVE MESSAGE block's Number data port, and a data wire has been dragged out of the RECEIVE MESSAGE block's Logic data port and into the SWITCH block. This setup forces the block to do a comparison of the two values (the one obtained by the Light sensor and the Number configured in the configuration panel). If these values are equal, a True value is passed to the SWITCH block. The True tab is shown in Figure 25-9, and it includes a MOVE block that will move SPOT2 forward eight rotations if Mailbox 3's value and SPOT2's Light sensor values are identical.

The SEND MESSAGE block and the RECEIVE MESSAGE block are absolutely essential for two or more NXT robots to communicate and share information. This chapter has barely scratched the surface of what can be done using these two blocks. I mentioned earlier that with a second NXT kit, you can build a remote control for your robot. In order to build a useful remote control, you need to use the SEND MESSAGE blocks in your remote control to send numeric values to the robot. These values could represent the number of rotations or degrees for motors B and C to spin, for example. Or they could represent the speed/power of the motors to spin. There are numerous ways to do this, and there really is no incorrect method—just pick the one that works best for you. And since you have three communication ports (1, 2, and 3), you could theoretically remote control up to three robots! Just remember to use BLUETOOTH CONNECTION blocks to specify the communication port number for each brick that you wish to send data. You can use the built-in Bluetooth controls on the brick's menu system, but using blocks will make it easier and faster to test as you create your program—no more fiddling with the buttons on the brick to find and link up to other bricks!

What's Next?

Well, we've got one more item to cover—it's called the My Block. And you're going to find it very useful for creating small programs that can be used over and over again in future robots.

CHAPTER 26

■■■

My Block Is Your Block

Don't go crazy looking for an actual NXT-G block on the palettes called "My Block." It doesn't exist. My Block is something that you are going to create. A My Block is a collection of NXT-G blocks that you have grouped together and may wish to reuse. My Block represents a feature that lets you build and reuse components. So let's jump right in and see how this approach of reusing components can help you.

Creating a My Block

Take a look at the following pseudo-code and the matching NXT-G program in Figure 26-1. (Adding comments to the blocks to make them a little easier to figure out which is which—it's a *lot* of MOVE blocks to keep track of.) If SPOT performs these movements, he should follow a square-shaped path and return to his starting position.

Me: SPOT, move forward three rotations and then turn left 90 degrees.

Me: SPOT, move forward another three rotations and then turn left 90 degrees.

Me: SPOT, move forward another three rotations and then turn left 90 degrees.

Me: SPOT, move forward another three rotations and then turn left 90 degrees.

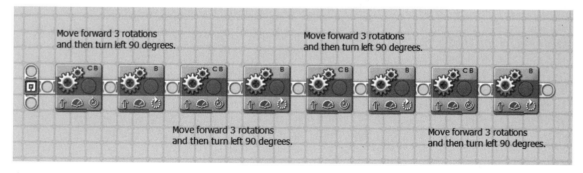

Figure 26-1. A simple movement program for SPOT

You could also place the first two MOVE blocks in the program in a LOOP block configured to loop four times, as shown in Figure 26-2.

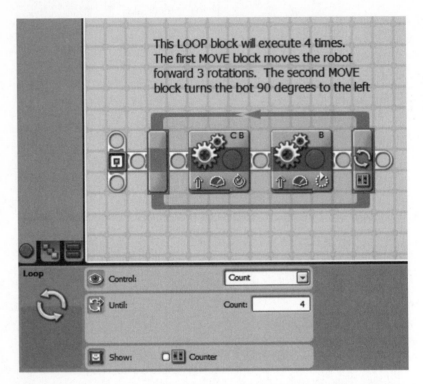

Figure 26-2. A simple movement program for SPOT using a LOOP block

But what happens if later you need SPOT to take a Light sensor reading after the second left turn? You would need to modify the two NXT-G programs. The first program (shown in Figure 26-1) isn't that difficult to modify; just drop in the Light sensor block in the middle of the program and you're finished. But for the second program (with the LOOP block), you have to modify the first LOOP block to run twice, then insert the Light sensor block, and finally create a second LOOP block for the final two movements. This is shown in Figure 26-3.

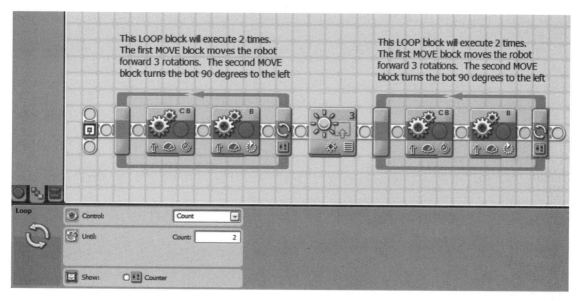

Figure 26-3. *The modified LOOP program*

Now, it wasn't that difficult to modify the program, but imagine if this program is getting larger and larger, with SPOT needing to perform not only left turns but right turns. The program can get quite large with all those MOVE blocks being added. This is where the concept of the My Block comes in handy.

Take a look at Figure 26-4, and then I'll explain what you are seeing.

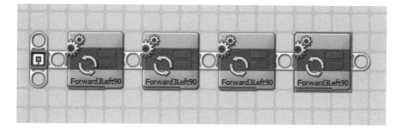

Figure 26-4. *A program using a bunch of My Block blocks*

In Figure 26-4, you'll see four My Block items. Each of these blocks contains two MOVE blocks. The first MOVE block moves the robot forward three rotations, and the second MOVE block turns it left 90 degrees. All you've done is take the program you saw in Figure 26-1 and group the pairs of MOVE blocks. Instead of eight NXT-G blocks (see in Figure 26-1), you now have four My Blocks!

Can you see the value of using My Blocks? Now you have a reusable NXT-G block that you can drop into this program (or any future program) anytime you want the robot to move forward three rotations and turn left 90 degrees. You could make a similar My Block that moves the robot forward three rotations and turns it right 90 degrees. The options are endless.

By using this concept, you can create collections of NXT-G blocks that perform very specific actions and then bundle them into a My Block and reuse them over and over again. Over time, your My Block collection will grow, and you'll save time by not having to recreate certain actions (such as turn 180 degrees, move forward two rotations, and take a reading on your Light sensor—all three of these actions can be bundled into a single My Block).

So, let me show you how you do this.

The first step is to create the repeatable actions you want to bundle in a My Block. To follow my earlier example, add two MOVE blocks as shown in Figure 26-5 that will be used to move SPOT forward three rotations and turn him left 90 degrees.

Figure 26-5. The start of creating a My Block

After you've created your small NXT-G collection of blocks that you want to make repeatable, click and drag to select the blocks, as shown in Figure 26-6.

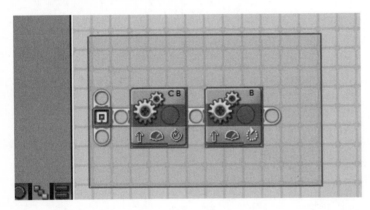

Figure 26-6. Click and drag to select the blocks you want to include in your My Block.

Next, click the Edit menu, and select "Make a New My Block" from the available options, as shown in Figure 26-7.

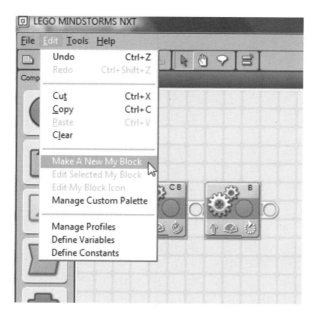

Figure 26-7. *Make a New My Block is selected from the Edit menu.*

■ **Note** If you are running NXT-G version 1.0, your edit menu may look slightly different as it lacks the Define Constants option at the bottom of the Edit menu.

The My Block Builder window will appear (see Figure 26-8).

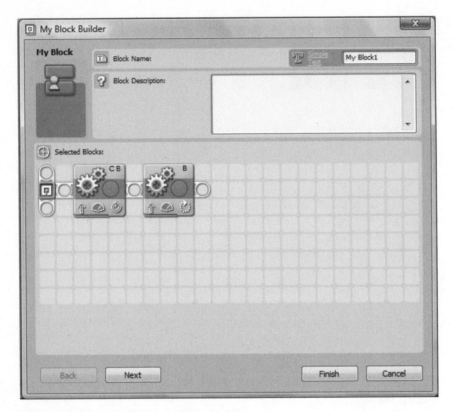

Figure 26-8. The My Block Builder window

Fill in the details as shown in Figure 26-9. Give the My Block a name that is useful to you in the Block Name field, and write a more detailed description in the Block Description text box. Click the Next button to choose an icon for your new My Block, or click the Finish button to complete the My Block creation process.

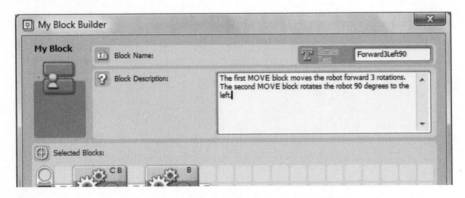

Figure 26-9. Provide a name and description for your My Block.

If you click the Next button, you'll see the Icon Builder screen, shown in Figure 26-10. You can drag and drop one or more of the small icons, which are located on the bottom of the window, into the Icon Builder pane. You can see a preview of your new My Block to the right of the Icon Builder workspace.

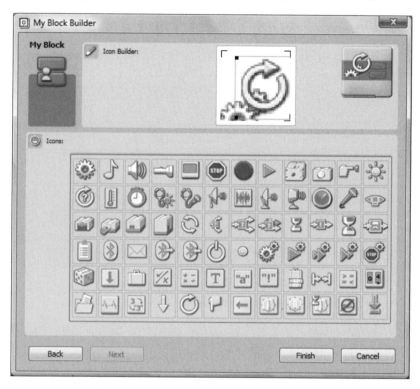

Figure 26-10. *Create a custom icon for your new My Block*

Click the Finish button, and that's it. The blocks you selected (in Figure 26-6) are converted to a single My Block that has the name and icon you specified (see Figure 26-11).

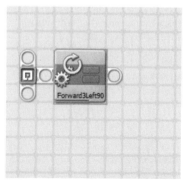

Figure 26-11. *Your finished My Block*

You can access your new My Block by clicking the Custom Palette and moving your mouse over the My Blocks palette tool, which is shown in Figure 26-12 (hover your mouse pointer over an icon and the name of the MyBlock will appear).

Figure 26-12. The new My Block appears in the Custom Palette.

You should also be aware that My Blocks can receive and send data via data wires. The key to making this work is that the blocks you want to add to a My Block *must* have their data wires configured before you select the blocks and choose "Make a New My Block" from the Edit menu. Any data ports that enter or exit the blocks you have selected will appear as data plugs in your new My Block after you've created it. Exercise 26-1 will provide you an example of how this is done.

Exercise 26-1: The MyBlock Plug

Create a MyBlock that will accept a single data wire to receive a number value. This number value will be sent to two RANDOM blocks to set their maximum value. The minimum value for the RANDOM blocks will be 1. Each RANDOM block will feed its generated number to the LCD display screen. Compare your solution against mine at the end of this chapter.

You're Ready to Go!

Well, that's it! OK, not exactly. Although I've covered all the NXT-G blocks available in your basic software, this doesn't mean you don't have anything left to learn. As more blocks are created by LEGO and third-party developers, you'll have the ability to add new NXT-G blocks to your palettes, and you'll need to play and experiment with them to learn all the functions and features they provide.

NXT-G is a great way to learn to program robots. Its drag-and-drop interface is easy to use, and you'll find that some very powerful programs can be created with it.

Keep learning, experimenting, and developing new ways to make your robots more responsive, more intelligent, and more impressive. Have fun!

Exercise Solution

Figures 26-13 through 26-23 show the blocks and configuration panels contained in the MyBlock named "TwoRandomsLCD" as well as the steps for creating the MyBlock. Remember, in order for a MyBlock to have a data plug included requires that a wire be run to one or more blocks inside the MyBlock selection area. Figure 26-13 shows how to drag a data wire from a VARIABLE block to the first RANDOM block.

The second RANDOM block gets the same value from the first RANDOM block using another data wire. Note also that in Figure 26-20 that you've selected all the blocks except for the VARIABLE block. You do not wish to include the VARIABLE block in the MyBlock because you want the MyBlock to be able to receive a number value via a data plug and you are not concerned about the source of the number value. The VARIABLE block is simply used to provide a wire so the final MyBlock will include an input data plug. Finally, the first and second DISPLAY blocks will provide the random numbers generated on lines 4 and 6, respectively.

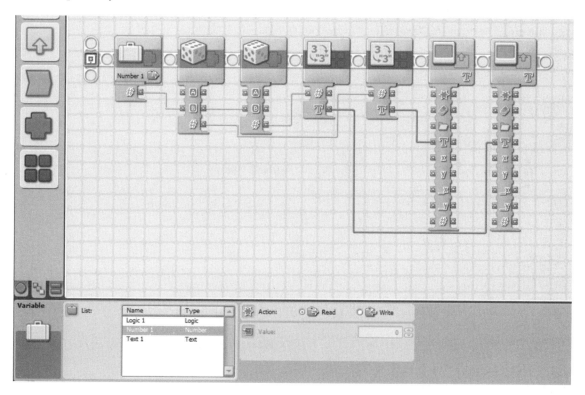

Figure 26-13. The full program and the VARIABLE block's configuration panel

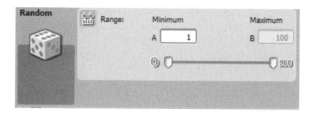

Figure 26-14. The first RANDOM block's configuration panel

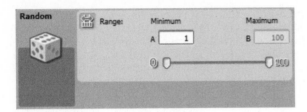

Figure 26-15. *The second RANDOM block's configuration panel*

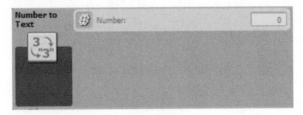

Figure 26-16. *The first NUMBER TO TEXT block's configuration panel*

Figure 26-17. *The second NUMBER TO TEXT block's configuration panel*

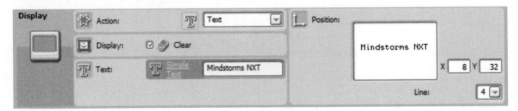

Figure 26-18. *The first DISPLAY block's configuration panel*

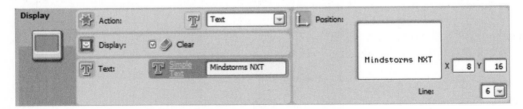

Figure 26-19. *The second DISPLAY block's configuration panel*

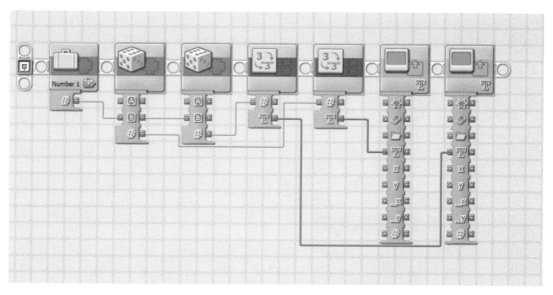

Figure 26-20. *All blocks selected for conversion to a MyBlock (minus the VARIABLE block)*

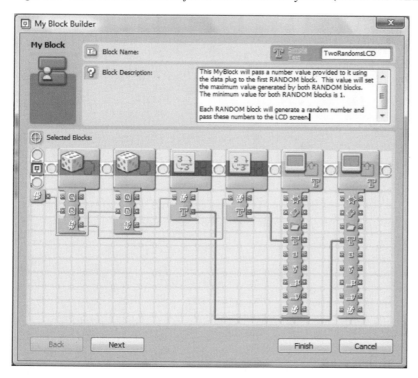

Figure 26-21. *Provide a name and description of the MyBlock*

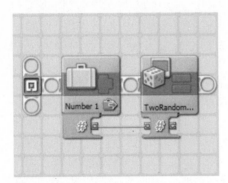

Figure 26-22. Blocks converted to a single MyBlock with a data plug

Figure 26-23. The new MyBlock is listed in the MyBlock flyout menu.

APPENDIX A

■■■

Math Basics for NXT

When programming your robots, you may find many times that you need to perform some basic math in order to properly direct them. While I don't have the space to cover every possible mathematical calculation you may need, I do want to focus on three very simple subjects that you might find useful. The first is converting between degrees and rotations; the second is calculating travel distance based on the number of degrees or rotations you configure; and the third is a very short discussion of how the X/Y coordinate system works on your Brick.

Converting Between Degrees and Rotations

When it comes to the MOVE block's Duration setting on its configuration panel, I've found that most people generally have a preference when configuring their robots to move a specified distance: some will use degrees, and others will use rotations. A rare few will rely on seconds (time-based movement), but if your robot relies at all on accurate movements, you simply cannot program your robot to, say, move forward for five seconds and know for a fact that it will move the exact same distance every time (the issue really comes down to batteries—as the batteries become weaker, the motor power is reduced, and those five seconds result in a shorter distance than in previous runs).

Whether you prefer degrees or rotations, you may find a time you need to use the other method; a book or an article might contain a robot you are duplicating, and the MOVE block settings might be in degrees, though you usually work in rotations.

Well, you'll be happy to know that the math for converting back and forth between degrees and rotations is very simple. Take a look at Figure A-1, and I'll give you a couple of examples.

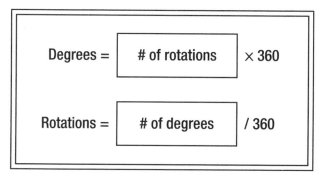

Figure A-1. Equations for converting between degrees and rotations

Figure A-1 contains two simple formulas. The top formula is for converting rotations to degrees, and the bottom formula is for converting degrees to rotations. Let me give you an example of each.

Let's say you want SPOT to roll forward 9.5 (nine and a half) rotations—easy enough. But your friend asks you to share your program with her and wants all the MOVE blocks configured in degrees. That's easy enough, too. You simply take a look at Figure A-1 and see that to obtain the value in degrees you need to multiply the number of rotations by 360. Using a calculator or doing it by hand, you'll find that the value in degrees equals 3,420. You go to the configuration panel on the MOVE block, change the Duration setting to degrees, enter the value of 3420, and then share your program with your friend.

OK, a week goes by and your friend e-mails you a copy of her version of the program with some modifications. You open the .rbt file and find that she's configured all the MOVE blocks using degrees, but you would really prefer the values to be in rotations. Again, it's easy to change. The bottom formula in Figure A-1 shows that all you need to do is divide the number of degrees by 360. In her first MOVE block, she's configured motor B to spin for 7,543 degrees. If you've done your calculations correctly, you'll find that the value of 7,543 divided by 360 is equal to 20.95277777! Will that work?

Well, the answer is that the MOVE block will allow you to enter only up to three decimal places. It would be safe to enter the value of **20.953** for number of rotations, but you'll find that the NXT motors are accurate only to the first decimal place. It's your call, and you'll want to experiment with accuracy, but in most cases, you'd be safe entering **20.9** or **21** as the value for rotations. Again, if accuracy is needed, you'll want to do a lot of testing to tweak that value. You might start by using a value of 21 and then reducing it by .1 for each experiment until you get the correct behavior from the motor.

Converting Degrees and Rotations into Distances

OK, you've programmed SPOT to move forward 720 degrees. But how far will that actually move him? What you need is the ability to convert rotations or degrees into inches or centimeters. Well, take a look at Figure A-2, and you'll see some more formulas.

Before I give you an example, remember that to calculate distance you need to convert the Duration value to rotations. So, if your MOVE block has the Duration set in degrees, use the first formula in Figure A-1 to convert it to rotations.

Now, let me walk you through how to use these simple formulas. In our example, we want to determine how far SPOT will travel if the Duration is set to 1080 degrees. We first need to convert that value to rotations, so we simply divide the number of degrees by 360. We end up with three rotations.

Next, according to Figure A-2, we need to determine one other value—the wheel circumference. This is easy, and I've given you a small picture to help you. You first measure the diameter of the wheel. The diameter is actually the distance between the two farthest points on the wheel (which happens to be the midpoint of the wheel as well). It doesn't matter if you measure the diameter in inches or centimeters, as long as you remember that the final distance you're going to calculate will also be in those units.

1. Circumference of Wheel = 3.14 × Diameter
2. Distance = Circumference × Rotations

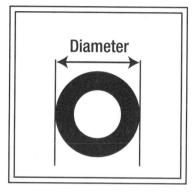

Diameter

Remember to convert Degrees to Rotations before calculating Distance!

Figure A-2. Calculating distance traveled using rotations

If you take one of the NXT 2.0 wheels and measure it, you'll find that the diameter of the wheel is approximately 1.75 inches (4.445 centimeters). (NXT 2.0 wheels are approximately 2.25 inches or 5.715cm.) Figure A-2 tells us to find the circumference by multiplying the wheel diameter by 3.14 (also known as pi; pi is a much longer number, but for our calculations, 3.14 is a safe enough approximation). If we've done our math correctly, we obtain a wheel circumference value of 5.495 inches (or 13.9573 centimeters).

Next, Figure A-2 tells us that we can calculate the total distance moved by multiplying the wheel circumference by the number of rotations. Once again, if we've done our calculations correctly, multiplying 5.495 inches by three rotations gives us 16.485 inches (41.8719 centimeters).

And that's it! You can now convert back and forth between rotations and degrees as well as calculate the distances your motors will spin (and that your robots will travel). There's one more small calculation I'll leave you with, but it will involve a quick visit to the Internet.

Would you like to know how to calculate the number of rotations or degrees required to turn your robots left or right? If you want your robot to turn in place without moving forward or backward, how do you calculate the proper number of rotations or degrees to spin one of the motors so that the robot turns left or right?

For the answer (and an example), point your web browser to the following URL:

http://thenxtstep.blogspot.com/2006/10/reader-question-submission-2.html

The X/Y Coordinate System in NXT

The final bit of information I want to provide is how to interpret the coordinate system used on your NXT Brick's LCD screen. The LCD screen has a horizontal resolution of 100 pixels and a vertical resolution of 64 pixels. This simply means you could place 100 small dots across the screen and 64 small dots down the screen. Values actually start with a zero, so the range of coordinates for X is 0–99, and for Y, the range is 0–63.

When using the DISPLAY block (or any block where you must specify a location on the LCD screen), you specify a location by using its horizontal value (X coordinate) and its vertical value (Y coordinate). So, to place a pixel (or dot) directly in the center of the screen, you would have a DISPLAY block place a Point (see Chapter 3 for details on using the DISPLAY block) with an X coordinate of 50 and a Y coordinate of 32.

Some people think there's a trick to using the coordinate system, but it's actually quite simple: coordinates start at 0, 0 in the lower-left corner of the LCD screen. Values for X increase as you move to the right, and values for Y increase as you move up the screen.

To summarize, the X/Y value of a pixel in the lower-left corner is 0/0. For the upper-right corner, the value would be 99/63. Remember, the Y value increases only as you move up the LCD screen, so the value of a pixel in the upper-left corner is 0/63, and a pixel in the lower-right corner is 99/0 (see Figure A-3).

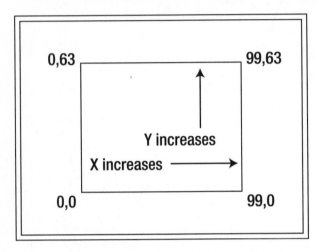

Figure A-3. *The Brick's LCD screen's X/Y coordinate system*

APPENDIX B

SPOT Building Instructions

You can always create a custom robot of your own to use while performing the exercises in this book, but I'd like to provide a very simple robot design in this appendix that can be built with both the 1.0 and 2.0 versions of the robotics kit. I call it SPOT. You'll find that you can easily build SPOT in less than 5 minutes, making it a great little robot for testing your NXT-G programs.

Figure B-1 shows the parts the make up the SPOT robot. Figure B-2 shows the completed SPOT robot— complete with 1.0 and 2.0 versions of the tires—from both sides. The images on the pages in between show step-by-step how to build the robot.

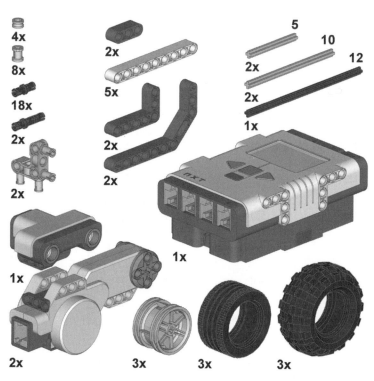

Figure B-1. Bill-of-Materials for SPOT

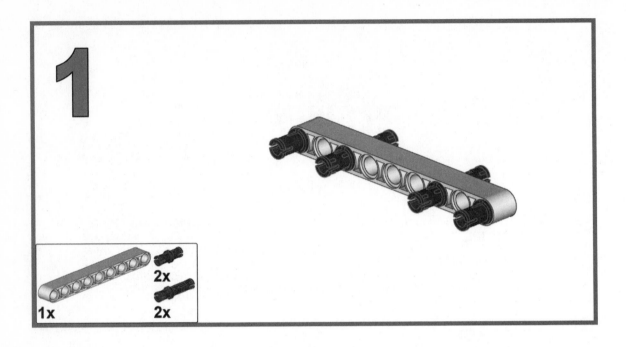

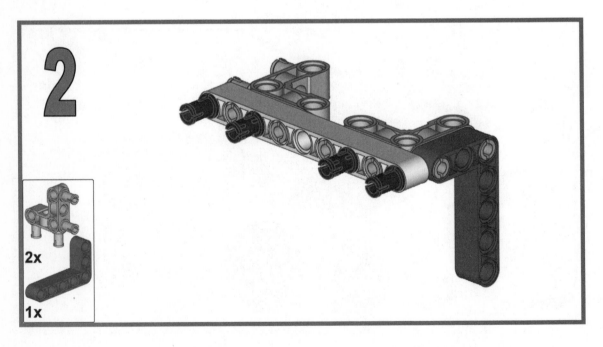

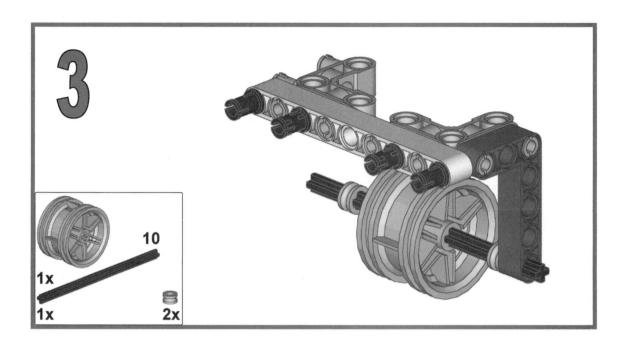

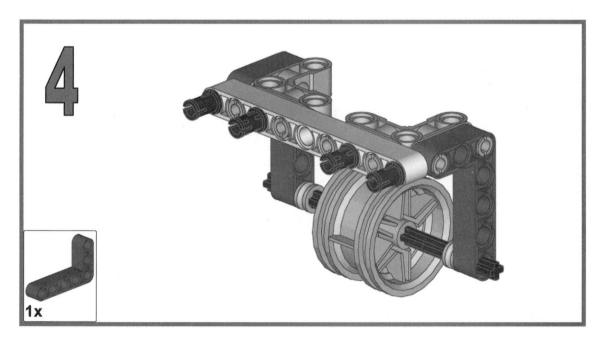

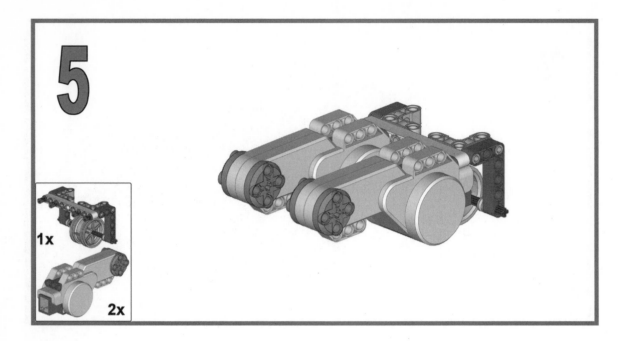

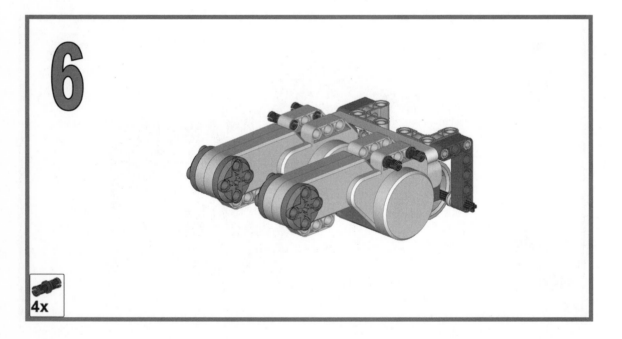

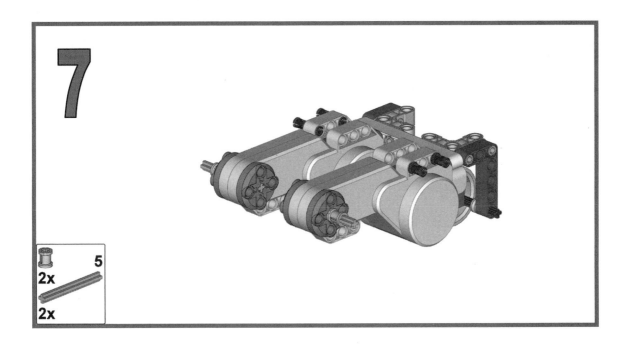

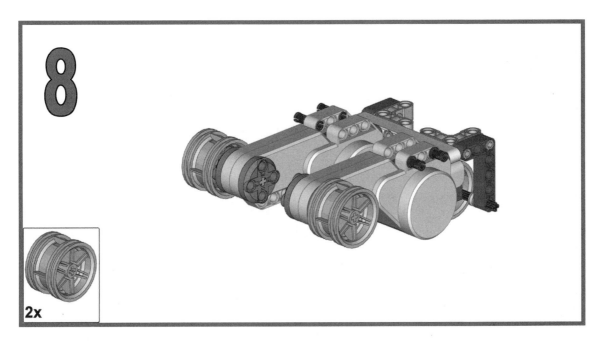

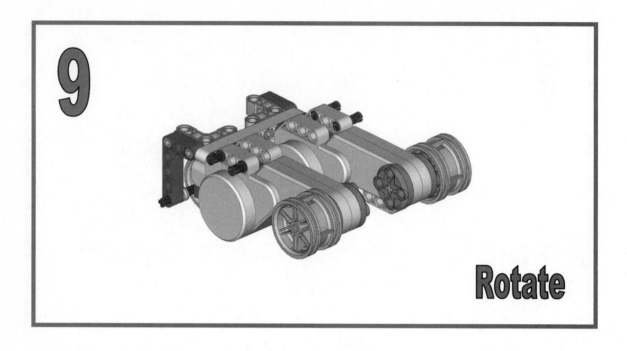

9

Rotate

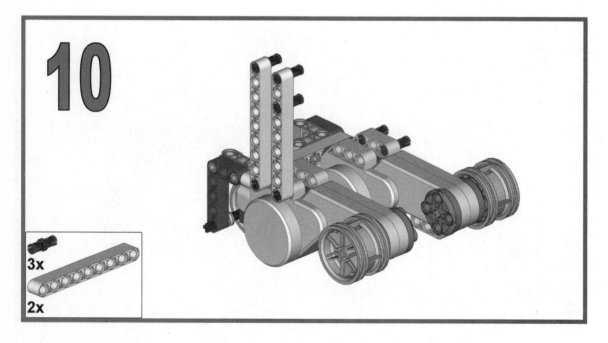

10

3x

2x

11

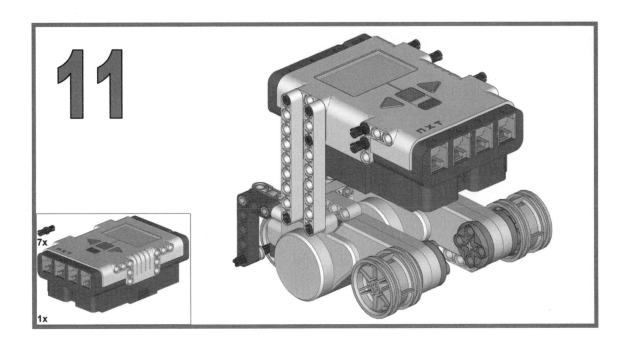

12

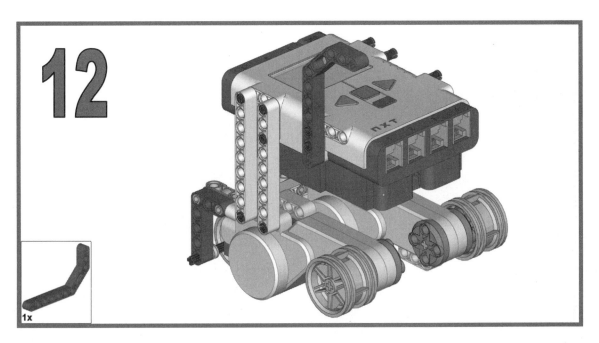

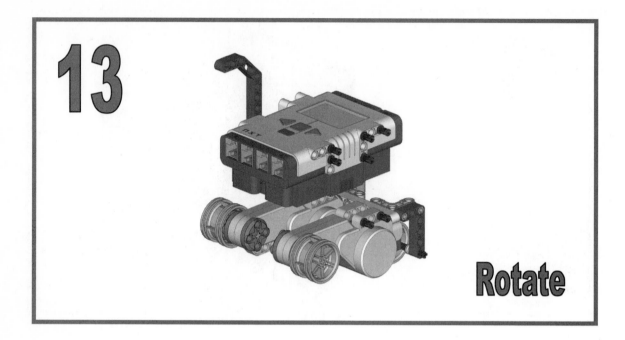

Rotate

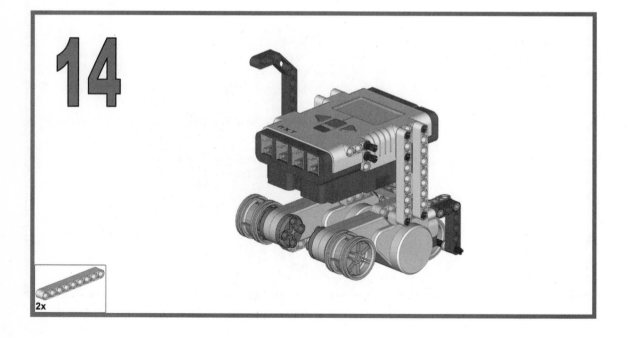

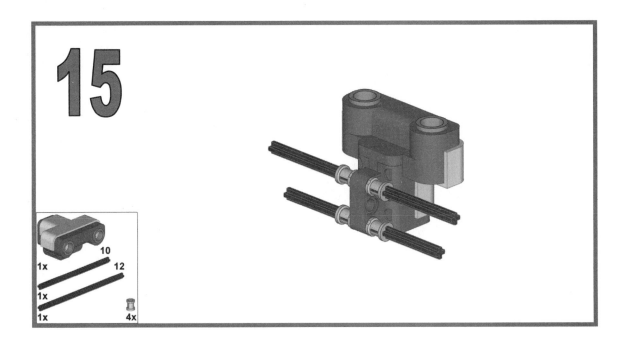

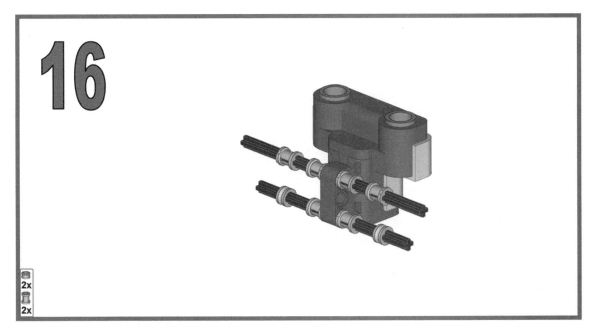

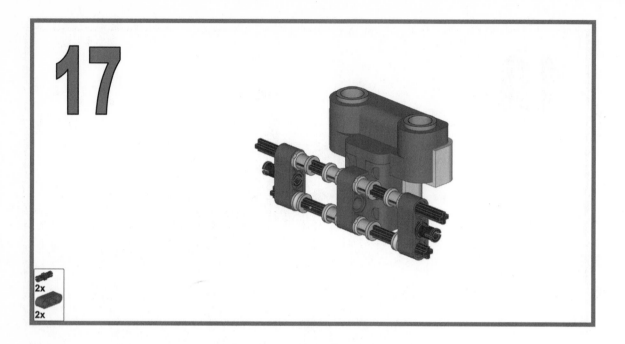

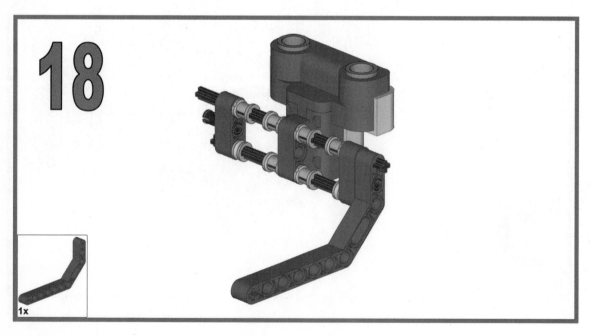

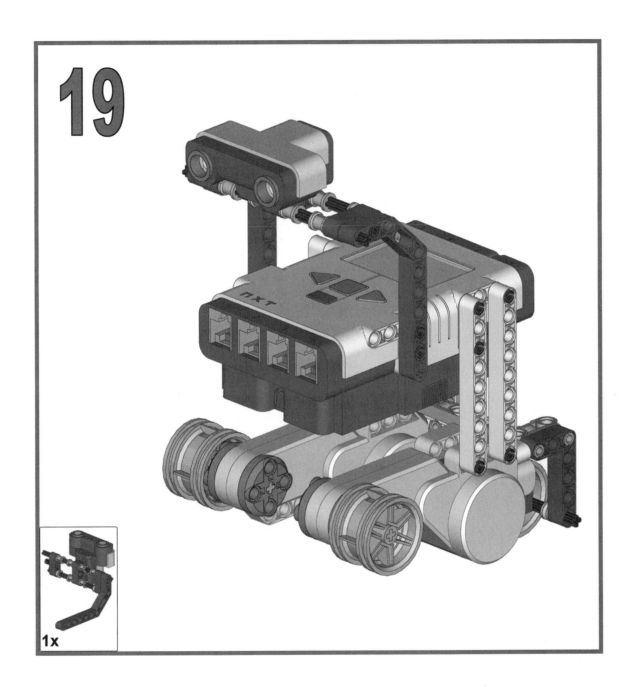

Figure B-2. *The completed SPOT robot*

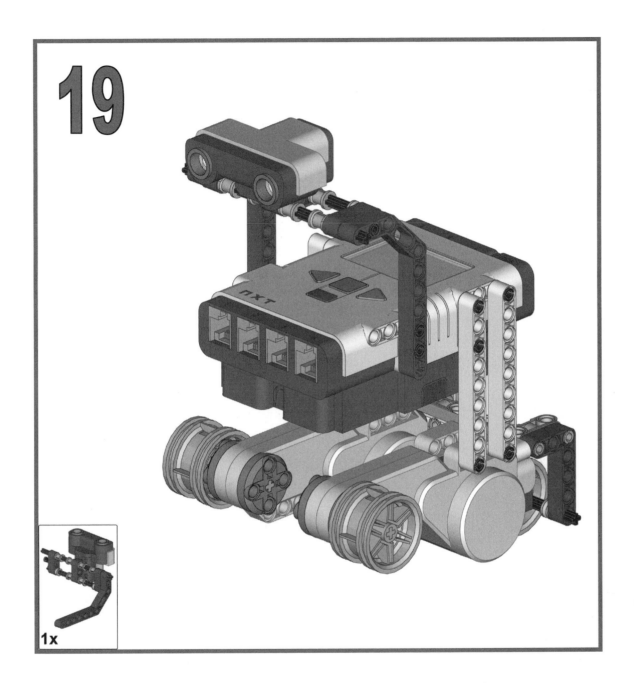

Figure B-2. *The completed SPOT robot*

APPENDIX C

■■■

Image Editor

I mentioned in Chapter 3 that the 2.0 version of the NXT-G software comes with a tool that will allow you to create your own small images that can be displayed on the LCD screen. That tool is called Image Editor and it's extremely easy to use. I'm going to walk you through creating a custom image in this appendix.

Opening an Image

After opening up your NXT-G software (version 2.0), click on the Tools menu and select Image Editor from the drop-down list. Figure C-1 shows the Image Editor tool open.

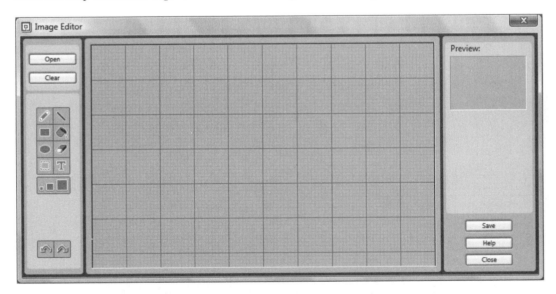

Figure C-1. The Image Editor tool allows you to create custom images for your programs.

One of the best ways to learn how to use this tool is to open an existing image and make some changes. To do this, click the Open button in the upper-left corner of the tool. You'll see a new window open that displays a list of the current images stored on your computer's hard drive, as shown in Figure C-2.

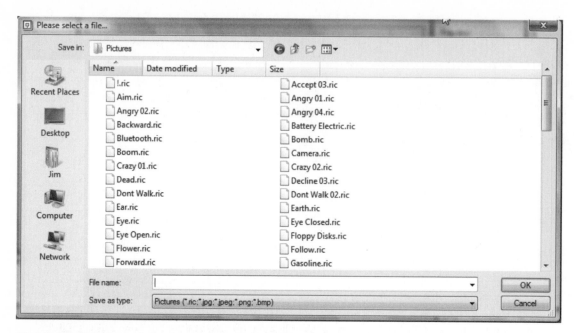

Figure C-2. Select an existing image to make changes to it.

I selected Boom.ric but feel free to select any image you like. After you've clicked on a file, click the OK button. The image will open in the Image Editor tool, as shown in Figure C-3.

Figure C-3. The selected image will be loaded into Image Editor.

■ **Note** Keep in mind as you edit existing images or create your own that the size of the image that can be displayed on the NXT brick's LCD screen will be limited to what's visible on the Image Editor workspace here. If you wish the image to appear on the screen, it must fit on the grid workspace.

Modifying an Image

I'd now like to edit the word "Boom" inside the image and change it to something else. To do this, I'll use the tools that are available as buttons along the left side of the Image Editor tool. In Figure C-4, I've selected the Erase tool, and I simply hold down my mouse button and drag the mouse pointer over any pixels I wish to remove.

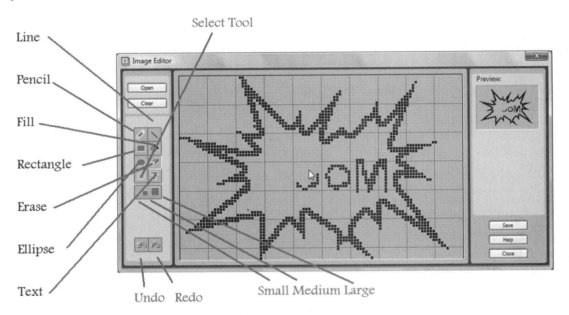

Figure C-4. The Eraser tool allows you to remove pixels from an image.

Next, I select the Pencil tool. While I'm holding down the mouse button, any pixel I move the Pencil tool over will be filled in. I can go back and use the Erase tool to fix mistakes. Figure C-5 shows my new image, which I'll call "Zap."

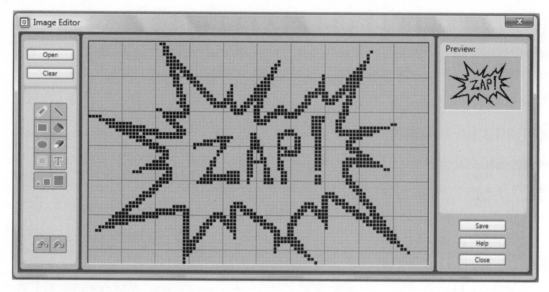

Figure C-5. The Pencil tool allows you to fill in pixels on the screen.

I can see the results of my editing in the Preview window in the upper-right corner of the tool. In addition to the Erase and Pencil tools, I have access to the Rectangle tool, which allows me to draw squares and rectangles, the Ellipse tool, which allows me to create circles and ellipses, and the Text tool, which can put text on the screen. There's a selection tool for circling a part of your image then moving that selected part around. Below the tool buttons are the Small, Medium, and Large buttons, which allow you to change the thickness of the edges when using the Rectangle or Ellipse tools. And finally, there's the Undo and Redo buttons at the bottom-left corner of the tool, which allow you to correct mistakes (click the Undo button) or add back in something you've removed like an erased bit of image) by clicking the Redo button.

Saving an Image

After you've created your new image (or modified an existing one), all you need to do is save your work. Click the Save button and give your new image a name, as shown in Figure C-6. If you're editing an existing image, don't overwrite the original—always remember to give your edits a new name. Figure C-6 shows I've saved this file as Zap.

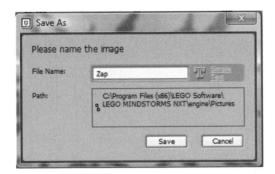

Figure C-6. Save your image by giving it a short but unique name.

After saving your image, click the Close button to close the Image Editor tool.

Using Your Image

Now all that's left is to use your new image with a DISPLAY block. Drop a DISPLAY block into your program and scroll down the File list until you find the name of your new image. Figure C-7 shows that I've located the Zap image and selected it to be displayed on the LCD screen.

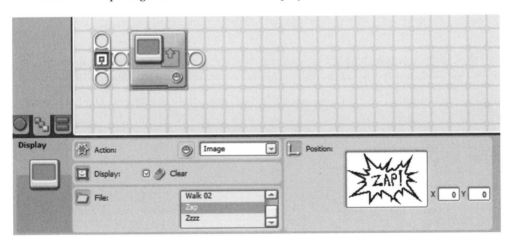

Figure C-7. Use a DISPLAY block to put your new image on the brick's LCD screen.

And that's it! I have a new custom image that I can use in my NXT-G programs to display a large "Zap!" on the LCD screen.

Index

■■■

You Need the Companion eBook

Your purchase of this book entitles you to buy the companion PDF-version eBook for only $10. Take the weightless companion with you anywhere.

We believe this Apress title will prove so indispensable that you'll want to carry it with you everywhere, which is why we are offering the companion eBook (in PDF format) for $10 to customers who purchase this book now. Convenient and fully searchable, the PDF version of any content-rich, page-heavy Apress book makes a valuable addition to your programming library. You can easily find and copy code—or perform examples by quickly toggling between instructions and the application. Even simultaneously tackling a donut, diet soda, and complex code becomes simplified with hands-free eBooks!

Once you purchase your book, getting the $10 companion eBook is simple:

❶ Visit **www.apress.com/promo/tendollars/**.

❷ Complete a basic registration form to receive a randomly generated question about this title.

❸ Answer the question correctly in 60 seconds, and you will receive a promotional code to redeem for the $10.00 eBook.

THE EXPERT'S VOICE™

233 Spring Street, New York, NY 10013

All Apress eBooks subject to copyright protection. No part may be reproduced or transmitted in any form or by any means, electronic or mechanical, including photocopying, recording, or by any information storage or retrieval system, without the prior written permission of the copyright owner and the publisher. The purchaser may print the work in full or in part for their own noncommercial use. The purchaser may place the eBook title on any of their personal computers for their own personal reading and reference.

Offer valid through 11/10.